ETURN

A Breton landscape

A Breton landscape

Grenville Astill
University of Reading

&

Wendy Davies
University College London

UCL
PRESS

First published in 1997 by UCL Press

UCL Press Limited
1 Gunpowder Square
London EC4A 3DE
UK

and

1900 Frost Road, Suite 101
Bristol
Pennsylvania 19007-1598
USA

The name of University College London (UCL) is a registered
trade mark used by UCL Press with the consent of the owner.

British Library Cataloguing-in-Publication Data
A catalogue record for this book is available from the British Library.

Library of Congress Cataloging-in-Publication Data
are available

ISBN: 1-85728-452-6 HB

Typeset in Bembo by Keyword Typesetting Services Ltd, Wallington, UK.
Printed by T.J. International Ltd, Padstow, UK.

For Morgan and Oliver, Edmund and Laurie

Contents

List of figures

List of tables

Preface

This book is the synthesis which concludes all the work undertaken in the course of the East Brittany Survey, a project jointly initiated and jointly pursued by both the authors (although most of the text was written by WD). We have learned a lot from nearly 20 years of working in Brittany and have taken great pleasure from being there; Marc Bloch remains a hero, as he was when we began.

The book has been long in the making; despite the "micro" approach, its subject is vast. We are conscious that we could write much more – months of work sometimes form the stuff of only one or two sentences – but in the interests of readability we have kept the text brief. For that reason too, we have kept references to a minimum, although we realise that there are many substantial and valuable works on which we could comment at length.

We remain indebted to all those named in our earlier book who contributed to the many aspects of the fieldwork; without them this final stage could not have been possible. We owe particular thanks for their assistance with this book to the archivists of the Archives Départementales of the Morbihan, Ille-et-Vilaine and Loire-Atlantique, and to the Service régional de l'archéologie de Bretagne (where the archaeological archive now rests); to Pete Addison and Lesley Ritchie, for their collection of essential data in the mid 1980s; to Patrick Chorley, Patrick Galliou, Pierre-Roland Giot, Michael Jones, Mary Saaler, Richard Smith and Noel-Yves Tonnerre for assistance with specific points; to Maurice Gautier and Gwyn Meirion-Jones for their generosity in supplying photographs; and to Steve Allen for completing a complex set of drawings. Others have helped us by reading different chapters: Hugh Clout, Martin Daunton, Mike Fulford,

Michael Jones again, and Bernard Merdrignac; and Liz Musgrave has very constructively read and commented on the lot. We are indebted to them all. We are also, of course, in a very practical sense indebted to the British Academy and to the Humanities Research Board for the final *tranche* of support which allowed us to complete the work.

The faults of course are ours. Although this book is one of synthesis, it is also necessarily an interpretation; some people may prefer to treat the raw data differently; we certainly hope that others will pick up and pursue, and perhaps overturn, some of the themes we have identified. Meanwhile, we feel that we are tyrannized neither by the spade nor by the word – and we enjoy working with both.

Abbreviations

AD	Archives Départementales
ADM	Archives Départementales du Morbihan
BMS	Baptêmes, Marriages, Sépultures
Car	Carentoir
INSEE	Institut national de la statistique et des études économiques
L	Liasse
Ruff	Ruffiac
S-N	Saint-Nicolas-du-Tertre
SRAB	Service régional de l'archéologie de Bretagne
Tr	Tréal

PART 1

THE APPROACH

CHAPTER 1

The problematic

L ooking at East Brittany in 1978, when we began work there, its rural communities of small farmers appeared timeless: strongly agricultural, committed to their localities, with limited external connections, living beside their work, and farming the land in a mixed regime. We knew, because of our familiarity with ninth-century texts, that this land was well peopled and intensively used before the year AD 1000, with an apparently similar mixed agricultural regime. Had there been no change?

In the first instance, therefore, we posed these questions: has land-use in eastern Brittany changed during the historic past, that is in the period since records began in northern Europe? Has the organization of human settlement in relation to the land changed during those two millennia? And if so, how, and how much, and when, and why?

Since there are no series of maps across the millennia, nor photographs, nor statistical data like that collected by the French state in the nineteenth and twentieth centuries, we thought hard about how to investigate change. Was it possible to use some of the approaches that have characterized prehistoric studies in the past couple of decades? Could modern field survey methods contribute anything that was not recoverable from documents?

In the second instance, therefore, we posed the question of how to establish a viable methodology for such a study.

Given each author's background of both historical training and archaeological experience, to draw upon written and archaeological data was obvious. But how to marry the two was not at all obvious. So, thirdly, we set out to test the parameters of interdisciplinary work. We wanted to explore the interface between documents and fieldwork: how easy (and

Figure 1.1 *The present landscape in the survey area: a view towards Carentoir, from the southwest*

how useful) is it to correlate several (and different) classes of evidence? Can one ever be a viable control on the other?

These, then, were the three problem areas that we set out to address: how much did land-use change in eastern Brittany in the last 2,000 years; how can such a set of issues best be investigated; and how far can useful interdisciplinary work be done?

We decided to look – at micro-level – at an area that had both good documentation across a long period and also the potential for an archaeological programme of extensive field survey. At an early stage, observing both the rate of decay of standing buildings and the resource that they offered for investigating sixteenth- to twentieth-century change, we also included a systematic study of standing structures in the area.

We chose the Oust–Vilaine watershed, in the Département of the Morbihan (Fig. 1.2). This allowed us to investigate a well-used landscape, in no way "marginal" or "peripheral" in the archaeological sense, with plenty of land under plough, giving us an opportunity to exploit modern fieldwalking techniques to the full. It is an area well supplied with written source material, from the early middle ages to the twentieth century, with a particularly rich corpus of localizable material relating to land-use from the later middle ages and early modern period.

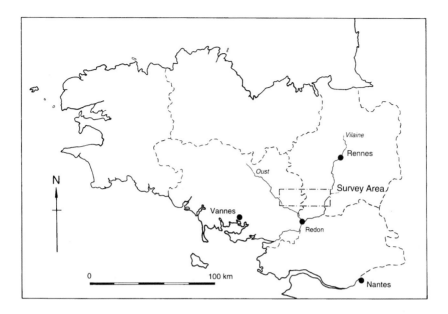

Figure 1.2 *Location of the survey area*

The project focussed on an area of 128 km^2, the four communes of Ruffiac, Tréal, Saint-Nicolas-du-Tertre and Carentoir, as a core for intensive study, with the communes surrounding the core sampled to take in the whole of the watershed. Sampling was organized by taking four transects, to north, east and west: Transect P ran west to the River Oust and Transect M ran east to the River Vilaine; Transects N and R ran, respectively, northwest and northeast (Fig. 1.3).

The landscape of the late twentieth century is gently undulating, open, with small patches of tree cover, some coniferous plantations and isolated trees – particularly fruit-bearing apple trees and pollarded chestnuts (see Fig. 1.1). While small streams are common throughout, it is only the larger valleys of the Vilaine, the Oust and its tributary the Aff that strike the attention of the visitor. There are very few permanent boundaries: large arable fields dominate the landscape although zones of pasture and temporary grassland occur too. A prominent menhir in Ruffiac, a modest alignment in Carentoir and a couple of dozen stone crosses (especially of sixteenth- and seventeenth-century date) remind us of the human past, but it is the number of settlements that signals the ubiquitous presence of people in this landscape (Gouézin 1994: 102, 48; Ducouret 1986).

At the time of the survey, in the 1980s, settlements in the core comprised the four principal villages or *bourgs* (the commune centres) and 348

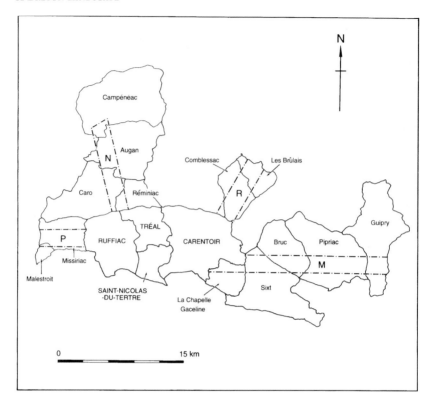

Figure 1.3 *The survey core, with sample transects*

subsidiary farms and hamlets: despite the central nucleations, a strongly dispersed pattern, with hardly anywhere more than 500m from a settlement; it is a pattern that is repeated in the sample transects. Carentoir, at 59.02 km^2, was by far the largest of the four communes, with a population of 2,495 in 1990; Ruffiac followed, at 36.47 km^2 and 1,381 inhabitants; then Tréal at 19.28 km^2 and 632 inhabitants, and Saint-Nicolas at 12.93 km^2 and 454; densities of population were therefore low, at between 33 and 43 inhabitants per km^2 (see further below, pp. 55–6, 52).[1] The nearest market towns are Malestroit, at the western end of Transect P and 3 km west of the Ruffiac border; La Gacilly, 1½ km south of the Carentoir border; and Guer, 6 km north of the Carentoir border. Though Guer is larger than the other two, all these are small towns, with populations of between 2,000 and 6,000. The capital of the Département, Vannes, lies 35 km to the southwest, on the coast; the regional capital, Rennes, lies 45 km to the northeast; and the town of Redon lies 18 km to the southeast.

Figure 1.4 *Rangée at Triguého (Tr)*

The survey area is notable for its distinctive vernacular architecture and for the use of siltstone orthostats (large upright slabs) as walling, both in buildings and in property boundaries. The buildings are, typically, single-cell dwellings, with ground floor living quarters and storage loft above, usually arranged in south-facing rows (*rangées*) of anything from two to twelve houses (Fig. 1.4). There are also some more substantial houses, *petits châteaux*, with implicit or explicit aristocratic associations, especially of early modern date (see Fig. 7.8) – often accompanied by walled garden and courtyard, with farm buildings and dovecot, and a landscaped aspect from the front of the house. Long-houses, with byre as well as domestic residence, and a common lateral doorway, are also notable. Some of the latter were converted into two-cell domestic dwellings in the nineteenth and twentieth centuries; plenty of two-cell dwellings were built afresh in the same period, while bungalows and modern two-storey multi-cell houses (typically built on mounds on the outskirts of settlements) characterize post-war housing. Other recent construction includes pig and poultry units, and modern farm buildings, whose number has increased noticeably since 1978.

****

It did not take long to discover that the aura of timelessness that first impressed us was completely misleading: the rate of change through the

Figure 1.5 *Collapsing building at Bois Neuf (Saint-Martin-sur-Oust)*

1980s was all too evident; the briefest look at the maps of the Napoleonic *cadastre* revealed a landscape that had been very different a hundred and fifty years before; and the visible decay of standing buildings suggested both changing settlement patterns and a once-larger population.

The image of the roofless and collapsing house has often been used to characterize inland Brittany and inland problems in the late twentieth century. It is an instant symbol of rural depopulation, of the desertion of the countryside and decline of local employment. Of course, the roofless house is a powerful image – but we think it is more powerful than it is useful. As we discovered, houses have collapsed and been left to rot for centuries; this is no new development of the late twentieth century. People forget that rebuilding happens close by and the collapsing house is part of a continuum of occupation. And although there certainly has been a decline of population in inland Breton communes, that decline can be as much a reflection of dynamic relationships and new opportunities as of dying communities (see below, pp. 52–4). Witness the 19 British families now domiciled in Ruffiac.

Rural Brittany has seen, and continues to see, a great deal of change. What is interesting is the relationship between the changing and the unchanging; as also what causes the changes and what makes them happen when they do: internal dynamic, external influence, or combinations of the two?

Notes

1. Densities in the sample transects were comparably low; however, they were higher in the vicinity of the towns of Malestroit and La Gacilly (i.e. in the communes of Missiriac and La Chapelle Gaceline), while they tended to be lower in communes to the north of the core and somewhat higher in communes to the east.

   Transect P: Missiriac 65 inhab/km^2; Transect N: Caro 29, Réminiac 32, Augan 32, Campénéac 22; Transect R: Comblessac 29, Les Brûlais 32; Transect M: La Chapelle Gaceline 66, Sixt 44, Bruc 37, Pipriac 57, Guipry 51.

CHAPTER 2

Method and methodology

This project was planned as a multi-disciplinary study. While drawing on the techniques of a range of specialists, the principal methods used were gathering and analysis of written data from archive collections, a staged programme of archaeological fieldwork and a systematic survey of standing buildings in the core communes. At an early stage of the project we also went through all the then available (high level and oblique) aerial photographs; and in 1996 we consulted the recent photographs taken by Maurice Gautier. Both early (1980–81) and late (1995) we consulted the records of existing sites and previous archaeological activity in the region; these were originally housed in the archives of the Direction des antiquités de Bretagne at Brest but are now at the Service régional de l'archéologie de Bretagne, in Rennes (hereafter SRAB).[1] We made no more than a modest use of place-name evidence since, although there are many excellent studies, place-names are difficult to use for microhistory when there are no, or few, dated early name forms.

Archives

The corpus of texts specific to the core communes and sample transects begins in the early middle ages with the collection of charters in the Cartulary of Redon. This is an eleventh-century collection of (largely) ninth-century documents about properties in southeastern Brittany in which the monastery of Redon had an interest (Davies 1990a); most of the properties lie north of Redon, and within 40 km of the present town. At least 65 of these ninth-century texts are about people and properties in the area of the four core communes, and there are at least a further 18 and 13, respectively, about properties in and near Transects N and M. The texts typically list the witnesses present at transactions, with place of performance and date – in other words, they tell us who was where, when. They also typically name the properties which were the subject of transactions, and localize them by *plebs* (a parish-like unit); sometimes they give measurements or detail boundaries, mentioning bordering properties, streams, roads and crosses, and sometimes they mention churches and houses. They give the value of sales and specify rents (usually in produce); and sometimes they define specific attributes of the land: woodland, or meadow, or – since Redon's interests stretched to the coast – saltpans, for example. Altogether they contain a mass of detail about local social and economic practice and procedures, as well as a large corpus of information about proprietorship (Davies 1988).

Although there are a few isolated texts – later Redon charters, Saints' Lives, other charter collections – from the intervening centuries, the next main corpus of relevant data begins in the thirteenth century. This consists principally of the many *aveux, dénombrements, hommages* and *minus* of feudal landlords, documents which describe the holdings and rights for which homage and fealty were due, often in very detailed terms. The texts are feudal statements, furnished by a tenant (usually noble) to a landlord, often at a key point in the transmission of an estate; but although they are technically statements about relationships and obligations, they are in effect estate surveys. For example, the *aveu* relating to La Boixière in Carentoir (later La Bourdonnaye), of 9 June 1708, begins by announcing that this is a declaration of the houses, land, *châteaux*, fiefs, rents, jurisdictions and other things owed to the king in the jurisdiction of Ploermel, made by the widow Dame Marie Anne Julienne de Porcaro following the death on 24 April 1707 of her husband M. Gilles François du Houx, *chevalier, seigneur* of La Gacilly and La Boixière. It goes on to list the *château* and house of La Basse Boixière, with its walls, chapel, grange and stable; the little garden and large garden (with measurements) and an enclosure planted with vines, with arable adjoining; two more areas of arable adjoining the park and below the *landes*; the meadow in front of the *château*; the *métairie* of Chesne Tort, with its house and stable roofed in slate, with a road in front and arable behind, and a garden, and two further fields (one uncultivated), with a meadow and pasture at the end of the meadow and with arable beside the pasture, and then another stretch of pasture (all with measurements), the rent for this *métairie* payable in grain and poultry; then further *métairies* with their appurtenances, a water mill, the forest of *Couettue*, and a long list of 143 minor tenancies with the rents due (largely in cash but partly in grain). Individual fields are sometimes named and measurements are given for most units.[2] The series is especially full from the late fourteenth until the early eighteenth century, inclusive. Since there were nearly 100 nobles at any one time in the core in this period, and there is a good survival of material, a large number of these documents is now preserved in the Departmental Archive collections at Nantes and Vannes.[3]

There are two other major types of record from the same period which supplement and enhance the evidence from these estate documents (all three of which were systematically searched, recorded, and indexed by Lesley Ritchie for the core communes of the project in 1985–7): parish registers and the continuing series of records relating to the monastery of Redon. The series of parish registers for the four core communes begins for Carentoir in the mid sixteenth century and for Saint-Nicolas late in the same century and becomes full for all four from the mid seventeenth century; the registers are particularly detailed for seventeenth and eighteenth centuries, recording material about occupations, epidemics and localities as well as baptisms, marriages and burials; they are now preserved in Vannes (Series 3E and 4E), and there are sometimes copies and additional material in the *mairies* of the local communes to which they relate (see below, pp. 170–1). Tréal was the subject of some especially detailed analysis since the modern commune is roughly coterminous with the medieval parish, unlike the other core communes.

The monastery of Saint Sauveur at Redon, which was exceptionally wealthy and powerful, thrived until the French Revolution; a very substantial archive of its papers survives in the Departmental collection at Rennes.[4] This includes estate surveys, rentals, lists of tenants, letters, bills, accounts, and descriptions of court cases and disputes (*procès-verbal*), and is especially rich for the fifteenth to eighteenth centuries. Most of Redon's properties in the survey area were managed during this period from its Priory at Ruffiac: *aveux* to or from the Prior characteristically specify lands in Ruffiac, Saint-Nicolas, Tréal, Carentoir, Augan, Réminiac, Saint-André and Sixt.[5] In the immediate neighbourhood of the Priory, for example, a Ruffiac Priory rent-roll for the period mid August 1649 to mid August 1650 lists some 40 tenancies and the rents received, paid in coin, wheat, oats and poultry; most tenancies have at least two tenants named and some have as many as 13.[6] Another local example is a contract of 1609, which records how two households from La Nouette and three from La Ville Marie (both near the Priory) came before the notaries of the court of Ruffiac Priory on 8 July and agreed to hold specified lands from the abbey of Saint Sauveur; the lands and land-use are then detailed, with names of fields, measurements and rents due.[7]

Other texts from this period have also been useful. These include records of different religious bodies, records of road-building and epidemics, and

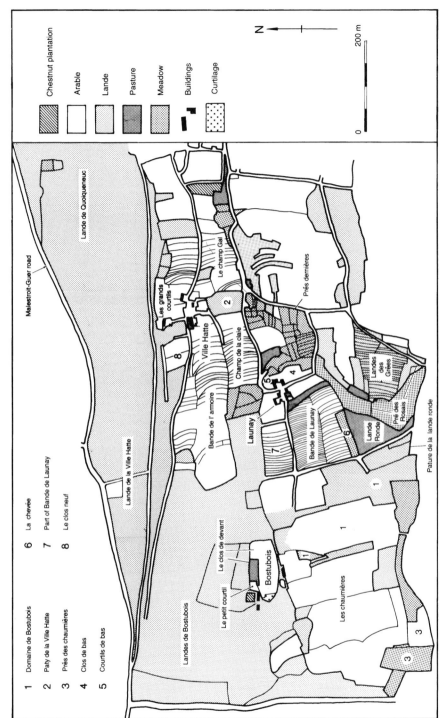

Figure 2.1 *The* ancien cadastre, *Tréal Section A₁, showing land-use and a sample of field names and field divisions*

1   Domaine de Bostubois   6   La chevée
2   Paty de la Ville Hatte   7   Part of Bande de Launay
3   Prés des chaumières   8   Le clos neuf
4   Clos de bas
5   Courtils de bas

Chestnut plantation

Arable

Lande

Pasture

Meadow

Buildings

Curtilage

N

0   200 m

Malestroit-Guer road

Lande de Quoiqueneuc

Lande de la Ville Hatte

Les grands courtils

Ville Hatte

Le champ Gal

Prés dernières

Champ de la claie

Bande de l' armoire

Launay

Landes des Grées

Bande de Launay

Pré des Rosais

Lande Ronde

Pature de la lande ronde

Landes de Bostubois

Le petit courtil

Le clos de devant

Bostubois

Les chaumières

13

records of the *fouages* – the hearth tax levied on all except the poorest peasant households, occasionally from the fourteenth century and regularly from the fifteenth.[8] For example, the *Réformation des feux* for the parish of Carentoir in 1447 lists 130 hamlets and two *bourgs*, with names of householders and vacant households in each; numbers per hamlet range from 1 to 12, with 14 at the *bourg* of La Gacilly and 29 at the *bourg* of Carentoir.[9] While these texts in theory record virtually all non-noble households, and are therefore at first glance of enormous significance for settlement history, the data are often incomplete and they do not localize the households in any precise way. Their principal value for us, therefore, is to contribute a broad-brush comparison both between hamlets at the time of any one survey and between surveys.

The third main section of the documentation is the corpus of cadastral material of the early nineteenth century. The records comprise detailed maps of all units of property (differentiating inhabited and uninhabited dwellings) and of roads within each commune, together with a series of ledgers listing ownership, field-names, land-use, land quality (in five grades), and resulting fiscal obligation. The maps are drawn to a large scale (varying between 1:1,000 and 1:2,500) and the record is comprehensive. One can therefore determine land-use, field shapes and the position of structures for the early nineteenth century wherever the original record (the *ancien cadastre*) survives, and correspondingly build up a picture of the total landscape and settlement pattern at that time (Fig. 2.1).

Over the period 1979–81 all the cadastral land-use, toponymic and settlement data for the four core communes were mapped. This material dates from the period 1825–9, is well preserved in the Morbihan Archives and is complete.[10] Subsequently, comparable data for all sample transects except Transect R were collected (finished in 1995). Recorded in 1825–48, the data are largely complete; however, most of the La Chapelle Gaceline records are missing, apparently misplaced when the commune was detached from Carentoir in 1874.[11] All of the cadastral material collected was summarized in electronic form in the early to mid 1990s.

The cadastral record allows us to see that nearly 200 years ago there were large expanses of marginal, uncultivated land in the survey area (the *landes*, see Fig. 2.1), settlements of very varied size and shape, and some extremely distinctive styles of land management, of which little trace remains today. Most of the arable land lay in large open fields, of irregular shape, divided into parcels, which were further divided into small sections (*bandes*), often strip-like, worked by different tenants and proprietors; however, some of the arable lay in large, rectangular, undivided fields associated with properties of noble origin. (Fallow land is marked in the arable fields.) Although there are plenty of tenurial "divisions" on the maps, neither boundaries between *bandes* nor between parcels leave much trace on the ground today. The properties of noble origin also had higher proportions of meadow than the norm, woodland plantations, tree-lined avenues leading to grand houses, and fishponds (see below, pp. 155–9). Outside these areas, meadow was usually water meadow, lying in the stream valleys, and – like the arable – was usually divided into small sections held by different farmers. There were some permanent pastures, although quite rare, and some chestnut plantations, some coppiced woodland and some more mature woodland. There are often very small fields, usually called *clos*, beside peasant settlements, almost invariably used for arable cultivation in the early nineteenth century. There are *clos* by former noble properties too, again usually used for arable, but often bearing names like "The Orchard" or "The Vineyard". Nearly all houses, however small, had an area of attached yard/garden, known as curtilage (*courtil*).

Government surveys and local records of the later nineteenth and twentieth centuries have also been especially valuable for refining the detail of agricultural and demographic change during the last 200 years. These records include the bulky and immensely detailed agricultural statistics required regularly by the state, census figures on population distribution and character, and local communal records about a wide range of matters – from clearance of the *landes* to road building and improvements.[12]

Archaeological survey

The main programme of archaeological survey had three different stages: (1) systematic fieldwalking of ploughed fields, at wide intervals, to note features and collect material from the surface; this was designed to achieve maximum coverage of the total surface area and to achieve a precise understanding of spatial relationships. (2) "Total surface collection" from a number of the fields already walked in Stage 1, together with geophysical and geochemical surveys, in order to investigate selected areas more closely and test the results from wide-spaced walking against fieldwalking the total surface, and assess the extent to which extrapolation from the particular to the general might reasonably be made. (3) Excavation of a selection of fields from which total collection had been made, in order to investigate surface/sub-surface relationships. All three stages were inter-related and interdependent, and all three were essential.

15

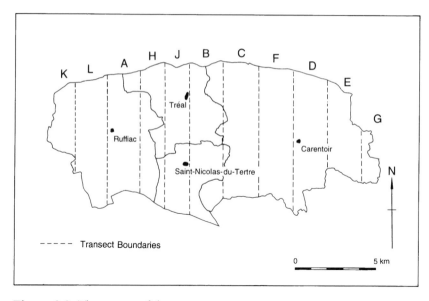

Figure 2.2 *The transects of the core survey area*

Fieldwalking

The initial phase of fieldwalking was organized within north/south transects, A–L, across the core communes, in the order KLAHJBCFDEG, from west to east (hereafter referred to as "transect-walking"). In this way, all available ploughed fields were walked in the four core communes in five Easter seasons, between 1982 and 1986 (Fig. 2.2). All transects except H, K and L were walked twice, with new fields walked in a second season, in order to increase the proportion of the surface area covered. The outcome was that 27% of the surface area of the core (3,454 ha, 1,949 fields) was walked (see Davies & Astill 1994 for detailed results). Sample transects M, N, P and R were walked in Easter seasons in 1986 and 1987, and the following proportions of their surface areas were covered: 18.7%, 18%, 8.5% and 14.6% (646, 203, 72 and 146 fields) respectively.

In transect-walking the interval between runs walked in each field was 50m and runs were divided into collection units 100m long. The fields walked were each given a unique number, in sequence of walking, by transect, with features recorded on a standardized recording form. Walkers were instructed to pick up all material that did not occur naturally: that is, sherds of modern as well as Roman and medieval ceramic; fragments of modern brick as well as earlier tile; slate and stone that had been introduced on to the fields. Collection was therefore not confined to ceramic data (although metal did not survive well and was very rarely picked up).

In most seasons there were considerable variations in the distribution of material recovered from the surface, and a set of standard conventions was devised in 1982, and applied consistently thereafter, in order to distinguish between greater and lesser concentrations of surface material and to provide a means of reference to them. A three-fold classification of "site", "probable site" and "possible site" was used to distinguish between the concentrations, the terms simply serving as tools for referring to larger and smaller quantities, without implying the presence of settlement or structure (see Davies & Astill 1994: 14, for precise criteria).

During each Easter season the collected pottery was processed and assigned to a broad chronological category, using three periods: pre-medieval, medieval and post-medieval; these classifications form the basis of discussions published between 1982 and 1989. The essential work of primary analysis of the forms and fabrics of the pottery began in 1983 and was completed in 1993; GGA's final, detailed description of the series can be found in Davies & Astill 1994: 167-209. The result of the analysis is a six-fold periodization of the material: prehistoric; Roman; medieval (tenth to fourteenth centuries); late medieval (fourteenth/fifteenth to sixteenth centuries); post-medieval (sixteenth/seventeenth to eighteenth centuries); modern (nineteenth and twentieth centuries). References to the pottery in all publications from 1994 onwards use this final classification; the first two classes equate – broadly – to the earlier working classification of "pre-medieval"; the next two to the earlier "medieval"; and the last two to the earlier "post-medieval". A master database of data derived from transect-walking, from both core and sample transects, was compiled by WD between 1991 and early 1996, incorporating results of the final pottery analysis, together with topographic and cadastral data; this initially used Reflex software, but was converted to Paradox in 1995 (see Davies & Astill 1994: 210-16).

The second phase of the main fieldwork programme was that of "intensive" or "total" collection. In this phase fields that had been previously walked at 50m intervals were gridded in 5m squares for walking the total surface. Fields were selected so that the complete range of preliminary surface results could be explored. They therefore included fields with surface concentrations of stone, tile and pottery; of Roman, medieval and post-medieval date; with dense and weak concentrations, and with none; on a range of different land-use at the time of the cadastral survey in the early nineteenth century: arable, meadow and *landes*, under both peasant and landlord management.

Total collection was undertaken in the three Easter seasons 1983–5, and also by special teams sent to the field for that purpose for three months in early 1986, two months in spring 1987 and one month in late autumn 1987. As a result total collection was made from 43 fields (see Davies & Astill 1994 for full detail of results).

Usually stone, and in a few cases pottery and tile, was weighed on site, but it was our normal practice to transport ceramic material to England for further study. Given the enormous amount of material collected, extremely useful results came from this programme, and we did enough to allow us to establish a relationship between collection at wide intervals and collection from the total surface of a field (Davies & Astill 1994: 217-21 and 271-80 especially). Ceramic data from total collection fields was subsequently manipulated using a variety of software packages, essentially Mapics during the 1980s and Uniras in the mid '90s; plots by period were thereby generated (Figs 2.3, 2.4, for example).

Excavation strategy

The third phase of fieldwork involved the small-scale excavation of selected fields from which total collection had been made. This work was designed to maximize the information recovered from a wide range of different locations, with the minimum acceptable trench size, and therefore in most cases involved a combination of machine-cut trenches and hand-digging. Excavation began in the Easter 1985 and Easter 1986 seasons and was continued in summer seasons in 1986 and 1988. Twelve different locations were investigated, in 46 trenches. Fields for excavation were selected in order to explore the range of surface results and to investigate surface/sub-surface relationships. They included fields with dense and weak concentrations of surface material, of varying periods, and of varying cadastral land-use. Excavation was also directed to increase understanding of the soils and sediments of the survey area, and accordingly involved the investigation of two lynchets and a bank.

Excavation tactics varied according to the type of site, although the basic approach was consistent. In those circumstances where the entire distribution of surface material of a particular field needed clarification, a series of equally spaced (at 30m) metre-wide trenches was cut by machine. Most of the plough soil was removed mechanically and then the sub-soil surface was excavated by hand and the sections cleaned and recorded. Small extensions were made to excavate more of particular features where it was felt that the work would help an understanding of the entire site. In those cases where a particular concentration of material needed investigation a 6m-square excavation module was consistently applied; the plough soil

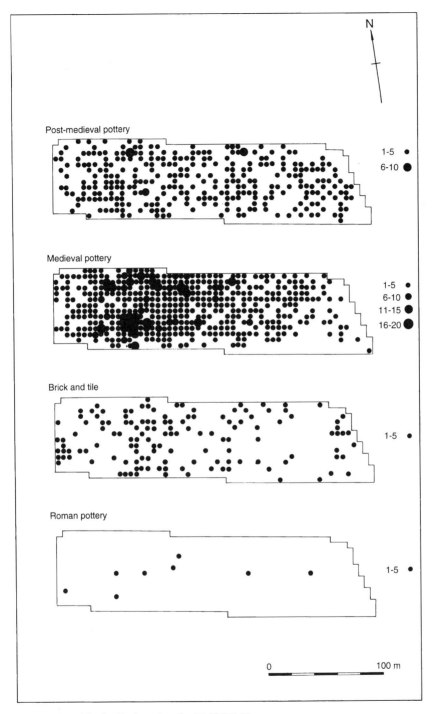

Figure 2.3 *Total collection plots for Field H132*

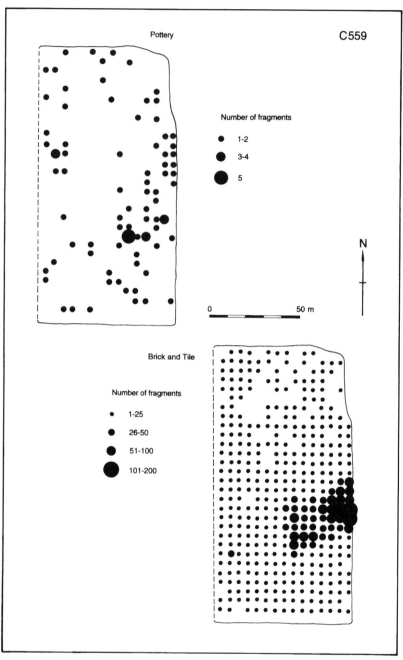

Figure 2.4 *Total collection plots for Field C559*

was hand-excavated in 0.1m spits and searched for material; and a 5% control sample was sieved.

In three particular cases excavation was essential for the overall survey results even though access was very limited. Here the fields were under crop and so, although some limited area excavation was possible, the wide-spaced machine trenching was not.

The main purpose of digging lynchets was to secure a sequence of land-use evidence, and this necessitated a more detailed recording of finds and environmental sampling. A preview of the depth of the lynchet and the occurrence of any underlying features was obtained from a metre-wide machine-cut trench. A similar-sized trench was excavated (stratigraphically) to one side in 1m squares and all the finds were three-dimensionally recorded; stone was recovered in 0.05m spits. Bone did not survive well enough to justify systematic collection.

Archaeological environmental work

At the outset of this project we had hoped to use the whole array of modern archaeological environmental techniques in order to elucidate sequences of land-use change during the historic period. To this end we commissioned a series of studies of different data sets (see Davies & Astill 1994: 37-8, 266-9).

As a result of Professor John Evans's helpful assessment of the potential of the survey area for producing good environmental results, we realised already in 1983 that the area is not ideal for environmental work, since its weakly acidic soils do not assist the preservation of bone and shell and it lacks peat bogs and lake sediments. While it was demonstrated that diatom floras did survive in soil samples taken from the Aff valley and from a swampy area south of La Danais (Carentoir), they were in a fragmentary state and did not suggest sufficient potential to merit further work.

There were usable results from a series of pollen studies, however: samples from Les Ajoncs d'Or in the Oust valley, just to the west of Ruffiac, showed zones of cereal introduction, elm and lime decline, and cereal and herb increase (Roggero 1984). Samples from the large expanse of early nineteenth-century *lande* 875m north of Le Rond Point in the southern boundary zone of Saint-Nicolas-du-Tertre clearly showed zones of cereals *previous* to zones dominated by grass and calluna heathland (Darley 1985); and further samples showed a similar profile. However, in other samples pollen had no clear zonation, or too few pollen grains to produce usable results, or pollen in the top 20cm only.

This was a very mixed record of sometimes good, sometimes poor pollen preservation and sometimes good, sometimes poor zonation – all undated. It was therefore difficult to locate any of the good zonations precisely in the historic period. However, the samples taken from the several areas of *lande* are of interest for their cereal zones; and it is clear from texts and pottery distribution that some areas of nineteenth-century *lande* had been cultivated in the late or post-medieval periods (see below, p. 129).

Anne Gebhardt also took a series of samples from excavated sites for micromorphological analysis of the soils. As a result of her analyses, she demonstrated that the soils studied had been subject to agricultural processes continuously since the first deforestation of the area (Gebhardt 1988, 1990, 1993). While this evidence that there was no regeneration of forest growth is useful, her arguments on the date of the initial deforestation do not stand against the evidence of archaeological excavation, of pollen analysis and of written records. These studies, which were sustained over the period 1985 to 1988, did not therefore yield any information about historic land-use that we did not already have from documentation or from fieldwalking and excavation.

There are therefore only a limited number of archaeological environmental results to feed into the question of land-use change. However, in the case of the excavated lynchets (T1 and T35) we nevertheless established a sequence of land-use over a very long period, and this was very precise about changes during the historic period. We did this by using standard excavation techniques, with meticulous attention to *all* material in the soil, including stone. This was a labour-intensive method, but it achieved results that are extremely useful.

Standing buildings

Many of the pre-twentieth-century buildings of the survey area are in an advanced state of decay, and deteriorated markedly over the period of fieldwork. A systematic survey of external features of all pre-1920s standing buildings in the four core communes was therefore undertaken – on foot – over the years 1984–5 by Pete Addison, for the project, in a year's full-time work. Where easy access was possible internal features were recorded too. The data were recorded on standardized recording forms, the forms themselves being adapted for the survey area from Brunskill's vernacular recording system (Brunskill 1965–6, 1976). Hence, wall, roof, window, door, and chimney attributes and materials were coded, as also special features characteristic of vernacular building in the *pays de Redon*.

The latter include detail of decoration, number of storeys and cells, external stairways, ovens and outshuts.

In the event, 4,589 structures were recorded on the forms, and a photographic record of 795 buildings or features was also made.[13]

Dating the buildings is critical if the corpus is to make a valuable contribution to the principal questions addressed by the project. Precise dates were recorded by Pete Addison for 6% of buildings within the four core communes of the study area; and he devised the framework detailed below for dating distinctive types of building (see Davies & Astill 1994: 254-63, cf. 237-41).

Precise dates ranging from the late sixteenth century to 1984 were recorded. There is nothing at present to suggest that any of the surviving buildings is of an earlier date, with the exception of the probable fifteenth-century seigneurial building at Couedic (Tr) (see below, p. 167, and Figs. 11.2, 11.3). The following paragraphs summarize Addison's main dating criteria for supplementing the precisely dated group.

Firstly, the round-headed doorway is an indicator of sixteenth-/seventeenth-century date: there is one three-voussoired example in a building dated 1579 and another has a date of 1633. In the survey area there are no dated three-voussoired, round-headed doorways later than c.1650 and, given the consistency of the type, it would be surprising if any of the undated examples are much later than this. Multi-voussoired round-headed doorways, on the other hand, tend to belong to the late seventeenth century: there are examples in buildings dated 1682 and 1697.

Secondly, some of the long-houses form a virtually identical group of such distinctive character as to be easily recognizable as a type. These buildings are unusually large, with lofts frequently a full storey in height, and they have massive dressings to all openings (Fig. 2.5). The distinctively large long-house, with "megalithic" jambs, appears to have a limited date range: four have dates in the seventeenth century and another is earlier than a building dated 1714. Other buildings, of single-cell type, share the distinctive characteristics and should be attached to the group. The type is therefore a useful indicator of early seventeenth–early eighteenth-century structures.

Thirdly, some of the long-houses have been converted to "long-house first derivatives" (by enlarging the hall window to make a second door); purpose-built examples of this type of converted long-house also occur and are a common nineteenth-century development.

Fourthly, nineteenth-century buildings, of the latter half of the century, typically have gables of uniform pitch without sprockets at eaves level, and have timber fireplace corbels and large, regular window openings of

Figure 2.5 *A "megalithic" long-house at L'Abbaye aux Alines (Car); photo: Pete Addison*

regularly dressed, though not squared, quoins (see Fig. 10.2). These buildings also, invariably, have timber lintels to all openings.

Finally, buildings Addison termed the "1920s" type typically have machine-cut quoins to doors and windows, gabled roofs with exposed purlins and rafters, gabled dormers (with cambered dormer lintels on earlier examples) and half-round ridge tiles (Fig. 2.6). This type of building has recorded dates from the late 1890s to post-1930.

Figure 2.6 *A "1920s" building at La Minardais (Car); photo: Pete Addison*

These typological indicators, together with sequential structural observations (for example, of buildings which must structurally pre-date a dated building), allow us to date an additional 19% of houses. Of the whole corpus, only one building is demonstrably of the sixteenth century; 65 are from the seventeenth into the early eighteenth century; 46 are eighteenth-century; 206 long-houses are largely of the seventeenth/eighteenth centuries; 464 (including 250 long-house first derivatives) are nineteenth-century; and 361 are twentieth-century.

There is therefore a datable core of about a quarter of the structures, as well as a tenth with pre-twentieth-century extensions. This is a usable proportion and is significant for assessing the ebb and flow of settlement size in the post-medieval period (see below, pp. 203–7). It should be said, however, that Pete Addison's framework was applied to the whole corpus by Mary Saaler, working for the project, in 1995, using the Reflex/Paradox database. Although dozens of tests were carried out on potentially diagnostic combinations of attributes, very few were consistent enough to increase the datable stock of buildings beyond the above. Conversions and reconstructions were evidently common in the nineteenth century and it is meaningless to attach precise single dates to many of the structures. Many are an amalgam of building and alteration, such that it is impossible to identify, and date, the earliest core without very detailed work on individual structures.

Notes

1. Reference to SRAB records relates to the records as at November 1995.
2. AD Loire-Atlantique B1957bis L2.
3. AD Loire-Atlantique and AD Morbihan respectively: Series B "Cours et juridictions avant 1790" and Series E "Féodalité, familles, état civil, notaires, corporations, communautés d'habitants avant 1790". There are also *aveux* in the Redon papers in Series H at Rennes, AD Ille-et-Vilaine. For the principal records used, see Appendix 1.
4. Series H, "Clergé régulier avant 1790", 3H in the Redon case; see Charpy et al. 1994 for this and other Ille-et-Vilaine material.
5. For example, AD Loire-Atlantique B1999; AD Ille-et-Vilaine 3H191[2] L2, 3H193.
6. AD Ille-et-Vilaine 3H187 L1.
7. AD Ille-et-Vilaine 3H188 L5.
8. AD Morbihan, Series G, "Clergé séculier avant 1790", for secular religious houses; AD Ille-et-Vilaine, Series C, "Administrations provinciales avant 1790", for road-building and epidemics; relevant *fouages* are mostly at Nantes, AD Loire-Atlantique, Series B, but there are also eighteenth-century *capitation* lists in AD Morbihan, Series C (21C).
9. AD Loire-Atlantique B2986.
10. Series P, "Finances, cadastre et postes (1800–1940)".

11. Transect P: 1829–36 (Malestroit) and 1840–42 (Missiriac); Transect N: 1826 (Campénéac), 1829–30 (Caro and Réminiac) and 1848 (Augan); Transect R: 1833 (Comblessac) and 1830 (Les Brûlais); Transect M: 1825 (La Chapelle Gaceline), 1830–32 (Pipriac) and 1831–33 (Bruc, Guipry and Sixt). Transect R and Transect M records (except for La Chapelle Gaceline) are in AD Ille-et-Vilaine, and are in a middling to poor state of preservation; the rest are in AD Morbihan.

12. AD Morbihan, Series M, "Administration générale et économie (1800–1940)", especially 6M and 7M, including nineteenth- and twentieth-century census material and agricultural statistics; Series W, "Archives administratives et judiciaires postérieures à 1940", especially 2W and 4W; Series O, "Administration et comptabilité communales (1800–1940)", especially $_2$O.

13. This building archive is available for consultation and is currently deposited in the Rare Books Collection of the Library of University College London; the data from the forms has also been copied into a Paradox database and is available on disks.

Principal archives consulted

Archives Départementales du Morbihan
21C513, 21C567, 21C583
E1604, E1646
4E33/1-11, 3E200/1, 4E200/1-7, 4E230/1-3, 3E253/1, 4E253/1-5
(Communal deposits: 3ES61/58 & /63, 3ES200/4 & /10, ES^{3}204, ES^{4}204, ES^{2}258)
G0981, G1066, G1311; 56G03
I745
34 J163
6M11, 6M14, 6M18, 6M21, 6M71, 6M252, 6M282, 6M305, 6M958, 6M964, 6M971, 6M980, 6M987-9, 6M1007, 6M1009, 6M1016, 6M1021, 6M1024-5, 6M1041
7M235, 7M238-9
$_2$O33/6
3P80, 3P106, 3P107, 3P109, 3P160, 3P193, 3P202, 3P259, 3P267, 3P293, 3P317, 3P326, 3P444, 3P352, 3P353, 3P355, 3P410, 3P453, 3P511, 3P519, 3P549, 3P572, 3P643, 3P910, 3P930-1, 3P974, 3P1884, 3P1999, 3P2649, 3P2722, 3P2934, 3P3141
2W10478
4W11563, 4W11761, 4W11783
1MiEC033R01-R15, 1MiEC200R01-05, 1MiEC230R01-03

Archives Départementales de Loire-Atlantique
B1957, B1966, B1988, B1991, B1999, B2988, B2986

Archives Départementales d'Ille-et-Vilaine
C1351-3, C1734, C1391-2, C2348, C2370, C3909, C4272, C4274, C4894, C4993
3H66, 3H187, 3H188, 3H189, 3H190, 3H191^1, 3H191^2, 3H192, 3H193, 3H194
7M132
3P457, 3P1177, 3P1940, 3P5277, 3P5358-1/2, 3P5445-1, 3P5552-1/2

A note on refuse disposal and manuring

Early stages of archaeological fieldwork soon demonstrated that many ploughed fields in the survey area had a scatter of introduced material – principally pottery, tile and stone – on the surface. These scatters could have arisen in a number of ways, manuring, middens, dumping and settlement debris being the most obvious likely causes. The ability to distinguish between these alternatives is of crucial importance in interpreting the results of fieldwork.

The evidence from excavation allowed us to identify types of scatter which derive from both sub-surface remains and from midden sites; and to identify specific scatters deriving from middens of the central to late middle ages sited on top of or in the neighbourhood of redundant buildings (Davies & Astill 1994: 271–2).

The evidence from totally collected and from excavated fields allowed us to identify surface scatters which derive from the disposal of domestic and other waste on arable fields. The many scatters with small quantities of sherds and of building material, evenly or haphazardly distributed across the surface of the field, must ultimately derive from refuse disposal: such material decreases with depth in the plough soil, and is not associated with sub-surface features; it was clearly introduced from the surface. Such scatters are in marked contrast to those which cluster on the surface of a field and which lie directly above or near structural remains. Even where the subsoil and structural remains had been ploughed away, as on parts of Field A116, material still increased with depth in the ploughsoil at sites where surface scatters related to sub-surface features.

Practice with regard to refuse disposal clearly changed over the centuries and we can be more confident about medieval and later practice than we can about Roman and prehistoric practices. The quantities of medieval and late medieval material on the fields are such that a high proportion of the debris from settlements must have been spread on them. This is in marked contrast to the Roman period, when only small amounts of pottery and building material are left on the fields; and is also in marked contrast to the early middle ages and the entire post-sixteenth-century period.

Although there is no direct evidence of fertilizing practice for the survey area during the central and later middle ages, it seems likely that the arable was fertilized both by the distribution of stable dung and by allowing animals to graze on the fallow; sherds of pottery and other household waste must have become mixed with farmyard piles of dung before its distribution on the fields. Practices which are known to have been common in inland Brittany in the eighteenth and nineteenth centuries – such as cutting fern from the *lande*, burning it with dung, and then distributing it on the arable (Clout 1973–4: 31) – may well also have been used.

For late prehistory and the Roman period, evidence for the survey area consists of very small quantities of surface material, unassociated with sub-surface features. In view of the small quantities it is reasonable to ask if the material got there by chance rather than in the course of distributing manure.

Iron-Age scatters are of extremely low density, but the presence of sherds in the early colluvium of the large lynchet T1 is important. This certainly indicates that Iron-Age sherds arrived on the field in or near the late Iron Age, and it is difficult to suggest an explanation for their presence – given the distance from the near-by settlement – other than through manuring (Davies & Astill 1994: 63–5).

Though Roman sherds are similarly rare, they are often accompanied by significant quantities of small fragments of tile (see below, pp. 77–9). Since this material occurs in discrete areas, at a significant distance (up to 500m) from settlement sites, its presence on the fields is best explained by intentional or unintentional distribution in the Roman period itself (the distance is too great for modern ploughing to have moved the sherds and in any case there were physical boundaries to prevent this). On Field A31/79 quantities of sherds were very small, the pottery was very abraded and the surface (but not sub-surface) material included small quantities of brick and tile. The sherds and tile are likely to have arrived on the fields as a result of surface distribution, at a period when first- and second-century pottery was being discarded. Manuring is again the best explanation for this type of scatter, although there is of course no way of knowing if all arable was fertilized in this way.

There is no evidence from the survey area to suggest the distribution of manure or household waste on arable fields in the early middle ages; indeed, the small number of surviving tenth-century sherds seems to relate to settlement sites rather than fields. However, in view of the discovery of early medieval pottery in post-Roman but pre-eleventh-/twelfth-century lazy beds at the site of Le Yaudet in northwest Brittany, it must in principle be possible that some material was similarly distributed in the survey area in the early middle ages (Cunliffe and Galliou 1995: 56–7). However, given that the Le Yaudet lazy beds were within an enclosure and very close to a settlement site, they may reflect gardens or an intensive infield system rather than the regular arable.

The frequency of late and some post-medieval sherds in the plough soil of some fields suggests that the medieval habit of distributing refuse on arable fields continued through the sixteenth and into at least part of the seventeenth century. Black roofing slate was also distributed with the refuse at this time. However, although roofing slate continued to be distributed on the arable until the later nineteenth century, known arable of the later seventeenth, eighteenth and nineteenth centuries usually lacks sherds of that period. It appears that the practice of spreading domestic refuse on the fields as a matter of course stopped; since plenty of sherds of this period are found near settlements, it looks as if the treatment of domestic refuse had changed and it no longer became mixed with stable clearings (see further below, pp. 186–9).

The distribution of black roofing slate on arable fields is interesting, particularly as gross quantities are extremely large and observations were systematically made for more than 1,000 fields. Basically the material began to be spread on arable fields in the late sixteenth century; it is found, with household refuse, on *new* arable of the early post-medieval period (i.e. in the seventeenth century); it was spread, *without* household refuse, on new arable of the eighteenth and nineteenth centuries; it was *not* spread on new arable of the twentieth century. The evidence of these changes is so consistent, and slate prevalence so striking, that it has to be considered whether or not it was being spread deliberately on new arable in the post-medieval/modern period – perhaps to break up the soil (for detailed discussion, Davies 1993: 345–9).

Perhaps as early as the early seventeenth century, household waste seems to have been dumped, and left, outside buildings – at greater or nearer distance (30-150m). Hence, fields that we *know*, from good written evidence, were arable in sixteenth, seventeenth, eighteenth and nineteenth centuries have large quantities of medieval but not post-medieval fabrics (see below, p. 188). It is exceptionally unlikely that farmers were experimenting with new forms of fertilization as early as the sixteenth and seventeenth centuries in this region; it is therefore likely that what changed was the method of domestic refuse disposal, not the manuring practice itself: domestic refuse was left in dumps and did not get intermixed with the dung (perhaps because there was greater differentiation between domestic and animal quarters – long-houses account for only 5% of the surviving housing stock – or because new types of flooring were introduced). Slate dumping was clearly not similarly differentiated. The dumps were sometimes located on the site of former medieval settlements (below, pp. 192–3) – although by no means all settlements of the early nineteenth century which had disappeared by the late twentieth attracted dumping in the same way (below, pp. 232–3; Astill & Davies 1984: 56, 1985: 96). Consciousness of public hygiene was clearly a Departmental and town concern in the second half of the nineteenth century: La Gacilly had a complex set of orders for street cleaning in 1887; the same concern was evident in the communes of the survey area before the First World War – witness the requests from both Ruffiac and Campénéac communes to sink wells in 1911.[1]

We know that by the early nineteenth century there was considerable interest in the region of Brittany as a whole in improved methods of fertilization and a lively trade in new fertilizing materials: Pierre Jauffret, from Aix, visited Lorient round about 1837 to demonstrate new methods to representatives from all five Breton Départements; and marling was adopted on a substantial scale (Clout & Phillips 1972). Though ash, lime, guano and bone-black[2] were being used in many parts of France by 1852, the cantons of the survey area record only the use of dung and ash and the purchase of street soil at that time (though, judging from the specification of La Gacilly's street-cleaning orders of 1887, street sweepings must have been rich in nutrients); it is clear from other evidence, however, that people in the neighbourhood of La Gacilly were already using bone-black and less pure burnt bone mixtures in 1857.[3]

The second half of the nineteenth century saw repeated legislation against fraud in the sale of fertilizers, and minute regulation of prices; La Gacilly was already ordering tests of samples of bone-black and other fertilizer by the Ponts et Chaussées engineer in 1857 and local dealers (one of whom was an innkeeper) were getting their material from the Mayenne as well as near-by Redon at that time.[4] By the 1890s the Station Agronomique was established in Rennes and was active in assessing and chemically testing preparations on sale. Nitrates, phosphates and potash were widely available in Brittany by 1900; it must be likely that the communes of the survey area were using them by the early twentieth century, although perhaps not much before. It is therefore likely that modern chemical fertilizing methods came into the survey area in about 1900, though it should be noted that animal dung still featured as a major fertilizer in the survey of 1929.[5]

Notes

1. AD Morbihan 3ES61/58; I745 (Rapport des commissions sanitaires, pp. 202, 204).
2. Burnt animal bones, rich in phosphate and carbonate of lime, and especially suitable for acid soils.
3. AD Ille-et-Vilaine 7M132; AD Morbihan 3ES61/58.
4. AD Morbihan 3ES61/63.
5. AD Morbihan 6M964; AD Ille-et-Vilaine 7M132; AD Morbihan 7M235, -8, -9.

CHAPTER 3

Context

Geography and geology

The modern administrative region of Brittany occupies most of the northwestern peninsula of France and comprises the four Départements of Finistère, Côtes d'Armor, Morbihan and Ille-et-Vilaine, with its capital located at the inland city of Rennes, not far from the eastern border of the region. In the later middle ages the dukes of Brittany mostly ruled from Nantes, to the south, on the Loire estuary; the southeastern Département of Loire-Atlantique, although in many ways distinctive, has often been associated with Brittany proper, has frequently been the seat of its governmental authority, and continues to provide some metropolitan services for the Morbihan, although it now lies within the French administrative region of Pays-de-Loire. In what follows "Brittany" and "the region" refer to historic Brittany of the traditional five Départements (that is, including Loire-Atlantique), not the modern four (see Fig. 3.5).

Brittany is a peninsula; there is a sense of the sea in many of its landscapes and it has long had a prominent role in the French fishing industry. The land itself has undergone many processes, from human as well as natural agencies: the rocks are well worn and nowadays the traveller will see a land predominantly composed of broad plateaux, mildly undulating and sloping gently to the sea. There are no great heights (the highest "mountain" is less than 400 metres) and such high land as there is concentrates in the west. Although the modern administrative region no longer stretches to the River Loire, the long valley of the Loire defines one of the major inlets of the French land-mass, clearly separating historic Brittany and northwestern France from the lands to the south; on the east,

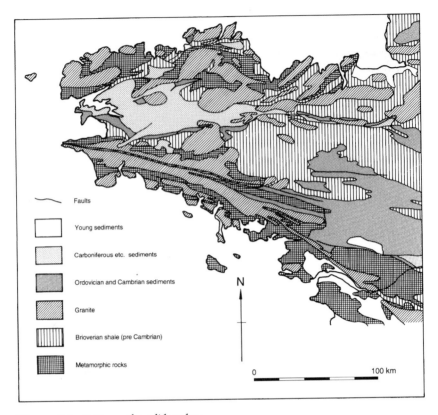

Faults

Young sediments

Carboniferous etc. sediments

Ordovician and Cambrian sediments

Granite

Brioverian shale (pre Cambrian)

Metamorphic rocks

N

0   100 km

Figure 3.1 *Brittany: the solid geology*

however, the peninsula is open, the Rennes basin being a western extension of the Paris basin (Le Lannou 1950–52; Meynier 1976).

Brittany is a land of old rocks, the oldest being the soft-weathering Brioverian (Pre-Cambrian), a silty shale which characterizes much of the peninsula. The Brioverian was intruded by granites and then overlaid with the shales and sands of younger sediments (Ordovician, Cambrian), subsequently toughened into slates and quartzites. Further intrusions of granite and deposits of Carboniferous slates and shales completed the rock succession. Today both the folds of harder rocks and the granite outcrops run largely along west–east alignments, and it is these long lines of low ridging that are the most striking feature as one travels from north to south (Fig. 3.1).

The complex of rock types in Brittany gives rise to very varied soils, from the shallow, stony, dry soils and the humus-iron podsols of the ridges to the deeper brown soils that lie over the softer shales and siltstones in the depressions. These brown soils are particularly susceptible to erosion but their great advantage is that the softness of the parent rock ensures a continuous supply of new material that needs little weathering before it becomes suitable as a growing medium. It has therefore been possible to work and rework this land for centuries. The stony soils and podsols of the ridges, on the other hand, have offered a sustained medium for cultivation only since the advent of twentieth-century machinery and modern fertilizers.

To many visitors, of course, whether modern tourist, early modern traveller or Celtic saint, Brittany is more memorable for its coast than its inland stretches. The peninsula has a long and heavily indented coastline. On the north coast estuaries are long and the tides are strong, retreating for kilometres at Mont-Saint-Michel bay in the northeast, and rising some 14m across the bay at Cancale. Salt marshes still characterize both northeastern and southeastern coasts and this resource, like the other resources of the sea, has been heavily exploited across a long period. In the historic past the coast has therefore always attracted the greatest density of settlement, as it still does today: as Le Guen (1985) pointed out, 50% of the population, in clinging to the coast, lived in a quarter of the territory in the 1980s.

The closeness of the sea influences the climate, which is prevailingly moist, especially in the west, although annual rainfall in Brittany is less than in many other parts of France. It rains little and often, and both drought and flood are uncommon. This is overwhelmingly a mild climate, although it can be very variable in the short term. Heavy frosts, thick snow and long periods of cold are therefore unusual. Winters are relatively warm and summers relatively cool, except on the southeastern coast, where it is both drier and warmer.

Brittany, then, is a land of gently corrugated plateaux with a very long coastline. Inland Brittany has traditionally been characterized as a land of *bocage*, woodland and *landes* – that is, of small enclosed fields, trees and long stretches of uncultivated upland. Nowadays there are a dozen or so small forests but tree cover occupies scarcely 10% of the surface area of the five Départements – less than half the French norm (Le Rhun & Le Quéau 1994: 18–19). In fact, recent environmental study very much suggests that woodland clearance was a fact of prehistory (early prehistory in coastal parts) and that there has been no extensive woodland during historic time (Marguerie 1992). Areas of *bocage* are also more difficult to find nowadays, particularly in view of the fact that there was clearance of field boundaries from the early 1960s (known as *remembrement*, involving the renumbering of properties for the modern tax register, as well as the removal of many banks and hedges); this attempt to consolidate small plots is now seen as

Figure 3.2 *Landes of the Monts d'Arrée; photo: Gwyn Meirion-Jones*

more environmentally damaging than agriculturally useful. But even before these twentieth-century changes, there were some large open arable fields in most parts of Brittany; *bocage* there certainly was, but it is easy to exaggerate its dominance (*Atlas* 1990: 20). The *landes*, by contrast, are well evidenced in the written and physical record and still characterize parts of Brittany like the relatively large expanse of the Landes de Lanvaux in the southeast, as well as smaller zones amid the farmland – heathland with light tree cover, furze, bracken, broom and gorse (Fig. 3.2). It is easy to demonstrate that the *landes* were once far more extensive, but it is misleading to present them as areas of desert and waste, as eighteenth-century commentators were prone to do: they had value and were always an integral part of the rural economy.

The survey area

The survey area lies inland, in the drier third of the peninsula, moist but not too wet for successful cereal cultivation and sheltered from the ocean winds. The core communes lie on Brioverian rock, the shale which breaks and decomposes easily, although there are some sandier areas within the Brioverian (*zones grèseuses*), which vary its silty quality. The predominating shale is sometimes punctuated by quartzose and conglomeratic outcrops, and its soft shaley character is sometimes hardened into a less flaky rock.

To the north and south of the four core communes, near the commune boundaries, the Brioverian is framed by narrow bands of the harder, folded sediments of the Réminiac Syncline to the north and the Malestroit Syncline to the south. Most of the core lies between the 20m and 60m contours; only 20% of fields walked rise above 70m.[1]

The Synclines are constituted, successively, of the blue/pink/purple siltstones of the Cambrian *Formation de Pont-Réan*, the sandstones of the Ordovician *Grès Armoricain*, the hard, black, slatey siltstones of the Ordovician *Formation de Traveusot*, the siltstones of later Ordovician formations and then the quartzites, sandstones and sandy siltstones of the

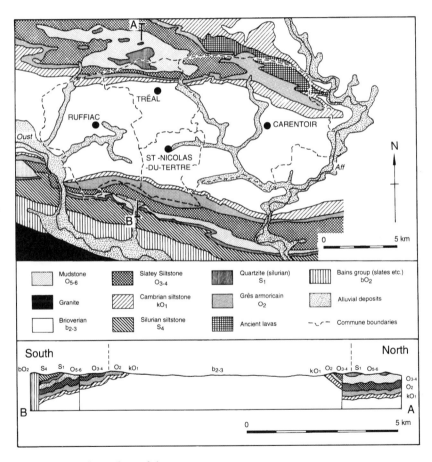

Figure 3.3 *The geology of the core survey area*

Silurian formations (*Carte Géologique* 1981). Two km to the south lie the shales and black slates of the Bains group, and 2 km farther south the granite *massif* of the Landes de Lanvaux itself (Fig. 3.3).

Beyond the core communes, sample Transects M and P run east and west across the Brioverian, until they meet the kilometre or so of alluvial deposits of the Vilaine and Oust valleys themselves. Transect N runs northwest across the upland of harder Cambrian and Ordovician siltstones, sandstones and slates of the Réminiac Syncline; and Transect R runs northeast, quickly crossing the edge of the Syncline before it too meets the Brioverian and runs across it. The sample transects therefore have a similar geological character to the core communes, although Transect N runs over the harder rather than the softer rock types. Transects M, P and R, like the core, lie largely between the 20m and 60m contours, with 5%, 12% and 9% respectively rising above 70m. Transect N, however, is quite different and most of it (71% of fields walked) lies above 70m.

Nowadays, as one might expect, plenty of Brioverian can be seen lying around the surface of the area or in buildings. Very large quantities of Ordovician and Cambrian siltstones (including the distinctive orthostats) are also distributed throughout the survey area, with some smaller amounts of Ordovician and Silurian sandstones and quartzites; slate from the Bains group is common too. Granite, however, is uncommon, except where a granite lintel occurs in a nineteenth- or twentieth-century building or a special granite feature occurs within a building or garden.

Because of the widespread occurrence of the soft shale bedrock, the potential agricultural value of the soils of the core communes and of three of the sample transects may be described as "dominantly excellent". The harder rocks of the higher ground, however, give rise to soils with lower agricultural potential; of these the podsols over the conglomerate are physically the poorest. The soils in low-lying positions are also poor, because they are so often water-logged.

Although nearly two-thirds of modern land-use is arable, the landscape is predominantly open (Fig. 3.4). The *remembrement* movement saw the removal of banks and hedges here as elsewhere in Brittany, especially during the 1970s, although the lines of earlier boundaries are sometimes still marked by low banks or by apple trees; and there were in any case plenty of large open arable fields in the early nineteenth century. In the 1980s the residue of property boundaries was very evident in *remembrement* mounds scattered across the landscape; these are much less evident in the mid '90s and clearance has clearly continued. However, despite the work of modernization and rationalization, there remain many small farming units and the proprietary and tenurial structures are still extremely complex. The practical consequence of this is that, in the mid 1990s, land-use in a large

Figure 3.4 *Arable landscape to the northwest of modern Tréal bourg*

open expanse can change frequently, even every 30 metres, as different farmers choose to grow different crops.

The region in historic time

In order to grasp the place of the survey area in the development of the region, we need some sense of the way Breton history unfolded over the last 2,000 years and of the moments when high politics touched the society and economy of the core communes.

The survey area lies at the eastern edge of the Département of the Morbihan,[2] a unit which reflects the extent of the medieval county of Vannes, and (more approximately) of the diocese of Vannes and the Roman *civitas* of the *Veneti* (see Fig. 3.5). Although there is some debate about the precise line of its early northern boundary, this is a unit which has kept its essential shape over some two thousand years and more. There has been an unusual degree of political continuity in the eastern Départements.

The first millennium

By the standards of the late Iron Age, pre-Roman Brittany seems to have been quite densely populated and numerous monuments survive. Already

39

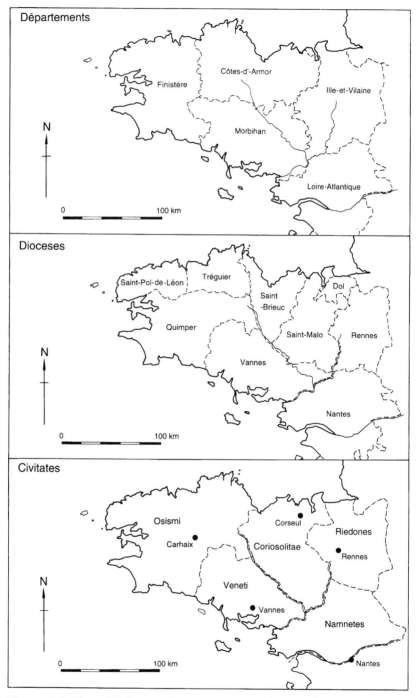

Figure 3.5 *The political geography of Brittany, I, showing départements, dioceses and Roman civitates (after Le Rhun & Le Quéau 1994, Pape 1995)*

in the second century BC the eastern tribes of *Veneti, Riedones* and *Namnetes* were producing coinage, and the western and northern tribes of *Osismi* and *Coriosolitae* followed them within a century. Roman conquest of the peninsula came in 57–56 BC. By the end of the first century AD the administrative structure of *civitates* (based on the five tribes) was in place, with *civitas* capitals at Vannes, Rennes, Nantes, Carhaix and Corseul; a good communication system had also been constructed: three major roads ran from east to west across the peninsula, supplemented by a network of smaller roads (Pape 1995: 21; Galliou and Jones 1991: 80) (see Fig. 4.8). Smaller towns and some industrial production developed; the greatest volume of production was, however, agricultural, as in most other parts of the Roman world, and the elaborate villa complexes which lay at the centre of the production units can be found in much of Brittany.

Roman Brittany suffered political and economic problems in the late third century, with severe raiding in the 270s and 280s. Although defensive action was taken, in the deployment of new troops and the establishment of the coastal forts of the Armorican Shore, our evidence for fourth-century Brittany suggests that it was not nearly as prosperous as in the preceding centuries; many scholars believe that villas were abandoned and that production declined. Local revolts there certainly were and the extent to which villas were abandoned in or before the fourth century, and the time of their abandonment, remains one of the most problematic issues of this period (Galliou 1983: 249–78).

Roman governmental control of Brittany did not survive much beyond the beginning of the fifth century. However, the eastern *civitas* capitals of Rennes, Nantes and Vannes retained their city identities, their bishops, and some political significance, in the succeeding centuries (Fig. 3.5). Although the circumstances and chronology of the migration are far from clear, in the fifth century and possibly before people left the island of Britain to settle in Brittany – so much so that by the late sixth century the peninsula, previously part of the larger northwestern tract of *Aremorica*, had come to be known as Little Britain (*Britannia Minor*). The detail of this major change is completely obscure and we know only that a prominent feature of the history of the very early middle ages was conflict between Britons and Franks – the new rulers of northern France. While Britons went raiding, repeatedly, to the Loire estuary, Franks crossed the River Vilaine and headed for Vannes. Both in the late sixth century and the ninth fighting often came to a head near the Vilaine – indeed, precisely in and around the eastern stretches of the survey's Transect M. The outcome was Frankish conquest, by the Carolingian emperor Louis the Pious, in about AD 820. There followed a period of complex political relationships between Frankish rulers and Breton leaders, of revolt and alliance, with alliance becoming more common in the context of increasing Viking attack. As a result, a Breton ruling family was elevated (whose political centres were at Renac on the Vilaine, 12 km southeast of the Carentoir boundary, and Plélan, 15 km to the north) and the political identity of the peninsula, that is of Brittany, was established. Although Frankish influence dwindled and family fortunes changed, the political experience of the ninth century shaped the framework of politics for the next 600 years.

The central and later middle ages

Having fled from the Vikings to England, the Breton leader Alain Barbetorte returned to lead glorious victories in the late 930s and then, as duke of Brittany, did homage to the king of West Francia (the predecessor of France) in 942. Although technically he held a duchy within the West Frankish kingdom, there was in practice very little contact between Breton duke and French king until the later twelfth century. The Bretons sustained their duchy and exercised a considerable degree of political independence, while the dukes themselves established an important base of landed property – although not without plenty of intra-Breton conflict. The greatest threat to the independence of the region came from the north: ever since the Norman conquest of England in 1066 the Breton dukes had often been closely associated with the Anglo–Norman kings, and some Breton aristocrats (including the duke) had acquired English lands as a consequence of the conquest. In 1156 the English king Henry II took over the county of Nantes and then proceeded to invade the whole of Brittany, confiscating property and taking castles. In the wider context of military conflict between the kings of France and of England, the French king displaced the English interest in Brittany in the early thirteenth century. In 1213 he appointed the Capetian count of Dreux to the duchy of Brittany, whose dukes thereafter acknowledged the French king.

The Dreux dynasty held the duchy for a century and a half and began to develop ducal powers and administrative systems to support them. Civil war over succession to the duchy provoked the personal intervention of both the English and French kings in the mid fourteenth century, and there was heavy campaigning at that time in the Redon–Malestroit–Ploermel region (with the survey area at its heart) and also farther west. Thereafter there was often campaigning in Brittany; both English and French could be involved, but the Breton dukes more frequently supported the French.

The later middle ages seems to have been a time of some significant demographic decline, in the early fifteenth century especially, following famines and epidemics of the previous generations; but it was also a time of notable development of the Breton textile industry, whose products joined the valuable existing trade in salt and wine. This was a period when Breton governmental and municipal institutions developed considerably, the dukes fostering taxation systems which yielded a significant income: not only the *fouage*, the hearth tax levied on the non-noble population (which was annual from 1420), but the sales taxes which reflected the growing commercial prosperity of the region as a whole (cf. Kerhervé 1987: 102–12). At local level, Brittany was divided into eight administrative seneschalcies, which lasted until the Revolutionary period; in the east not only were the leading cities of Vannes, Rennes and Nantes the seats of seneschals but Ploermel – about 12 km northwest of the core survey boundary and only 5 km west of Transect N (see Fig. 3.6) – was too.

Although the Breton *parlement* is first mentioned in 1288, this was not the *parlement de Bretagne* of later history; the word was used to refer both to the *cour de parlement*, a ducal court, and to meetings of the "estates" of clergy, nobles and *bourgeois*. The *états*, although still an institution somewhat dependent on the duke, nevertheless did meet and did consent to taxation, and representatives of the towns regularly joined the two higher estates from the fifteenth century.

The late medieval dukes were powerful, and in effect independent, rulers whose duchy was administered from Rennes, Nantes and Vannes, until focussed in Nantes in the late fifteenth century. Anne became duchess of Brittany in 1488; shortly afterwards she married Charles VIII of France, and then – following his death – Louis XII of France. As a consequence, the duchy was annexed to France in the early sixteenth century.

From Duchess Anne to the French Revolution

Annexation or not, the sixteenth and seventeenth centuries are nowadays seen as the "golden age" of Brittany (Croix 1993). By the late middle ages Brittany's central commercial position – particularly in relation to the oceans – had brought enormous wealth to the region. Francis I of France (1515–47) and his successors appointed governors for Brittany and, from the late seventeenth century, a new kind of royal official, the Intendant. However, despite royal appointment of top officials, until the French Revolution some Breton institutions continued to run as established in the later fourteenth and fifteenth centuries: Breton customary law, for example, continued to be administered; the seneschalcies continued to provide the framework of administration; and meetings of the *états* (a body of under 200 members) continued and became regular, discussing business and policy until January 1789. The Breton *parlement* (based on a small group of 32 *conseillers*) was founded in 1554 as a superior court of justice and continued to meet until 1788. Both *parlement* and *états* were in conflict with the king from time to time (the early 1720s, for example), although the "third estate" (of townspeople) often clashed with the first and second estates of clergy and nobles.

These were no mere high-level activities, unrelated to agricultural life in the parishes. The politics of Brittany touched the survey area both through its nobles who participated in government and – increasingly in the eighteenth century – through the proactive benevolence of government. The *seigneur* of Coëtion (in Ruffiac) was *conseiller au parlement* in 1661, as was the *seigneur* of Peccadeuc (in Carentoir) a century later.[3] Nobles like the Marquis de la Bourdonnaye (Car) played a very active role in the fight against epidemic in the late eighteenth century, supported by some government funds for the purchase of food and meat and the payment of medical officers. By this time the Intendant had representatives in the localities (for example, in Malestroit and Redon) and these *subdélégués* provided a genuine link between parish and government. Officials made regular enquiries into local disasters (like the hailstorms in the summer of 1765 in Carentoir, Ruffiac and Missiriac) and provided assistance to deal with the worst. The late eighteenth century was also a period when government gave attention to major communications, handled for the Intendant by the local sub-delegations. The bridge by the *château* of Bodel (just north of the Ruffiac border) was a constant troublespot in the attempt to improve the route from Rennes to Malestroit, between 1758 and 1782 especially, and there survives a large bundle of letters, complaints and bills for repairs at this spot.[4]

If regional government retained a strongly Breton flavour in the early modern period, and reinforced the sense of Breton identity for the participants, Bretons nevertheless became involved in western European wars. The French Wars of Religion of the late sixteenth century brought the French to fight on Breton soil again and it was at Nantes that the Edict of Toleration, following the end of the Religious wars, was proclaimed (in 1598). The armies of the Catholic League were deployed in the Morbihan in 1592, their leader the duke of Mercoeur moving north from Vannes to Josselin in May of that year in advance of the battle of Craon with the Royalist troops. Many Bretons supported the League, although different towns took different sides: Rennes, for example, was Royalist and Malestroit – partly within the survey's Transect P – was staunchly so. The *bourg* of Malestroit declared for the king in 1589. It was attacked twice in 1591 and in July 1592 was besieged and fell to the League; however, two months later the Royalists arrived to relieve the town, the walls were repaired and the river diverted around the settlement to create an effective defensive system. Malestroit representatives went to the Royalist *États*, meeting in Rennes, at the end of the year.

Although the conversion of the king to Catholicism in 1593 began the series of events which led to the end of the wars in France, the Bretons nevertheless still suffered warfare from time to time in the next 200 years. Civil revolts, like the so-called *papier timbré* revolts of 1675, were disruptive.[5] The English also attacked the coast, particularly in the mid eighteenth century, and this had consequences inland: the men of Malestroit mobilized, for example, when the English attacked Lorient (on the Morbihan coast) in 1746.

After the Revolution

For all the many continuities from the eighteenth into the nineteenth century, there is no denying that the French Revolution was a watershed in Breton as in French history. Properties of the clergy were sold (like the sale of Ruffiac Priory lands and houses in 1790–92); nobles lost their titles and status; and the feudal language of proprietorship was finally abandoned. Fighting in the streets of Rennes in January 1789 gave vent to anti-noble feelings, but although Breton *parlement* and *états* had both been involved, at different levels, in opposition to the French king in 1787–9, there were nevertheless royalist and counter-revolutionary movements in Brittany during the period of the Revolution. There was also some panic and a good deal of suspicion at local level, like the pro-Royalist insurrection at Préclos, in Tréal, imagined by the revolutionary authority in Malestroit in 1791 – an episode which remains strong in local memory (Marsille 1911).[6] The peasant risings of the Chouannerie, though focussed south of the Loire, disturbed the eastern Morbihan in the 1790s: October 1790 saw attacks on enclosures at Sérent (just west of Malestroit), March 1793 saw Redon, Ploermel and Rochefort attacked by guerilla bands, with 165 people subsequently arrested and 33 executed; and in 1796 thousands of guns were surrendered at Josselin, Questembert and Pontivy, to the west of the survey area (Sutherland 1982: 261–3).

Despite the violence, the administrative reforms that came to France with the Revolution came to Brittany too; the network of local communes was created on the basis of the ecclesiastical parish structure in 1790, with groupings of communes in cantons (Fig. 3.6), as the seneschalcies disappeared and were replaced by départements (Fig. 3.5; see further below, pp. 57, 220). At regional level Brittany lost its publicly recognized identity – not regained until the twentieth century – as the ideology of the indivisible Republic began its course.

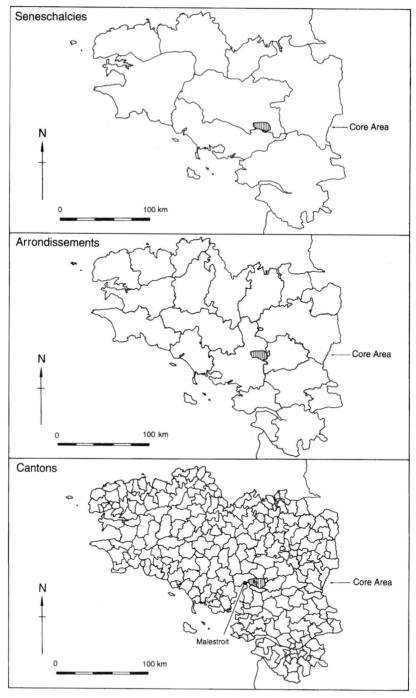

Figure 3.6 *The political geography of Brittany, II, showing seneschalcies, arrondissements and cantons (after La Borderie 1896, Le Rhun & Le Quéau 1994)*

The nineteenth century saw a major collapse in the textile industry and the beginning of the large-scale migration out of Brittany that was to influence mid and later twentieth-century development: over a million Bretons (a third of the population) left the region between 1851 and 1951, a process assisted by the coming of the railway to western Brittany in the 1860s. It also saw a movement, with government encouragement, of sustained *défrichement* of the *landes*: though this had begun in the eighteenth century, between 1850 and 1950 there was a substantial expansion of the arable and, consequently, loss of uncultivated heathland on 25% or so of the land surface. Government initiatives also launched a series of enquiries into the land and people of France, of astonishingly comprehensive detail, and, reaching to the very roots of Breton culture, took action against the Breton language. Instructions to destroy the Breton "idiom" had gone out already in January 1794 (since it was considered incompatible with the unity of the Republic), and laws that education should be conducted only in the medium of French were repeated during the nineteenth century; however, from the 1880s the strategy to exclude every language except French from the schools became effective (a strategy which continued until the 1950s). This was a strongly sustained political programme, from the centre, a key aspect in the drive to consolidate the unity of the French State; government administrators, like the *sous-préfet* of Quimperlé, in 1831, found Brittany utterly alien when they arrived to govern it: "La Basse-Bretagne, je ne cesserai de le dire, est une contrée à part qui n'est plus la France" (Favereau 1993: 128, 145–6).

Despite the onslaught, many Bretons died fighting for France in the First World War, a fact which contributed to the notable demographic decline of the early twentieth century, and many did noble work for the Resistance in the Second World War. Government attitudes did not change until the 1950s, when permission to teach the Breton language was finally given. In 1976 President Giscard d'Estaing chose Ploermel to announce the Charte Culturelle, formally and publicly recognizing the place of regional languages and cultures throughout the French state. By 1990–91 there were about 300,000 Breton speakers and 500,000–600,000 who could understand the language; there are targets for a modest increase in bilingual pupils by the year 2000. While the separatist political movements that surfaced in the late nineteenth century continue, support for them is small-scale. But though that support remains limited, what *has* happened in Brittany in the late twentieth century is the development of mass support (of the order of 80%) for Breton language, culture and identity – *Bretonnitude* – within the French state (Favereau 1993: 124–40).

The region now

Demography

In 1990 the population of France was 56,615,155, that of Brittany 3,847,821 and of the Morbihan 619,945. In 1982 nearly a third of the population of Brittany lived in small villages and hamlets, each with fewer than 50 residents, as against the tenth living in such settlements in the whole of the rest of France. Hence, in the late twentieth century Brittany remains a land characterized by dispersed settlements (Le Rhun & Le Quéau 1994: 22–3).[7]

Notwithstanding the pattern of dispersal, Brittany is traditionally a region of high population, high birth-rate and high fertility – high, that is, relative to the rest of France. In 1990 the Breton population was more dense,[8] at 113 inhabitants per km^2, than that of the rest of France (104 inhab/km^2), although heavily concentrated round the coast (Fig. 3.7) and – it should be said – rather less dense than that of most English counties (see below, p. 52). However, the character of the population is changing: as older Bretons return to retire, younger Bretons go to neighbouring regions and to Paris to work; the population is ageing.

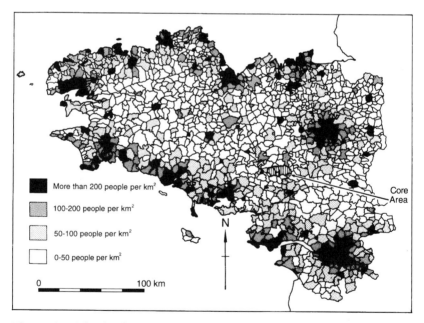

Figure 3.7 *The distribution of population in Brittany in 1990 (after Le Rhun & Le Quéau 1994)*

Between 1954 and 1962 30% of 20-year-olds left the region. The level of out-migration of the young has declined since the '60s, but future trends are uncertain: what happens next depends on a complex of local, national and international factors.

There is of course considerable regional diversity within Brittany, in age-profile as in other demographic aspects. It is in western (Lower) Brittany that the ageing population is most evident. And it is in the centre west and the north that growth rates have been small or negative since 1975, with the higher growth rates focussing on the eastern cities of Rennes and Nantes and their environs. The larger towns have attracted migrants from all over Brittany in the twentieth century, drawing particularly from the western inland communes. The rural/urban balance has therefore changed dramatically since the Second World War, although it was not until 1960 that the size of the urban population overtook that of the rural. Despite substantial urban growth in the mid and late twentieth century, Brittany is still weakly urbanized by French standards: in 1990 only 57% of its population lived in towns as against the national mean of 74%. There are only nine towns with populations over 50,000, and all the large and moderate-sized towns (except Rennes and Pontivy) are coastal (Fig. 3.8).

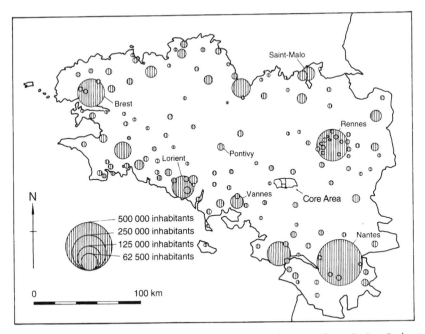

Figure 3.8 *The towns of Brittany in the 1990s (after Le Rhun & Le Quéau 1994)*

Of inland towns, only the two exceptions of Rennes and Pontivy have more than 10,000 inhabitants.

Agriculture

Agriculture remains at the heart of the Breton economy, and of Breton wealth, as it has done for centuries. Notwithstanding a decline in agricultural employment, the intensity of agricultural production has increased considerably, especially in the northwest,[9] and there has been enormous growth in the food-related (agri-food) industries since the 1950s. Seventy-five per cent of French-produced cauliflowers and artichokes come from Brittany, 78% of *crustacés*, 54% of pigs, and 48% of poultry, to name the most prominent cases. As production has increased, the number of farms has reduced by two-thirds and their mean size has accordingly increased; in the 1990s that mean is approaching 30 ha (still small by French standards), although there remain plenty of 1-5 and 5-10 ha units.

Despite the importance of Breton vegetables, in fact a large majority of the agricultural surface is devoted in one way or another to animal products. The most striking change in land-use in Brittany in the twentieth century has been an increase in temporary grassland and in cultivation of animal feedstuffs, coupled with the virtual disappearance of buckwheat, rye and oats. The loss of cereals for human consumption has been replaced by the introduction of maize for cattle and by new products like oil-seed rape. However, in terms of the *value* of the end-products, it is pork, poultry and milk that have the greatest shares, the latter declining in recent years.

Employment

The change in employment patterns (and in people's lives) has been dramatic since the Second World War. Barely 12% of the working population of the region worked in agriculture and fishing in 1990, as against 53% in 1954. (Less than a tenth of this sector worked as fishermen, though this is more than half of the French total.) The number employed in industry grew considerably in the 1980s, particularly in medium-sized towns, and nearly doubled in Côtes d'Armor and the Morbihan; there has also been a modest increase in industrial production, particularly in the neighbourhood of small towns (Philipponneau 1993: 13).[10] The rate of growth of service industry employment has been even more striking, rising from 27% of the population available for work in the region in 1954 to 53% in the 1990s, a higher rate of growth than that of the rest of France. This arises particularly through the activities of the state and the municipalities (educational, medical and social) and of banking, catering, automobile and leisure services. Tourism, alive since the coming of the railways, is important for the region, but it mostly affects a small proportion of – largely coastal – communes. However, the "green" tourism of inland Brittany is on the increase in the '90s.

Bretons said a resounding "yes" to the referendum on the Maastricht treaty in September 1992, proclaiming their support for the new Europe of wider markets, linguistic diversity and regional opportunity (Fig. 3.9). Many Bretons now see the third millennium as a period when they will look outwards while retaining their distinctive cultural identity.

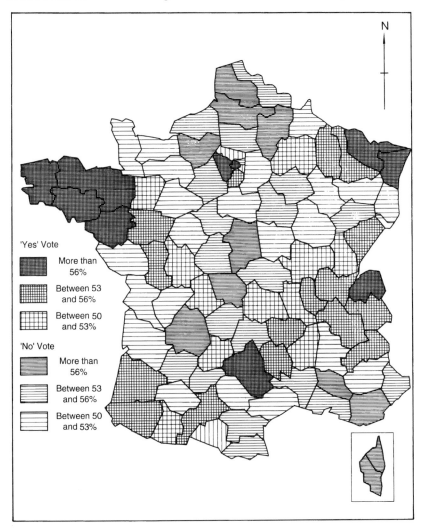

Figure 3.9 *The "yes" vote, 1992 (after Ouest France 1992)*

51

The survey area

Lying in the centre south of the peninsula, the Morbihan has a more positive demographic profile than some other parts of the region. In 1990 it had the highest fertility rate of the five Départements and was less characterized by an ageing population than some western areas.

The survey area, lying inland, demonstrates population growth, if at low rates. Density of population is well below the mean, at 43, 41, 39 and 33 inhab/km^2 respectively for Carentoir, Ruffiac, Saint-Nicolas and Tréal in 1990. Sample transects N and R have even lower densities, M a little higher, and P – being in the neighbourhood of Malestroit – considerably higher (see above, p. 9, n.1). These levels compare with, for example, south Shropshire and west Devon in 1991, at 40 inhab/km^2, although it should be noted that both these English regions are well below their county means of 120 and 150 inhab/km^2 respectively.

Despite the current very modest growth in the survey area, all four core communes have exhibited the long decline in inland rural population of the twentieth century (see Fig. 10.1). Carentoir's population was as high as 4,069 in 1896 (its highest during the period of regular census returns); Ruffiac 1,877 and Tréal 1,179 in 1906 (their highest); and Saint-Nicolas 724 in 1901 (its highest). By 1975 Carentoir had suffered a reduction of nearly a half to 2,355, Ruffiac was down by a quarter to 1,478, Tréal down nearly a half to 637, with Saint-Nicolas down a third to 504. Ruffiac and Saint-Nicolas continued to drop through the 1980s, Tréal remained stable, while Carentoir rose a little (INSEE n.d.; INSEE 1990).

The survey area is – obviously – rural and the towns just beyond the western and southern extremities of the core are very small (that is, Malestroit at the western end of Transect P and La Gacilly now 1½ km south of the Carentoir border). Malestroit, although quite densely populated, had no more than 2,502 inhabitants in 1990 and La Gacilly had 2,269. 15 km farther to the south lies Redon, with 9,260 inhabitants in 1990; 12 km to the north of the Ruffiac border (and 5 km west of Transect N) is Ploermel, with 6,996 inhabitants; 6 km to the north of the Carentoir border (and 3 km west of Transect R) is Guer, with 5,800 inhabitants; and the departmental capital of Vannes, with just over 50,000, is 35 km away to the southwest (see Fig. 3.8). The nearer towns (especially La Gacilly) have some influence on the employment pattern of the survey area and provide some services, but none of these is large or near enough to influence the organization of the countryside itself – there is no "periurbanization" here.[11] However, the facelift given to Carentoir and Tréal centres since 1991 reflects the new policy of the canton, and of the mayor of La Gacilly and *conseiller général* in particular, to develop rural amenities (Philipponneau 1993: 370–71).

The Morbihan has seen some of the most successful industrial development of the last generation, particularly in rural communes, and this growth continued through the 1980s without the levelling-off experienced in Brittany as a whole; the increase has continued in Vannes, Ploermel and La Gacilly; and in the survey area and its surround, from Redon to Ploermel, Yves Rocher has created 14 new establishments (perfume and toiletry factories), employing some 3,000 people locally. One – a small one – is in Carentoir.

The Morbihan's rate of growth in tertiary sector employment since 1954 has been spectacular (134%). While its flourishing tourist industry is concentrated on the coast, some of the greatest volume of Breton river tourism travels up the Oust, passing through Malestroit.

In agriculture, Ruffiac, Saint-Nicolas, Tréal, Carentoir and the sample transects have their due share of the Morbihan's large number of pig units, which are common all over. Poultry units are also extremely common, though more so in western communes and less so in eastern, especially in Transect M. Cattle-farming is at one of the highest levels in Brittany, especially in Carentoir (> 175 cattle per 100 ha in 1988) and rather less high in Transect M. Much of the survey area has shared with other inland areas the shift away from cereal domination since 1955. In fact, cereal cultivation still predominated in Carentoir, Tréal and Transect R in 1988; but it was animal fodder that predominated in Ruffiac, Saint-Nicolas, Transect P and Transect M; and cereals *and* permanent grassland in Transect N (Canévet 1991: 170–71).

Despite the prominence of animal products, these are communes of mixed farming regime, without striking specializations or very intensive use – unlike many parts of inland Brittany – although Saint-Nicolas had a higher degree of intensive production in the late '80s (Le Rhun & Le Quéau 1994: 81). There is a milk product factory at Malestroit but the area otherwise has no big agricultural co-operatives and no big agro-industrial producers. It remains a zone of small, independent farmers and still has a significant proportion of small farms – the mean size of farms in the core in 1988 was 17–21 ha, well below the Breton mean (Canévet 1992: 327).

Although the populations have declined over the nineteenth and twentieth centuries – in characteristic inland fashion – there has not been the major shift to employment in service and other industries that has marked some other localities. In Carentoir 61% of the population available for employment in 1990 worked in the commune; but in Ruffiac only 50%; in Tréal 44%; and in Saint-Nicolas 45% (INSEE 1990). Although agriculturally dominated, significant proportions of the working population of these communes now go outside to work. Moreover, the communes are well placed for future employment opportunities: they lie within easy range (in today's mobile world) of Malestroit, La Gacilly, Guer, Ploermel and Redon, and within working range of Vannes and Rennes; and they lie in a region eligible for EU development assistance (Le Rhun & Le Quéau 1994: 204–9). That there is plenty of potential for the future is emphasized by the success of the five brothers of Carentoir – still in their 30s – who have developed a software business with an international clientele.

Notes

1. Contours are here (and below) related to our fieldwalking statistics (Davies & Astill 1994); given the ubiquitous ploughing of upland in the late twentieth century, these are a fair reflection of the overall topography.

2. Virtually all of Transect M and all of Transect R lie in western Ille-et-Vilaine.

3. AD Ille-et-Vilaine 3H193; *ibid.* 3H189 (1761) and Tréal BMS 1762.

4. AD Ille-et-Vilaine C1353 (epidemics); C3909 (calamities); C2370 and 2348 (roads).

5. The revolts were sparked off by a government requirement that all public acts be recorded on special paper or parchment, a requirement that had considerable cost implications for the population.

6. A rumour that M. de la Ruée of Préclos was plotting an insurrection reached Malestroit. Forces were sent out; there was shooting; and 37 people were arrested at the *château du Préclos* on 29 June 1791. Nothing came of it.

7. In this paragraph, as in the whole of the last section of this chapter, we are indebted to the collection of data in the excellent collaborative publication, Le Rhun & Le Quéau 1994, as also to other recent works emanating from Skol Vreizh.

8. "Breton" population here and below refers to the whole population of Brittany, not just the Breton-speaking population.

9. The revenue per Breton farm was slightly higher than the French mean in 1991 (102:100) but the mean conceals the regional diversity, with the Finistère index at 132 but that of the Morbihan and Ille-et-Vilaine at 85 (Le Rhun and Le Quéau 1994: 82–3).

10. The relative employment share of the different sectors in 1990 was: agriculture and fishing 12.5%; industry 19%; building and public works 7.5%; the tertiary sector (i.e. commerce, transport, public and other non-market services) 61% (Philipponneau 1993: 16).

11. See Le Rhun & Le Quéau 1994: 170–71, where the influence of middle-class people is seen to displace that of agricultural workers on rural councils, leading to changes in the visible landscape of the communes and in local amenities – for less than 10 km round the smaller towns and 25–30 km round great cities like Rennes. Contrast the appearance of the *bourg* of the rural commune of Saint-Avé, 4 km from Vannes, with that of Ruffiac.

A note on parishes and communes

The administrative geography of the survey area has changed over time, but there were groupings that expressed local community identities already in the ninth century and there have been strong continuities since then.

In the ninth century there were *plebes*: groups of people, primarily units of civil association, with responsible officers such as machtierns and priests, each with a clear sense of identity; the word *plebs* referred to the territory inhabited by the group as well as to its population, a territory of the order of 40–50 km^2 (large parish size); it was common for a church to be associated, giving the *plebs* an ecclesiastical dimension too (see further below, pp. 92–3). Many of the present-day communes of the survey area were *plebes* in the ninth century: Carentoir and Ruffiac; Caro, Augan and Campénéac in Transect N; Comblessac in Transect R; Sixt, Pipriac and Guipry in Transect M.

The moment of creating the ecclesiastical parishes, with the full apparatus of tithe and baptismal rights, is usually obscure, but most of the *plebes* were clearly parishes by the eleventh or twelfth century (see Vallerie 1986: 83–7, 105–6, for some suggestions about origins). The early parish of Ruffiac included the present territories of Tréal, Saint-Nicolas-du-Tertre and Saint-Laurent; and that of Carentoir included La Gacilly, Quelneuc and La Chapelle Gaceline (Fig. 3.10). Tréal became a separate parish in the central middle ages, perhaps as early as the eleventh century, although its boundaries were not quite those of the modern commune: part of eastern Ruffiac lay in Tréal in the early sixteenth century; Saint-Laurent became a parish *c.*1422, while Saint-Nicolas became a *trève* of Ruffiac in 1576 (i.e. an annex to a parish, with a separate church) and a separate parish in 1802. (In

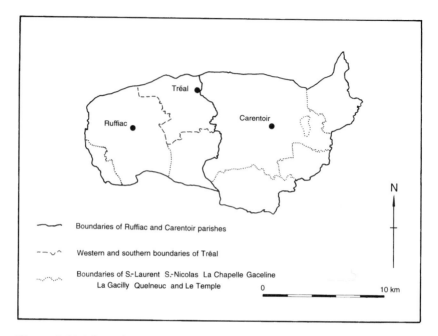

Figure 3.10 *The early parishes of Carentoir and Ruffiac*

effect, Saint-Nicolas seems to have functioned as a separate parish from the sixteenth century, with its own *bourg* too.) La Gacilly, Quelneuc and La Chapelle Gaceline were all *trèves* of Carentoir, as also La Haute Boixière (by La Bourdonnaye *château*) in the eighteenth century, and all but La Haute Boixière became separate parishes, in 1802, 1842 and 1844 respectively. The small zone of Le Temple *within* eastern Carentoir (including the hamlets of La Gilardais, Le Bois Faux, Le Haut du Bourg, Le Bourgneuf de Haut and Le Bourgneuf de Bas, Le Chauffaut, La Porte Juhel and Les Landes) was a separate parish from 1387: this arose because a community of Knights Templar was established at Le Temple in the twelfth century, which became the centre of an important Commandery in the early fourteenth (see below, p. 119).

While it is possible that Bruc in Transect M was a *plebs* as early as the ninth century, it was certainly called a *vicaria* in the early twelfth century, a reference that could well derive from a late ninth-century text, and was certainly a parish by the twelfth (Planiol 1893–4). Réminiac in Transect N and Les Brûlais in Transect R became parishes in the central medieval period and 1820 respectively. Malestroit (at the end of Transect P) became a separate parish from Missiriac in the later twelfth century, but was re-united with it in 1432, to be re-established as a separate parish in 1802.

The modern civil administrative structure of communes was created at the time of the French Revolution. Hence, Tréal, Saint-Nicolas, Ruffiac, Carentoir, La Gacilly and the then parishes of the sample transects became communes in 1790. So did Le Temple, but it soon gave up separate commune status and joined Carentoir in 1802. The parishes of Quelneuc and La Chapelle Gaceline acquired separate communal status in, respectively, 1863 and 1874 (Fig. 3.10).

In 1790 the Morbihan was divided into nine "districts", themselves divided into cantons; Ploermel district included a canton of Caro, which included the communes of Ruffiac and Saint-Nicolas (Kerrand 1988); the district of Rochefort included a canton of Carentoir, which included the communes of Carentoir and Tréal. Districts were abolished in 1800 and *arrondissements* were in place by 1801 (see Fig. 3.6); at that time the number of cantons was also reduced and Ruffiac and Saint-Nicolas went into Malestroit canton (see Fig. 3.6); Carentoir remained head of its canton until 1837, when La Gacilly became the civil head.

The four core communes therefore now lie in two different cantons, Carentoir and Tréal in La Gacilly, and Ruffiac and Saint-Nicolas in Malestroit; all four now lie in the *arrondissement* of Vannes, although Ruffiac and Saint-Nicolas were in the *arrondissement* of Ploermel in the nineteenth century.

Part 2

Changing land-use in the landscape of east Brittany

CHAPTER 4

Romans and provincials

Although we did not set out to study prehistory, fieldwork generated some new and interesting prehistoric data; what happened in the later Iron Age, in particular, has a major bearing on the early historic period and is an essential preface to the "Romans" (Davies & Astill 1994: 229–34, 269–71).

Prehistory

The surviving data in the survey area for the earlier prehistoric periods comprise some worked flints and prehistoric monuments, which appear to have a late Neolithic date centring on the third millennium BC. One kilometre to the south of Transect M there is a remarkable concentration of monuments around Saint-Just (Ille-et-Vilaine), where there are at least five groups of menhirs and eight megalithic graves; recent fieldwork has demonstrated that this was a place of considerable significance in inner Armorica during the Neolithic era (Le Roux et al. 1989; Briard et al. 1995: 146–52). In most of the communes of the survey area, however, no more than a single menhir or megalithic grave is recorded, although those to the north and northwest of the core, in or near Transect N, have noticeably more: three gallery and one lateral-entry grave, and a menhir, at Caro; a menhir, an alignment and at least three graves in Monteneuf; two (perhaps three) graves in Augan and one in Campénéac (Gouézin 1994: 48–50, 78–80, 39–40, 47). There is a standing stone near Digoit (Ruff) in the core, but although total collection was made from the surrounding field (L500) and the field 250m to the east of it (L26), no worked flint was recovered, although some quartz which may have been worked was noted.[1]

The surviving megalithic graves – like the lateral-entry grave at Sigré in Carentoir, or the large graves at Augan, or the grave recently excavated at Beaumont (Saint-Laurent-sur-Oust) – are of a type and size which could well have had some significance for the majority of the population in the third millennium BC. Both menhirs and graves tend to be sited in dominant positions on higher land, visible from some distance, often in areas which were later to become *lande* (although the menhirs at La Minardais in Carentoir and Bodel in Caro were on the upper (pasture) slopes of stream valleys).

While their precise function continues to be debated, the menhirs clearly reflect human use of the land surface, a point also demonstrated by recent analyses of pollen cores (Giot et al. 1979: 407–8). Dated pollen sequences from the Landes de Lanvaux, the wetlands near Redon and the Saint-Just area all show that these places were heavily wooded in the early and middle Neolithic; but in late Neolithic times we have the first significant evidence of clearance (Marguerie 1992: 234–5; Marguerie 1995).

The fact that some flintwork was picked up on some 60% of total collection fields – in a range of different topographic locations – is testimony to the widespread exploitation of the survey area in the Neolithic and Bronze Ages. Most zones within this area were, or could have been, subject to human control at that time, that is, at a date millennia before the start of the historic period. While most of the flint assemblage itself is undatable, the few diagnostic elements suggest a late Neolithic/early Bronze-Age date. The occurrence of flint is rare; but flint was scarce in the interior of Brittany, and the excavation of the grave at Beaumont confirms the use of local *grès* as an alternative in this area (Tinevez 1988). Despite this use of local stone, material was obtained from a wide geographical range, from river gravels and coastal areas of Brittany, Plussulien (Côtes-d'Armor) and perhaps Montbert (Loire-Atlantique), as well as from Grand Pressigny in the Touraine (Tingle 1994: 230–31).[2]

In common with many parts of eastern Brittany, there is little settlement evidence to discuss other than to note that two fields, L80 (near Kerhal, Ruff) and H132 (beside Le Château de la Ruée), yielded relatively large quantities, and a wide variety (in terms of cores and flakes), of worked flint, including an arrowhead and a worked piece of local metamorphic stone in the shape of an axe (L80). The worked stone did not cluster on the surface of H132.[3]

From the end of the third millennium BC there is prolific evidence for the exploitation of mineral resources in Armorica, especially tin and lead, particularly from the west and centre of the peninsula. The distribution of metal artefacts shows that the region was in touch with other areas of Atlantic Europe, a network lasting at least until the eighth century BC. In the middle Bronze Age production and use of bronze increased, as indicated by the vast number of metalwork hoards, and also spread eastwards (Giot et al. 1995: 27–197).

Although coastal areas seem to have been most touched by external contacts, there is increasing evidence that the interior, including the survey area, was also affected. In Campénéac megaliths were re-used at the beginning of the second millennium to create a large early Bronze-Age tomb; stones from a megalithic alignment were used to form a similar grave at Saint-Just, and a dolmen was re-used for burial (Briard 1989: 29–40; Le Roux et al. 1989; Briard et al. 1995). In Augan a middle Bronze-Age gold torque, as well as a late Bronze-Age hoard of 200 socketed axes, has been discovered (Giot et al. 1995: 57, 95, 114, 186; Briard 1989: 114–19). There seem to have been wealthy people living in and around Transect N at this time.

Later prehistory

The later prehistoric periods, that is the later Bronze and Iron Ages, can be recognized both in the ceramic record and from excavated features in the survey area.

The prehistoric pottery falls into two chronological groups: fabrics which are probably of late Bronze-Age/early Iron-Age date (Fabrics 86 and 150), and those which are of later Iron-Age date but also regularly occur with early Roman wares (Fabrics 13, 14, 15, 30, 31 and 45). All appear to be local products (Davies & Astill 1994: 172–8). Sites from three potentially distinct periods of settlement and land-use have been identified: later Bronze-Age/early Iron-Age, later Iron-Age and later Iron-Age/Roman; and half of the 12 excavated sites produced occupation evidence from one or more of these phases, mainly consisting of pits and ditches (Davies & Astill 1994).

Excavation of B409 (Le Bois Guillaume, Car) produced three phases of Iron-Age occupation, each of a different character. An agricultural phase was followed by one of pit digging, perhaps to quarry the underlying mudstone, and finally the area was covered by a dump, probably the remains of a collapsed wall or bank. Of the excavated pottery 38% was pre-medieval, and the vast majority of this (some 31% of the total) was of the earlier Iron-Age Fabric 86; 6% was later Iron-Age and 1% Roman. The occupation phases thus appear to be associated with the late Bronze/early Iron Ages, and the later material may have been brought on to the site in the course of cultivation, particularly when a Roman villa 250m to the southeast was flourishing (Fig. 4.1); the Roman pottery decreased with depth.[4]

Figure 4.1 *Superimposed ?Roman enclosures beside La Touche au Roux (Car), from the west; photo: Maurice Gautier*

The results of this excavation suggest some settlement desertion or shift *during* the Iron Age and the reversion of the occupation area to agricultural use, certainly during the Roman period, and probably in the later Iron Age.

The later Iron Age

Excavation has demonstrated later Iron-Age occupation in three cases; there were notable amounts of the earlier Fabrics 86 and 150, although it was rarely possible to associate these wares with excavated features and therefore postulate early Iron-Age occupation on the same sites. At K445/446 (Béculeu, Ruff), 43% of the total pottery assemblage was prehistoric. Fourteen per cent of the total was prehistoric at A116 (Les Viviers, Ruff) and in the near-by lynchets (T1 and T2). In T1, a trench through a large lynchet, the pottery in the lowest colluvium indicates Iron-Age cultivation, and perhaps the cutting of the boundary ditch at the base of the lynchet, and thus by implication some setting out of fields.

In the trenched field H80 (La Hattaie, Ruff), prehistoric pottery constituted 78% of the total excavated assemblage; the fills of two pits contained Fabrics 86 and 150 only, suggesting earlier prehistoric occupation. Since this site produced extensive later Iron-Age evidence, continuity of occupation during the Iron Age is clearly possible.

Evidence for later Iron-Age land-use and settlement mainly consists of ditches. At H80 the excavations located the periphery of a later Iron-Age settlement, as shown by large pits with building debris (daub, tile and siltstone), with an extensive network of associated field ditches to the east. The evidence from A116 is more limited because the features were buried under 0.7m of colluvium, but they contained small quantities of both earlier and later Iron-Age pottery. The intercutting ditches could have been field boundaries, or alternatively residues from human settlement or animal folds, given that high phosphate concentrations were recorded without a correspondingly high quantity of any later group of pottery.

Both sites, and also K445/446, demonstrate some kind of continuing use during the whole of the Iron Age. Further, and most significantly, there are two kinds of evidence suggesting the desertion of these settlements (like B409 above) in the later Iron Age. Firstly, the proportion of Roman pottery from all the sites is very small; it is not associated with tile scatters; and it comes from surface collection not excavation. Since the majority of the Roman material occurs only on the surface, it is best interpreted as manuring debris: the earlier settlement sites must have become fields. Secondly, since excavation located Iron-Age ditches, any long-term continuity of settlement or land-use should have been shown either by the ditches being recut or by the appearance of Roman pottery in the upper fills of the ditch silt. Neither occurred. Since the late Iron-Age fabrics and forms found on H80 also occur at the near-by Roman site of A92 (Les Landes de la Ruée, Ruff), it looks as if the change of use occurred in the later first century BC, in the context of the "Romanization" of the area.

Late Iron-Age and early Roman ceramics overlap at A92, but Iron-Age and Roman scatters do not often coincide; this may be an additional indication of settlement disruption. Some similar results come from other parts of eastern Armorica: an aerial photographic survey in the Rennes basin, linked with some fieldwalking, has shown a very low coincidence (3%) between enclosures interpreted as of Iron-Age and those of Roman date (Provost & Priol 1991: 70, 76). This should not be seen as a sudden "rupture" associated with the trauma of Roman conquest: most of the evidence from eastern Armorica indicates that the abandonment and relocation of settlements took place over some time (Pape 1995: 107); while the process of Romanization clearly modified the settlement hierarchy and some settlement form, its full effects may have taken 200 years to become apparent. The occurrence of Roman *tegulae* on a bare 12% of "later Iron-Age" enclosures, for example, suggests that Romanization was a slow and perhaps incomplete process (Daire et al. 1991: 177–8).

The sequence from A31/79 (Le Petit Madou, Ruff) makes this long-term point. Here, there was a trace of late Bronze-/early Iron-Age activity, for a few sherds were of Fabrics 86 and 150 (8% of the prehistoric pottery, itself 20% of the excavated assemblage). This was followed by a sustained period of agricultural use, demonstrated by ditch systems and a possible lynchet, starting in the late Iron Age and continuing into the early Roman period.

By contrast, excavation at A92 clearly demonstrated the existence of a substantial Roman settlement occupied from the late first century BC until the second century AD, and perhaps later (see Fig. 4.7). The field also yielded some unstratified late Iron-Age pottery (16% of the excavated assemblage), some of which was similar in fabric and form to the material excavated from the purely Iron-Age H80, 1 km to the east. There is no indication of Iron-Age occupation at A92 but there is a ditched enclosure 250m to the northeast which may locate an Iron-Age settlement (Fig. 4.2); it is likely that farming introduced the Iron-Age material on to A92 before the construction of the Roman villa.

The same sequence is suggested by six total collections: A159, B282/283, B324, D61, D142 and D221. In all these cases a small proportion of later Iron-Age pottery was recorded, ranging from 0.01 to 0.1 sherds per 5m square, and a larger quantity of Roman pottery with brick and tile. The implication is that Iron-Age arable fields became Roman settlement sites.

Figure 4.2 *A ditched enclosure northeast of Les Landes de la Ruée (Ruff), from the south; a double-ditched trackway is visible just to the north of the enclosure; photo: Maurice Gautier*

In other cases, it looks as if fields farmed in the later Iron Age continued to be farmed in the Roman period: 19 intensively walked fields had small quantities of both later Iron-Age and Roman pottery (average 0.001–0.01 sherds per square); where excavated, the quantities of pottery declined with depth, and none of the fields had Iron-Age or Roman features.

Wider perspectives

Firstly, the significance of surface material: in view of the low survival rate of friable prehistoric pottery on the surface, and the depth of soil which often masks Iron-Age deposits, the occurrence of small numbers of prehistoric sherds on the surface could be regarded as an indication of underlying prehistoric occupation. However, the presence of surface material does not invariably point to the date or presence of underlying features. On four sites small proportions on the surface (respectively 0.01, 0.1, 0.01, 0.03 sherds per 5m square) decreased with depth on excavation;[5] indeed, no prehistoric pottery at all was recovered from H132 and G74 excavations, even though relatively large amounts were found on the surface of G74 (La Métairie au Joly, Car). Since other fields with small surface quantities *did* produce occupation evidence (A116, H80 and K445/446), it has to be said that crude surface quantities of Iron-Age pottery are no sure guide to sub-surface features.

The *character* of the assemblages, on the other hand, can be important. Total collection from A91 (Bernan, Ruff) yielded an assemblage in which nearly a quarter of the pottery was prehistoric, and 6% Roman. Since the assemblage included domestic debris such as a distinctive loom weight, two spindle whorls, a whetstone and 11 fragments of granite millstones, this is sufficient to propose a late Bronze-Age/early Iron-Age settlement continuing through the Iron Age, and perhaps into the early Roman period.

While there is little justification for attempting an interpretation of the overall distribution of prehistoric material, given the rarity of its recovery in transect-walking, there certainly tends to be more found near the north of the core; further, nine of the 14 findspots of later Iron-Age pottery in Transect N are within 2 km of the northern commune boundary of Ruffiac, and there is a large promontory fort (*oppidum*) near Le Mur, on the edge of northeast Carentoir. The high ridge which forms the southern boundary of Ruffiac, Saint-Nicolas and Carentoir was devoid of pottery finds, as was the low-lying area to the south of Ruffiac *bourg* (Fig. 4.3). Only one field in each of the sample Transects R and P produced any Iron-Age pottery, but seven did in Transect M; two fields in M (M262, M527, both near Le Hil and not far from the Château de la Boulaye, Bruc) are

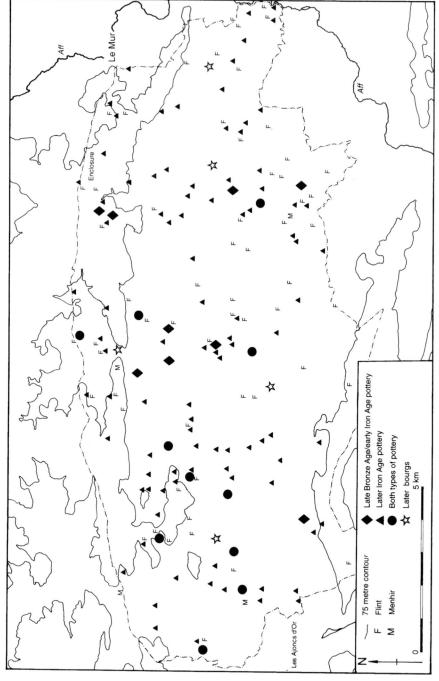

Figure 4.3 *Distribution of prehistoric material in the core survey area*

notable for producing more Iron-Age and more Roman fabrics than any field in the core.

Although we cannot recover the complete Iron-Age distribution pattern, it is clear that prehistoric material is found in the full range of topographic zones of the survey area. Material is not exclusively found in the main arable areas of the historic period (indeed the subsequent colluvial deposits bias the sample against these zones), but is found in areas that were *landes*, and on high ridges as well as valley bottoms. Moreover, the zones where no prehistoric material was found are topographically no different from those where Iron-Age material *was* collected. This does not have to mean that the survey area was fully exploited, but it does mean that by this time different ecological zones had been brought into use: the medieval pattern can be glimpsed in its infancy in the first century BC.

The distribution of material derived from Iron-Age fields and settlements leaves next to no room for any extensive tracts of woodland, let alone forest. The pollen sequences from the Landes de Lanvaux and the Redon area in fact indicate increased clearance and continued expansion of arable in the Iron Age (Marguerie 1992: 237–8); and the sequences from near-by Beaumont (Saint-Laurent) suggest that the *lande* was forming in the later Iron Age, as a direct result of these processes (*ibid*.: 194; cf. Visset 1994: 4, on Kerfontaine (Sérent), just to the west of the Oust). The same expansion is indicated in the survey area by fields like H11, north of La Thiolais (Ruff). This field produced a notable quantity of later Iron-Age pottery (0.1 sherds per 5m square) but no historic-period material. This must mean that the field was uncultivated in the middle ages, and we know it was *lande* in the early nineteenth century. A new area of cultivation of the later Iron Age was therefore not sustained into the historic period.

Recent aerial survey has extended knowledge of the character of later Iron-Age settlement in Brittany, with the recording, and sometimes excavation, of roughly curvilinear enclosures; typically they have an area of less than 1 ha (Giot et al. 1995: 258–61; Daire et al. 1991: 168–9). Within the survey area parts of several ditched enclosures have been recorded as cropmarks, similar to enclosures noted in other areas of Armorica. Two such enclosures have been observed in north Carentoir, at Les Landriais and Le Bois Faux; one partial enclosure is recorded from Transect R at Les Croix in Comblessac, and another in Transect M, at La Ville Janvier in La Chapelle Gaceline; there is a further enclosure in Transect N, in Augan, located, like many of these, on a ridge;[6] more were recorded during flights in 1995 and 1996. A rescue excavation of another Augan enclosure recently took place in advance of road construction at Bellevue, 4.5 km to the east of Transect N. It demonstrated a ditched enclosure dated to the mid third century BC, revealed as part of a larger settlement by aerial photography. In the mid second century the enclosed settlement was rearranged but occupation ceased after the second century BC (SRAB 1993: 22–7). The material assemblage from the excavation was extremely sparse, an interesting result when one remembers the paucity of surface prehistoric material throughout our survey area.

The re-establishment of contacts across the continent after the Bronze Age seems to have taken a long time. It is not until the late second century BC that the increasing occurrence of imported Italian *amphorae* shows that the region was being drawn into a Roman commercial network (Galliou 1990). That this was part of a more profound change, political as well as economic, within Iron-Age Armorican society is suggested by the introduction of tribal coinages, first among the *Veneti*, *Riedones* and *Namnetes*, and then the *Coriosolitae* and *Osismi*. An Iron-Age hoard of some 600 coins has been found at La Tenille (Pipriac), in Transect M – overwhelmingly of the *Veneti*, with some coins of the *Riedones* and *Pictones* too – indicating some participation in the development, at least in the eastern parts of the survey area (Pape 1995: 138–9).[7] However, no imported or fine wares of Iron-Age date have been recovered from any part of the survey area; and the most recent distribution maps of imported Italian *amphorae* show blanks not only for the survey area itself but also for the middle and lower reaches of the rivers Vilaine and Oust (Galliou & Jones 1991: 57). This suggests that not all parts of Armorica were equally influenced by long-distance contacts.

The Iron-Age ceramic assemblages from the survey area are very local in origin. The sources of the stone which was used during this period – the mudstones (B409) and the siltstones (H80) – are also very local and are all derived from within it. This is a marked contrast with the earlier prehistoric period when worked stones were brought in from Plussulien, the coastal regions and the Touraine, and with the succeeding (Roman) period when again a greater diversity of stone was used and pottery was imported.

Roman settlement

Our knowledge about land-use and settlement in the survey area during the Roman period is based largely on the detailed information derived from excavation and total collections.

Two Roman sites were sample excavated, A92 and A31/79. Total collection from A92, near Les Landes de la Ruée, located a concentration of tile over an area of some $11,700m^2$, on the extreme northern edge of the field, on a ridge (see Fig. 4.7); the concentration clearly extended farther north, at least over the rest of the ridge (and under a track), as cropmarks have recently confirmed (Fig. 4.4).

Despite extensive plough damage, the excavations produced a sequence of early Roman ditches which had been sealed by a thick destruction level of Roman building material, in particular tile and large stone blocks, some of which had been dressed. Field A92 is therefore hard by a substantial Roman building or buildings. The tile assemblage not only included roofing tiles, but also flue tiles and thick floor tiles or hypocaust *pilae*. The

Figure 4.4 *A ?Roman enclosure on the ridge to the east of Les Landes de la Ruée (Ruff), from the west; photo: Maurice Gautier*

Roman pottery assemblage included some 32% of imports, 5% of Central and Southern Gaulish samian and the remainder of *terra nigra*. Local fine or table wares, including bowls and flagons, increased the total of table wares in the assemblage to 44%. The quality of the material culture would therefore point to this site being a villa, that is a substantial house at the centre of a large farm.

Three neighbouring fields were transect-walked (A93, A94, H74) and these produced a significant amount of tile (over 1 kg each), associated with Roman pottery (see Fig. 4.7). These tile scatters allow us to estimate the minimum extent of the settlement: approximately 5.5 ha. Fieldwalking in Transect P, around Bermagouet, where previously a bath-house had been excavated, also produced a scatter of tile about 5 ha across, clearly indicating its status as a similarly large villa (Sanquer 1977: 346–7).

The other "Roman" excavation site – A31/79, near Le Petit Madou – appears to be peripheral to the actual Roman settlement. The excavated sequence was: a late Iron-Age/early Roman phase of agriculture, shown by a series of field or enclosure ditches, and then another phase of ditches and pits which were filled with settlement debris, brick, tile and stone, presumably from a demolished building. There may thus have been some rearrangement of the settlement, the focus of which lay to the west of A31/79, at a time when the majority of the fields and enclosures remained in use.

There was a significant similarity between the pottery assemblages from both Roman sites. A high proportion of the 16 Roman fabrics which have been identified for the survey area was found in the excavations, 10 and 12 fabrics for A31/79 and A92 respectively. The proportion of imported wares, 32%, was the same, although A31/79 had a higher proportion of Central and Southern Gaulish samian (12%, compared with 9%) and local fine and table wares (16%, compared with 12%); both sites thus had a pronounced element of fine or table wares. The building debris from both was also similar in character. The stratified tile from A31/79 not only included roofing fragments but also floor and probably flue and *pilae* tile. The building stone, which demonstrated that new sources of harder stone were exploited in this early Roman period, was mainly quartzite, but quartz, granite, conglomerate and sandstone were also present. The assemblage from A31/79 is therefore of a similar, villa-like character to that from A92.

Although tile scatters might in theory be of post-medieval to modern date, where Roman pottery is associated with a concentration of tile it must be likely that such scatters represent settlement debris of the Roman period (as demonstrably the case at A92). Surface finds of Roman pottery are rare and brick/tile is uncommon in the fieldwork assemblages; only a tiny minority of fields (4%) yielded more than 500g – and some of that minority had enormous quantities, up to 95 kg (Davies & Astill 1994: 224). Surface tile is therefore a useful clue to the location of this type of Roman settlement; and, since it is very difficult *not* to notice dense concentrations of tile when fieldwalking, it is likely that a high proportion of the total number of such settlements has been identified.

Eight of the total collection fields are best interpreted as on, or close to, Roman settlements.[8] In some cases their tile concentrations were large. C559, near Serre (Car), is somewhat similar to A92: here a dense tile scatter occurred as a diagonal band across the field, covering some 2,400m^2 (see Fig. 2.4). The tile was not associated with the small amount of post-medieval pottery, but on the eastern edge of, and within, the tile scatter there was a cluster of Roman pottery (covering 225m^2). The smaller field at D61 (500m southwest of Les Cormiers, Guer) had a dense concentration of brick and tile extending over 1,680m^2, which was matched in area by a dense scatter of Roman pottery (maximum 17, average 2.3, sherds per square) (see Fig. 5.4). The eastern half of the concentration also produced high phosphate readings (900 ppm). Other fields had much smaller concentrations – for example, 375m^2 at B347, 500m^2 at D221, 625m^2 at B282/283 – with smaller quantities (2.4–6.4 pieces per square). The concentration at B282/283, however, is part of a large potential settlement area of 26,000m^2 (2.6 ha), and was probably one element in a pattern of dispersed settlement. The assemblages from B282/283 and D142 included very high proportions of imports, 53% and 39% respectively; most sites, however, produced between 10% and 20% of imported pottery, while C559 only had 2%.

Further settlements are suggested by enclosures identified as cropmarks. Sixteen recent examples in the survey area are listed in the SRAB Sites and Monuments Record, and more were photographed during 1996. In no case has a complete plan been recorded: most consist of lengths of ditches forming two or three sides of potential enclosures. These cropmarks have been interpreted as Roman enclosures on the basis of their rectilinear shape, an interpretation which is convincing where previous or subsequent fieldwalking has produced *tegulae* or Roman pottery. For example, the cropmark showing an enclosure which extends beneath the *château* of La Guichardais in Carentoir lies in a field (D247) that had produced tile and Roman pottery (Fig. 4.5); two second-century coins have also been found nearby (SRAB Carentoir 8H). In fact, tile was collected from seven of the 16 fields with enclosures and Roman pottery from two of these and one other; no Roman finds were recovered from the other eight, whose Roman nature remains to be tested (Table 4.1).

To put these settlements in a wider context, a cautious comparison can be made with the plans of Roman settlements, which have been discovered

Figure 4.5 *Elements of ?Roman enclosures beside the Château de la Guichardais (Car), from the south; photo: Maurice Gautier*

Table 4.1 Rectilinear enclosures in the survey area recently identified as cropmarks

Commune	Slope	Contour	Transect	Field	Finds	SRAB ref
Comblessac	NE	75	R	R13	No	4
Comblessac	NE	85	R	R14	No	5
Comblessac	S	60	R	–	No	3
Les Brûlais	Ridge	80	R	–	tile	2H
La Chapelle	Ridge	50	M	M26	Ro pot	2H
Sixt	Ridge	45	M	M211–213	tile	2H
Pipriac	S	60	M	–	tile	21
Pipriac	N	50	M	M600	No	20
Augan	S	60	N	–	No	15H
Augan	S	75	N	–	No	9H
Augan	Ridge	75	N	nr N199	tile	8H
Campénéac	Ridge	80	N	N161–162	tile	1H
Campénéac	NW	70	N	–	No	7H
Ruffiac	N	25	L	nr L78	No	9H
Ruffiac	Ridge	40	A	A306	tile/Ro pot	10H
Carentoir	Ridge	70	D	D247	tile/Ro pot	–

by aerial photography and then fieldwalked, within the Coriosolite region to the north (Langouet 1988: 129–49). The largest villa complexes, such as at Boulienne in Saint-Père-Marc-en-Poulet (Ille-et-Vilaine), were formally arranged around courtyards, extended over at least $7,500m^2$ and appear to be part of tile scatters of at least 250m in diameter (5 ha). The 5.5 ha extent of the tile scatter around the settlement A92 would place it in this category. Smaller building groups, as at Lehon, Saint-Suliac (Côtes-d'Armor), were still arranged around yards within enclosures and were some $4,000m^2$ in area, with a tile scatter of 130–150m diameter; sites such as C559 or D61 are probably of a similar size. A survey of the southern Vilaine valley, which is close to the survey area, has noted that the largest sites are not so frequent as they are in the Rennes basin or the north, and the most common sites have left tile scatters of 100-150m in diameter. The smallest villa type, for example Pluduno, Le Fossé Châtelet (Côtes-d'Armor), often consisted of a single, multi-roomed building about $500m^2$ in extent; sites such as D221 or B347 in the survey area may be similar. A fourth pattern is that of the ditched enclosure, usually interpreted as a farm: these were mostly under 1 ha in extent and were the most numerous of all Roman settlement types (Gautier et al. 1991: 62, 58–9).

There is no reason to insist that all Roman tile scatters in the survey area reflect villas. D61 is located in the extreme north of the core, on poor soils (extensive cadastral *lande*), on a major Roman road, and about 3 km from a large Roman settlement at Le Mur (see below, pp. 81–3); its total tile scatter stretched over $11,193m^2$ (see Fig. 5.4). Though few fields were walked in its neighbourhood, there was no sign of any surrounding manuring scatter. In these circumstances we should consider the possibility of a non-agricultural, more specialized, settlement at this site.

Now, the material collected in transect-walking can be used to suggest the overall distribution of Roman material (Fig. 4.6). Some 34 concentrations of tile weighing more than 1 kg were found, with a pronounced concentration in the northeastern part of the core survey area; six had more than 10 kg. Just over a third (12) were not associated with Roman pottery and could be of a later date (Davies & Astill 1994: 224). There are also a further 90 locations where transect-walked fields yielded Roman pottery without, or with less than 1 kg of, brick or tile. When quantities are so small, interpretation is difficult: only six of the fields, for example, produced more than one Roman fabric (one of these fields had three, but that was the greatest number). One possible interpretation is that these small quantities derive from Roman fertilizing of the arable. However, of the 15 total collections whose Roman assemblages have been interpreted as manuring scatters (below, pp. 77–9), 12 produced no Roman pottery at all when the fields were transect-walked. Another possibility, therefore, is that

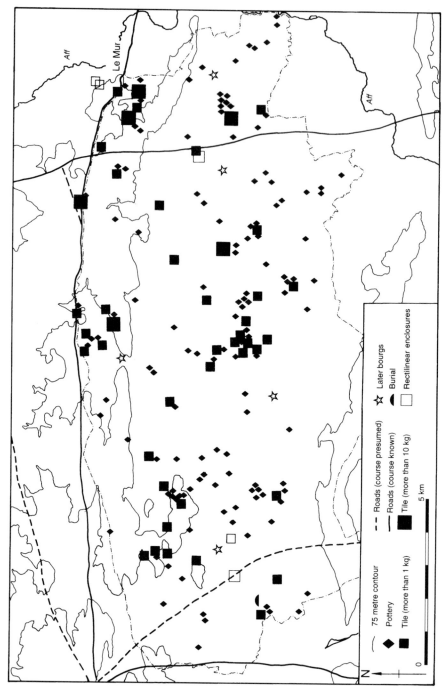

Figure 4.6 *Distribution of Roman material in the core survey area*

the pottery locates Roman settlements which were built of non-ceramic materials and, by implication, represent a different standard of occupation from the stone and tile structures. None was sampled by excavation, but the scatters may represent the kind of small farm that has been recognized from aerial and other survey in Brittany. Although often referred to as "indigenous" farms in the literature, we have no indication of their ethnic origin or social status; they were almost certainly, however, possessed by people less wealthy than the villa owners. Although some of these settlements were converted into villas in the second century, others retained their unsophisticated character, even when they were sited on the more fertile soils (Galliou 1983: 93).

Roman arable

Just as one can locate the position and extent of Roman settlements by fieldwork, so the same methods can be used to estimate a minimum area fertilized from the settlements. The distribution of very small quantities of tile around a denser scatter is a useful pointer to the minimum extent of the arable farmed from a villa (see above, p. 75).

Nine fields were transect-walked within 500m of A92 (Fig. 4.7). Only one of the fields had Roman pottery, but six produced notable quantities of brick and tile. Some of the fields farthest from the villa had none, while others as far as 530m (for example A308) had a very small quantity of tile (5g). A steady decrease of tile with distance from A92 was observed (Table 4.2), which suggests that at least lands within 500m of the villa were fertilized, representing an area of about 78 ha.[9] This *decreasing* pattern of tile is very unlikely to have been caused by later ploughing across the villa since the quantity of tile is too great to have been spread such a distance by plough action alone (see above, pp. 28–9). Of course, some parts of this notional fertilized area may not have been cultivated, while fields beyond 500m may well have been. The 78 ha area is thus a conjectural minimum of land under arable cultivation.

A pattern similar to the distribution of tile round A92 can be seen around three other Roman sites (Table 4.2). Relatively large quantities of tile were recovered up to a distance of 350m from B347 (Le Cleu, Tr), apparently a comparatively small settlement site. In fields beyond, 370–550m from B347, there was a significant decrease in the amount of tile; most fields produced none or very small quantities. It looks as if the settlement's main arable was an area of about 350m radius. A similar, but less complete, pattern may be seen around D221 and D142 (La Meule and La Certenaie, both Car); both settlements seem to be comparable in size to B347. In the case of C559, one of the largest Roman sites which the survey has found,

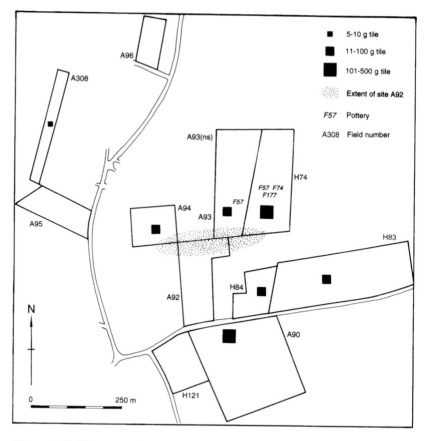

Figure 4.7 *The extent of the tile scatter surrounding Field A92 (Les Landes de la Ruée)*

Table 4.2 Tile spreads in relation to selected total collection fields

Total collection fields	Number of surrounding fields	Weight of tile 100–350m	Weight of tile 370–550m
A92	9	300–350g	5–85g
B347	22	150–480g	10–60g
C559	4	300–1434g	0
D61	12	0–20g	120–350g
D142	16	300–400g	13–114g
D221	18	200–350g	0

no fields beyond 300m of the site were walked, but the large quantities of tile from the nearer fields did not appear to be decreasing with distance.

Excavation enabled us to check the light scatters of Roman material which came from several total collection fields.[10] In all instances there were no obvious concentrations of Roman pottery on the surface, the pottery decreased with depth, and no underlying archaeological features of demonstrably Roman date were found. In such circumstances the most likely explanation is that this material came on to the fields in the course of agricultural activity. In comparison with the two occupation sites of A31/79 and A92, these scatters have a limited variety of Roman fabrics and a low proportion of imports: six of the fields had five or fewer fabrics and the percentages of imports ranged from 0% to 20%, with the majority between 8% and 14%.[11]

The remaining "Roman" total collections share the characteristics of small quantities of brick and tile and of Roman pottery;[12] average number of sherds per square ranged from 0.01 to 0.04. Since transect-walked fields within 200m yielded no pottery and very small quantities of tile (between 10 and 200g), these too are likely to have belonged to arable zones.

Some of these tile scatters are part of extensive, low-density but discrete, scatters: A159, for example (La Touche Gourelle, Ruff), lay within a tile scatter of 18 ha, and B324 (near La Ruaudaie, S-N) of 14 ha. The low density of these scatters makes them look like Roman arable, although the areas are significantly smaller than that surrounding A92, and could in some cases indicate dispersed settlements rather than fields.

The wider Roman context

The Roman conquest of Armorica in 57–56 BC in the long run introduced a pattern of colonization that was seen elsewhere, namely the superimposition of an administrative framework upon pre-existing, late Iron-Age, political structures. Control of territory and population was exercised through the acculturation and integration of the leading members of the tribal groups. The identity of the original tribal areas was retained in the *civitates*, whose boundaries may have been defined by the major rivers, in continuation of an Iron-Age political pattern (Pape 1995: 20–30; Galliou 1983: 37–40; below, p. 90, n.18). The administrative centres – the *civitas* capitals of Rennes, Corseul, Carhaix, Vannes and Nantes – were developed from Iron-Age settlement foci, and in the course of the first century AD they were rebuilt as Roman towns with regular street systems and public buildings, although none was sufficiently important to receive the patronage of the imperial house.

Epigraphic evidence shows that the smallest Armorican *civitas*, of the *Riedones*, was subdivided into at least three smaller administrative units, *pagi*, and it has been assumed that the other *civitates* of Armorica were treated in the same way (Pape 1995: 30–33). Each *pagus* would have had a central settlement, perhaps a *vicus*, which was an administrative and religious focus for the locality; unfortunately few *pagi* have been identified.

The administrative structure was integrated by an extensive road system, the main arteries of which linked the *civitas* capitals. Some of these routes may well have existed prior to the colonization (Eveillard 1991; Pape 1995: 80–81).

The survey area was crossed by at least three Roman roads (Fig. 4.8). The first, about which we know most, was the east–west route between Angers and Carhaix, now thought to have been the pre-eminent road in Armorica (Eveillard 1991: 20). For the most part it forms the northern

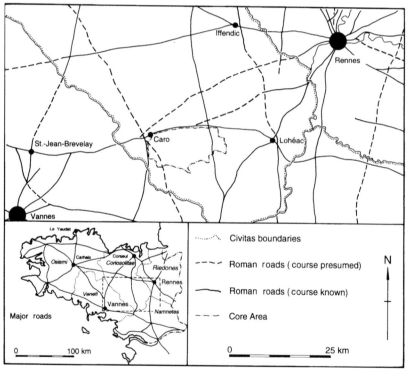

Figure 4.8 *The Roman roads in eastern Brittany with (inset) the major roads of Armorica (after Eveillard 1991)*

commune boundaries of the core – of Ruffiac, Tréal and Carentoir. A second, north–south, route connected Corseul and Rieux and crosses the present northern boundary of Carentoir. Its course south probably passed some 250m to the west of Le Temple, and just to the east of La Chapelle Gaceline (cf. below, p. 224). The third road ran from Le Yaudet on the northwest coast to Nantes and intersected the Angers–Carhaix road at or near Caro. The course of the route has not been located exactly, but it crossed Ruffiac, running west of the present *bourg*, through the Tréleu and La Hiarnaie vicinity, and forded the Oust near Saint-Martin-sur-Oust. A fourth road, connecting Rennes and Vannes, joined the Angers–Carhaix road 3 or 4 km west of Le Mur. Traversed by three important arteries of the road system in Roman Armorica, the survey area can hardly have been isolated; indeed, it was in many ways at the centre of Roman communications across Brittany.

Two of the roads (Angers–Carhaix and Corseul–Rieux) crossed in the valley of the River Aff, very close to the junction of the modern commune boundaries of Carentoir, Comblessac and Quelneuc, near the most northeasterly point of the core (see Fig. 4.10). Overlooking that junction, on the slopes of a volcanic intrusion, was the Iron-Age *oppidum* of Le Mur, also a large Roman settlement complex.

The site at Le Mur is known only from what survives above ground and what has been found in the near vicinity. Within the *oppidum*, on a dominant promontory overlooking the river, is an earthwork interpreted as a Roman trapezoidal enclosure. Just to the east are recorded two temples, one with a small heptagonal *fanum*, presumably of "Romano-Celtic" type, the other of rectangular plan with two rooms (Fig. 4.9). Both were set within a single walled enclosure, beyond which was a long, narrow building, similar to the gallery of a villa (Galliou 1983: 201–4). Pottery, including samian and *terra nigra*, and a white terracotta statuette, have come from the site, as well as 57 coins which range in date from mid to late third century (Guennou 1981: 73–4).

In 1987 two fields (R7 and R8) were transect-walked close to this settlement. Both fields produced very large quantities of brick and tile and small amounts of Roman pottery. In R8 were identified the ploughed-out remains of a hexagonal building approximately 7m across, within a circular wall with a diameter of about 15m (see Fig. 4.10). This structure was over 300m to the west of the site location recorded on the 1:25,000 map, and could be the remains of a third temple. This clearly indicates a much larger and more diverse settlement than previously recognized, especially as the remains of another stone structure, about 50m^2, was noted in the adjacent field (R9). Both fields R8 and R9 also produced large amounts of tap slag

Figure 4.9 *Temple area at Le Mur (Comblessac), showing two temples (one overgrown) within an enclosure incorporating a long rectangular building; photo: Maurice Gautier*

and furnace bottoms, indicating the smelting and smithing of iron. The fields containing these buildings bordered the east–west Roman road.

At the very least Le Mur was a defensible site with a large religious complex comprising temples and subsidiary buildings, some of which were of an industrial character. It appears to have been in use from the first century to at least the end of the fourth (Sanquer 1977: 345).

The roads and the fort appear to have exercised a strong influence on the Roman settlement pattern of the area. The distribution of the "Roman" tile scatters of the core survey area has a pronounced northern and eastern bias (see Fig. 4.6). The densest, and invariably some of the largest, tile scatters are to be found on, or within 1 km of, the Roman roads, especially the Angers–Carhaix road.[13] Three of the densest scatters were located within 4 km, and two within 1 km, of Le Mur.[14] In fact, almost half of all tile scatters in the core (16 of 34) are within 1 km of the Roman roads.

Proximity of villas to known Roman roads is repeated in the sample transects. The villa near Bermagouet, in Transect P, confirmed by the

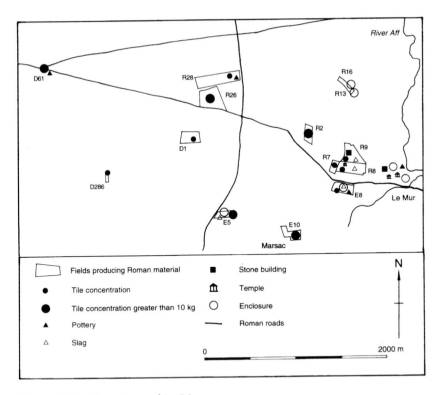

Figure 4.10 *The environs of Le Mur*

excavation of the bath suite, and by a dense tile scatter (P46, P71), is close to the crossing of the Oust (Pape 1995: 97). Two heavy tile scatters in Transect R (R2, R26) are close to the Angers–Carhaix road, and not far from Le Mur. The distribution of Roman pottery and tile in Transect M, from Carentoir to the Vilaine, is notably uneven. A dense scatter was found at Le Château du Boschet, near the modern boundary between Carentoir and La Chapelle Gaceline, in the vicinity of the Corseul–Rieux road. The next 3 km east, where Transect M passes through the commune of Bruc, is devoid of Roman material (cf. the medieval pattern, below, p. 131). Farther east, there is more Roman pottery and a clutch of extensive tile scatters just to the south of Pipriac;[15] all four lie within 1.5 km of the course of a road from Rennes to Rieux (Eveillard 1991: 21–2). Only one further dense tile and pottery scatter was recorded in the transect, on the western slope of the Vilaine valley (Les Émailleries, M573/574/575).

This association between villas and roads was common elsewhere in Roman Armorica, as indicated by a large-scale survey of Gallo-Roman settlement in eastern Brittany (Galliou 1983: 92; Langouet & Jumel 1986: 103). Most tile scatters reflect the presence of large estate centres – villas – whose inhabitants appreciated the economic advantage of living near a major road. These settlements were not always located on the most fertile land of the area: the distribution of tile scatters as a whole is remarkable for the lack of coincidence with the arable core of the survey area in the medieval period (see Fig. 6.1). Those in the north and east of the core were located on higher land and poorer soils (some 44% were on or above the 70m contour), although tile scatters are notably close to water sources (87% within 300m). Their siting seems to have been determined more by proximity to the communications system than by proximity to the best soils.

There were of course some tile scatters farther south, such as the group in the centre of the survey area, near La Ruaudaie (S–N); these are less extensive than those to the north, and within the zone settlements seem to be closer together, usually 0.5 to 1 km apart compared with 1 to 1.5 km in the northern zone. There are also some settlements which seem to have been more specialized: Le Mur is clearly the best evidenced case, but there are others which bordered the roads – D61 and E8 (near Le Mur), for example. Total collection from D61 produced a clear settlement assemblage, which had every Roman fabric, except two, that has been found in the area. The total collection also yielded discrete building scatters and finds such as the leg of a clay figurine. The neighbouring fields did not show any signs of the characteristic manuring pattern associated with agricultural settlements. Moreover, the junction between the Rennes–Vannes and the Angers–Carhaix roads was located close to D61, which, with the major road and river crossing near Le Mur, must have made the area an important focus (Fig. 4.10).

Settlements such as Le Mur, D61 and E8 may therefore have had a regional importance and provided services for those who used the roads – one could well have been a resting place (*mansio*). Their more specialized character will have made them dependent on commodities supplied from the surrounding villa estates. Comparison with other parts of northwest Gaul would encourage us to think of this area as an economic and religious centre, perhaps including a settlement similar to a *vicus* (cf. Galliou 1983: 84–7). After all, it was a considerable distance from all the *civitas* capitals of eastern Armorica. The presence of at least two temples at Le Mur is reminiscent of rural sanctuaries identified elsewhere, combined worship and recreational centres. Is it indeed conceivable that Le Mur functioned as the centre of a *pagus*?

As might be expected, the distribution of fields with Roman pottery but no tile mirrors that of the tile scatters, but only in part. There are zones where the pottery occurs without the tile, often located on the fertile soils of what were to become medieval arable areas; that to the east and southeast of Ruffiac, which has A31/79 at its centre, is one such. The other notable zones of Roman ceramics are to the south of Carentoir, and in that commune's present southeastern tip (densely settled in the early modern period).

The sites which only have Roman pottery often have a different kind of location from that of the villa tile spreads. The most significant difference between the two is that the vast majority of pottery sites (83%) is located below the 60m contour compared with only 56% of tile scatters. This association with good arable land (and *dis*association from big villas) makes it likely that this material comes from small farms, as suggested above (pp. 75, 77), although the paucity of the pottery makes it impossible to discuss the size, let alone the character, of such settlements. The limited material culture of the survey area suggests that the majority of the local population was neither sufficiently mobile nor sufficiently resourced to sustain the civic lifestyle which the specialized sites symbolize.

Despite the above possibilities, some areas were completely devoid of Roman-type settlement and land-use (see Fig. 4.6). The best evidence for this is the absence of Roman pottery and tile on seven total collection sites.[16] Some are located in areas that were "blank" in the medieval to post-medieval periods (see below, pp. 119–22); and some are found within zones that have plenty of evidence for settlement, both Roman and later. The pattern of Roman settlement and land-use therefore looks patchy, but it is important to note that – as in the case of Iron-Age material – the zones that were clearly utilized are not topographically differentiated from those that were not. Roman pottery finds were exceptionally few in Transects N, P and R, emphasizing that settlement in the core – though patchy – was nevertheless significant in the Roman period.

Change in the Roman countryside

So far the entire Roman period has been approached without any real consideration of the dynamics of change over some five hundred years. This is to ignore discussion about what happened to Armorica in and after the late third century. Unsettled conditions, particularly in the 270s and 280s, which had been produced through a combination of political and military instability, social unrest and extensive coastal raiding, are thought to have been widespread. This instability is believed to have had a profound effect on economic relationships, illustrated by the apparent abandonment of the vast majority of excavated villas at this time, and also by the contraction of urban areas behind newly built town walls. For some commentators, this is evidence of an irreversible collapse in the rural economy of Armorica: the countryside was deserted as part and parcel of a general population decline. Reports of some field surveys suggest that 75% of the rural settlements identified by tile concentrations were abandoned, since no fourth-century material was recovered; and the few pollen analyses have been used to argue for a widespread cessation of cereal cultivation (Langouet 1988: 216–17; Marguerie & Langouet 1993). Others have taken a less extreme view and argued that there was a regrouping of settlement, so that farming activities were organized from large, concentrated estate centres (Galliou 1983: 113).

Much depends on whether the currently available data are regarded as truly representative of the total situation. In eastern Brittany imported pottery – mainly Argonne ware, but also *céramique á l'éponge* – is the only ceramic indicator of fourth-century occupation. These ceramics have a mainly coastal and (limited) riverine distribution, which may be as much an indication of wealth or status as of the presence or absence of settlement (Davies & Astill 1994: 178-80). The absence of fourth-century imports from earlier Roman settlement sites cannot necessarily be indicative of desertion in the later third or fourth century (Provost & Priol 1991: 78); indeed, someone must have been receiving the fourth-, and even fifth-, century coinage found in inland Brittany. We still need to discover if there were locally produced wares in the east in the fourth century; this is certainly the case in Finistère, where villa sites like Kervéguen and towns like Carhaix have produced assemblages (smaller than those for the first to third centuries) of local pottery associated with Argonne ware (Ménez & Galliou 1986: 55–6).

We also need to be aware that post-third-century occupation may have had a different, less substantial, character, which is more difficult to recognize. The return to timber construction is indicated in villa excavations from Finistère, for example at Keradennec. In the past this has been interpreted as "squatter" occupation or "barbarization" (Galliou 1983: 113), but the excavation at Le Châtillon-sur-Seiche, in the Rennes basin, has demonstrated extensive fourth-century use in the form of timber buildings associated with metalworking, which can hardly be interpreted in such a pejorative way (Pape 1995: 116). Meagre though the evidence is, it could indicate a major change in the way villa properties were used in the fourth century; if so it must also indicate a change in the way important landowners managed their property, for instance by selling, or by leasing to tenants and moving elsewhere, perhaps to the towns and even perhaps away from the region altogether. Though we could do with some more dated pollen cores of the late Roman period, the balance of the present evidence is that there was some decline in cereal pollens in the Late Empire

(Marguerie 1992: 241–2). This pollen evidence does not necessarily indicate complete abandonment of the land; it could just as well reflect extremely localized changes, or changes in agricultural strategy, for example from cereal to animal husbandry (see below, pp. 114, n.13).

Although villa owners no doubt exerted a great influence on the way farming was conducted, they were in the minority, and therefore any conclusive discussion of what happened in the fourth century should include the smaller farms, and settlements without ceramics. This cannot be done at present for lack of evidence. However, it is worth recalling the numerous enclosed sites revealed through aerial photography. A surprisingly high number of the rectilinear enclosures discovered in the Rennes basin – some 38% – was not associated with any tile scatter. Such enclosures may well have contained buildings without ceramic roof tiles, built in a different way from, but nevertheless contemporary with, those which did have tile. There is also the possibility that those without tile were built when the material was no longer available, that is after the later third century, and that these sites represent a horizon of late Roman settlement which was little affected by Romanization.

The material assemblage from the survey area shares many of the general problems: it allows us to discuss Romanized land-use only during the early Roman period, because we have yet to recognize material that is peculiar to the later Roman period. None of the pottery, and perhaps none of the ceramic tile, can be dated later than the mid third century because most of the local pottery is dated by association with imports, and no later Roman imports have been identified.

The following possibilities have therefore been considered: that the later third and fourth centuries were aceramic, and therefore invisible to archaeological fieldwork; that the fabrics and forms of the pottery remained virtually the same for the whole of the Roman period, with minor changes in the fourth century (accompanied by a general diminution in ceramic use), which is what appears to have happened in the west; or that the survey area suffered a dramatic demographic decline in the later third and fourth centuries. This last possibility must be unlikely since more than a quarter of the core has been subject to detailed archaeological fieldwork, and this has failed to find even one late Roman site. There is no positive evidence from our area for the rapid contraction in the agricultural economy which has been postulated for the later third century (Langouet 1988: 216–17; below, pp. 110–11).

There is, however, some late Roman evidence: there is a cemetery at Foucherel in western Ruffiac. The inhumations were laid within settings of tiles, and some were accompanied by white and blue glass vessels and some metalwork (Marsille 1912; Galliou 1983: 217–18; Guennou 1981: 77).

"*Tegulae* inhumation" is thought to be a late Roman practice which spread from the south of Gaul, and is usually dated to the later fourth and fifth centuries (Galliou & Jones 1991: 113). The cemetery is close to a tile scatter (L111/117), which might be the forerunner of a settlement contemporary with the cemetery, situated close to a major Roman road.

Small pieces of evidence from the surrounding communes also point to some late Roman activity: the pottery from Comblessac (from Le Mur) extends into the fourth and the coin series into the late third century, as did a large hoard from Missiriac (Guennou 1981: 73–4, 76); and two milestones were erected in Caro in the late third century. A large villa at La Démardais (Porcaro), near Augan, was certainly occupied until the fourth century, with no sign of a violent end, and the site had substantial re-use several centuries later (SRAB 1993: 42–53; Blin 1993: 21–2; below, p. 110). Little takes us beyond this point. Two sherds of Argonne ware, however, have been found in Pipriac, one from Transect M (M447).[17]

But this still leaves us with a problem: we cannot produce any evidence for a period of significant settlement relocation or change in the third and fourth centuries. The available evidence will allow us only to argue that identifiable Roman-period settlement was at its maximum extent in the late second and early third centuries, and that imports – on the whole – stopped in the fourth century. This is significant because it suggests a decline in the area's contacts with the rest of Gaul; and it appears that this is generally true of the southern Coriosolite territory (Gautier et al. 1991: 57). While most of the population may never have had access to imports anyway, there was always a minority that did; the Argonne ware from Pipriac may suggest the continuation of that – perhaps declining – minority nearer the Vilaine. This relative isolation was to continue throughout the medieval period (see below, pp. 138–9, 243).

We have some evidence for the continued use of some sites between the later Bronze/early Iron Age and the Roman period; there is also evidence for the construction of Roman settlements on areas that had been cultivated in the Iron Age, as there are some clear examples of the abandonment of both settlement and fields during the later Iron Age. The impression of both continuity and change within the overall framework of exploitation is established for the late Iron Age and is typical of the middle ages; it may well also be typical of the Roman period. It should be noted that Carentoir is a Gaulish name; it is also the case that the Oust–Vilaine watershed has a significant number of commune names which end in Latinized Gaulish -*ac*, and that within the core there are at least a further seven -*ac* settlement names (Addison 1983: 21–2), and another is evidenced in Ruffiac in the ninth century. The form is widespread in Late Antiquity in Gaul and its continuation in the local toponymy of the survey area must indicate an area with strong continuities between the late Roman and later periods (cf. Vallerie 1986: 216–21); six of these Gallo-Roman names lie in Carentoir, four are near the northern road and one was used to refer to Le Mur in the early middle ages (below, p. 110).[18]

★★★★★★★★★

Three things are striking about the survey area in the Roman period, and all have more than local significance. Firstly, excavation and total collection located rather less Roman pottery than that of the Iron Age; since Iron Age fabrics were overwhelmingly of local origin and Roman only partly so, something seems to have happened to the local pot-making tradition during the first centuries AD. Secondly, northern Carentoir lies on major intersections of Brittany's Roman communications network, while eastern Carentoir, northern Ruffiac/Tréal and western Ruffiac all lie on major roads. This must have given the settlement at Le Mur, and other settlements in that sector, a regional importance. Thirdly, while ideas of desertion and depopulation in the late third and fourth centuries are barely credible, there do seem to have been some major changes in and around the big villa sites in that period. It certainly looks as if villa *owners* may have relocated, bringing significant changes to property management in the area. This need have no demographic implications at all; indeed, it is precisely the area of the big villas that provides the strongest indications of continuity into the early middle ages. Unlike most parts of northwest France, Comblessac has a recorded history in the immediate post-Roman period – just as it has a very prominent material history in the Roman (below, p. 108).

Notes

1. Nor was any flint recovered from the transect-walked fields 250m to the west and 400m to the south of the menhir, L18-24.
2. Cf. the similarly diverse range of stone in the Neolithic period at Beaumont and around Paimpont (Tinevez 1988: 65–77; Briard 1989: 107–9).
3. Maximum recovered from any 5m square was three pieces of flint, although 13 were found during excavation.
4. Total collection: 3% each of prehistoric and Roman pottery; 46% of prehistoric pottery was Fabric 86: being less well fired, it would not have survived surface exposure as well as the later wares.
5. D153, Bot Colin (0.2% of the total pottery assemblage); G74 (0.7%); H132 (0.2%); L26, Digoit (0.6%).
6. SRAB Carentoir 21H, 22H; Comblessac 2; La Chapelle Gaceline 1H; Augan 7H.
7. SRAB Pipriac 023.

8. A159, B282/283, B324, B347, C559, D61, D142, D221.

9. For comparison, we calculate that in the central middle ages a minimum of 50–60 ha around some settlements was manured; below, pp. 122, 125.

10. A116, B409, D153, G74, H80, H132, K445/446 and L26.

11. Two of the six – A116 and B409 – had the highest amount of tile (1.2 and 5 pieces per 5m square). This occurred in weak concentrations and was not in the same areas as the Roman pottery; it looks as if the material was of post-medieval or modern date. The other fields had less, 0.2 to 0.6 per square, but the tile was more evenly scattered over the surface.

12. A96, A107, B319, B408, D282, E89, E227, F187, F212, G60/61, G217, G500, H145, J97, J158, L80; Davies & Astill 1994: 221.

13. ›10 kg of tile: C559, D61, E5, E10/230; E263 was close to the Corseul–Rieux road; L17/111 and A331 were near the Le Yaudet–Nantes road.

14. E5, E10/230, R118/119.

15. Le Château du Boulaye, M260/261/262/263/266; Le Château Gaillard, M400/447/448/450; La Rigaudière, M315/341 (cf. SRAB Pipriac 012H); Le Pâtis de la Porte, M405/406/407/408. Cf. also SRAB Pipriac 010 (Les Carrées) and 026 (La Roussière).

16. B216, B236, B242, B500, E500, J165, L500.

17. The other is not precisely provenanced (Galliou 1983: 175).

18. There has been much published discussion of what is perceived to be a discrepancy between the boundaries of Iron-Age tribes and Roman *civitates* of *Veneti* and *Coriosolitae* (thought to have followed the courses of the rivers Oust and Vilaine), and the boundaries of the medieval dioceses of Rennes and Vannes, located slightly to the north (see Fig. 3.5). The disputed zone lies precisely in our survey area. Since the 1940s it has been suggested that the discrepancy had its origin in a reallocation of territory between the *civitates* as part of late Roman defensive arrangements: there is no evidence that this took place, let alone for the date of such an arrangement, although there is a late Roman "military" burial at Guer (Langouet 1988: 6–8, 219–20; Pape 1995: 29–30; Petit 1970).

CHAPTER 5

The problem of the early middle ages

The early middle ages present us with some serious problems: there is hardly any surviving material from the survey area which is securely datable to this time, that is from the fifth to the early eleventh century, and hardly a feature that can confidently be assigned to the period. Paradoxically, there is an unusually large amount of written data about the ninth century (large, that is, by comparison with other parts of northern Europe), but only about this single century. This means that there is virtually no evidence of any type from the period AD 400–800 and that key questions about settlement location and land-use can be approached only from written evidence and only from a single 100-year time-span.[1] Although it is undoubtedly useful to do this, the data cannot be localized precisely. We can therefore discuss each commune in a generalized way, and zones of each commune, but we do not know the precise spot where a named hamlet or residence was located and we do not know the precise spot where this or that named field was worked, although many properties have their boundaries detailed in the record. To talk about relationships between settlement and land-use is therefore near impossible.

Despite the frustrations arising from our inability to localize, the ninth-century texts are rich in local social, personal and economic detail. There also survives a very small quantity of tenth-century pottery, distributed across the core study area and sample transects. Although there is a danger that the quantities are too small to bear any kind of interpretation, the material can hardly be ignored; and, in fact, the corpus of tenth-century evidence does look significant when viewed as a whole. We shall therefore treat these two categories in turn, before concluding with a look at some possibilities for the ninth and tenth centuries, and some even more hesitant thoughts about the 400 years before.

The ninth century

Our knowledge of the ninth century derives from the fact that a monastery was founded in the year 832 at Redon, 20 km to the southeast of the core survey area, on the navigable waters of the River Vilaine. This foundation grew to be rich and powerful within a generation of its creation and had a major and lasting impact on the entire region. It benefited from gifts of property throughout southeastern Brittany, from large and small donors; records of those grants, as well as of the sales and leases that involved the abbot by the 860s, were kept in the monastery's archive, to be copied into a cartulary in the eleventh century (de Courson 1863). This cartulary survives: not only does it contain records of transactions to which Redon was a party but it also has records of transactions affecting some properties prior to their acquisition by the monastery. In other words, the abbot acquired a bundle of "title deeds" when he acquired a new property. The texts therefore tell us about far more than the monastery and its interests; and they begin round about the year 800 (Davies 1990a; Davies 1988: 1–4, 26–8).[2]

In the ninth century there were two *plebes* – communities – in the core area: that of Ruffiac and that of Carentoir; there are 21 texts relating to Carentoir and at least 44 relating to Ruffiac. Ruffiac included the modern commune of Tréal, which was already at that time an identifiable area within the *plebs*, and Saint-Nicolas-du-Tertre and Saint-Laurent (neither separately identified); Carentoir included modern Quelneuc, La Gacilly and La Chapelle Gaceline, none of which was at that time separately identified (see above, pp. 56–7). The sample transects crossed further communities: Caro (including the identifiable area of Réminiac), Augan and Campénéac in Transect N; Comblessac in Transect R; Sixt, Pipriac and Guipry in Transect M.

These were communities with very clearly defined identities: the *plebs* (*plou* in Breton) was a recognized unit of social cohesion and civil organization, very similar to the civil parish or rural commune in later European history. People identified themselves and their properties with reference to this or that *plebs*, did their business in public meetings within the *plebs* and settled nearly all their disputes in a court within the *plebs*. Each of the two core *plebes* had a focal church as well as a scatter of small monasteries. The focal churches were served by small groups of local priests, most of whom had hereditary property interests in the locality, who performed a range of secular services for the lay communities in addition to their spiritual roles. Each *plebs* also had a "machtiernship", a hereditary office in the hands of a minor aristocratic family; the machtiern usually presided at public meetings, sometimes took action in response to complaints and occasionally used his residence – the *lis* – for the performance and recording of public business. Whatever his origins, by the ninth century he was a kind of permanent, hereditary local chairman, who had high status and more wealth than the comfortable peasant; he was, in other words, a petty aristocrat.

The machtierns' communities were communities of peasant farmers, whose interests were overwhelmingly agricultural and whose lives were largely played out within their home *plebes*. Because of the number of local records, we are in the fortunate position of being able to assess the public business range of the free adult males of Ruffiac and Carentoir and some of the communities beyond: we can count the individuals who went to meetings within and beyond the *plebs*. For more than half the free male population, we have no evidence that they ever travelled beyond the confines of the home *plebs*; about a fifth would travel to the neighbouring *plebs*: Ruffiac men to Carentoir or Pleucadeuc, Carentoir men to Ruffiac or Sixt, Augan men to Guillac or Guer; another fifth might move about in three or four *plebes*; and only the remaining tenth would go to the lengths of making the 20–30 km journey to Redon, as some certainly did to present their gifts on the altar of the monastery (Fig. 5.1).

"Free" and "male" are used advisedly. These were societies in which public business was done by men and in which some of the work was done by unfree people, although this does not mean that peasants did not themselves engage in agricultural labour. The unfree were owned by their peasant masters (and sometimes – though rarely in the communities of Ruffiac and Carentoir – by aristocratic lords); they were usually attached to the land they worked, and therefore changed owners as land was bought and sold. When the priest Driiunet bought two farms in Carentoir, very early in the century, he bought them "with pasture, meadow, house and the man called Posidhoia who looked after them, and his sons Anauhoiat, Iudmin and Iudmorin, and whatever offspring they should have, from generation to generation" (de Courson 1863: no. 166). But although these people had no powers of negotiation, they were not subject to especially onerous service demands. They worked the lands for which they were responsible according to their own schedules and paid relatively high annual renders to their owners, handing over the bulk of the produce they created and keeping only sufficient for their own subsistence needs. They were markedly silent – no serf ever spoke at public meetings or gave evidence at dispute hearings – and this stands in marked contrast to the

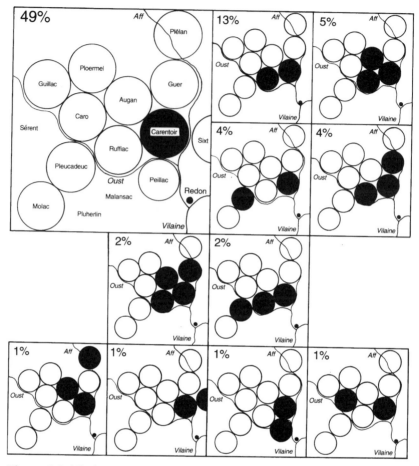

Figure 5.1 *The business range of Carentoir people in the ninth century*

vociferous arguments of the free peasants. In eastern Brittany as a whole, Ruffiac and Carentoir are distinguished by the relatively small proportion of serfs in the peasant population: maybe 25% in Ruffiac but as low as 10% in Carentoir, although in Augan to the north (Transect N) the proportion was probably as high as 50% (since there were major aristocratic landowners there whose property was predominantly worked by serfs). Not all the free were proprietors, of course: at least a fifth of the peasant population in both Ruffiac and Carentoir owned their own land, and probably quite a lot more than a fifth, but some of the free were tenants, who could negotiate the terms of their tenancies and terminate them if they wished.

There is not the slightest doubt that – for a pre-industrial economy – the lands of ninth-century Ruffiac and Carentoir were intensively worked. Judging from the number of different free adult males named in a single generation, the total population of Ruffiac (with Tréal, Saint-Nicolas and Saint-Laurent) in the mid ninth century may well have been in the order of 1,200 or 1,300 persons, about a third of its level in c.1900 (Davies 1988: 46; cf. Tonnerre 1994: 120). In this area, unlike some other parts of eastern Brittany, the property units were contiguous: again and again we read that one unit had a similar unit on each of its four sides, just as the holding Ranworocan, near Quoiqueneuc in modern Tréal, was bounded by Randronhael, Ranpeniar, Ranconon and Lostwiel. The *ran*, the most common Breton word for the unit, was usually discrete, had separate fields within it and seems to have had a mean size of about 25 ha, although properties could be larger or smaller and there are cases in which two or three *rannou* agglomerated to form a larger unit called *villa* or *tref* (Fig. 5.2a). The basic unit, then, was like a smallholding and its mean size is comparable to those of the late twentieth century (see above, p. 53); the occasional agglomerations were like small farms. The *ran* usually included house and arable – sufficient to support one household – and might also include meadow, pasture and some uncultivated land (Fig. 5.2a), although the latter were sometimes located beyond a larger arable zone (Fig. 5.2b); farmwork was organized in relation to the *ran*. Hence, it was the normal pattern for a household to control its own labour and its own economy, which meant that virtually every household provided its own food: even the Ruffiac smith, Carantcar, had his own plots of land. If a family acquired more than one property unit, then it would get free tenants or unfree serfs to work them, although only a tiny proportion of the adult male population, about 5% in each community, owned several – two, three, four, or five at most. Both tenants and serfs also seem to have worked from their own households, managing the daily round in much the same way as did the free peasant proprietors.

This was mixed farming land, with no specialization of crop in these particular *plebes*. Rents and renders characteristically cite both cereals and livestock: wheat, oats and rye were grown; sheep, pigs and some cattle were reared; and men gathered fruits, bedding, firewood and building materials from the uncultivated land. We hear of a meadow near Lodineu, south of Ruffiac *bourg*, of orchards and gardens, and of small patches of woodland. There is a strong sense that arable activities were predominant in these villages west of the River Vilaine, for there is more reference to cereals than to animals and land measurements tend to be expressed in sowable areas.[3] Given the paucity of surviving early medieval pottery,

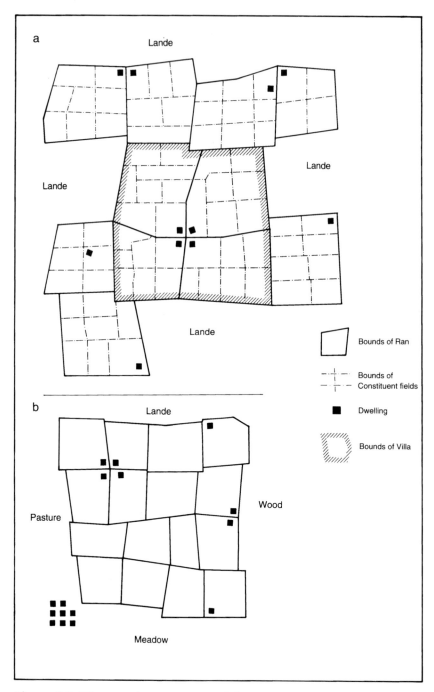

Figure 5.2 *Diagrammatic representations of the ran, the basic farming unit, showing (a) rannou including mixed land-use (b) arable rannou*

household waste cannot have been distributed with animal dung on the arable; or, if it was, the waste cannot have included durable potsherds.

Although we can rarely localize features that are mentioned in the texts, one can nevertheless derive a sense of the physical landscape in these areas from written references. There certainly does not seem to have been much *bocage*. Occasionally we hear of a bank or ditch that marked a property boundary – like the *fossatella* ("little ditch") that ran along one side of Ranconmarch and Ranhaelwal in Carentoir – but banks or ditches did not *surround* properties. More usually, it was the properties themselves that constituted boundaries, without special signs, just as nowadays you can walk across an unmarked field in Carentoir and be told by the locals that you have walked from M. Hercouet's land to M. Joly's. Patches of trees sometimes lay on these boundaries and small stands of woodland were sometimes included within the properties themselves; but there is nothing that suggests large areas of woodland, much less of forest, in these communes – although not far away, west of the River Oust in Pleucadeuc and south by the Landes de Lanvaux, there were larger stretches (cf. Tonnerre 1994: 113–14). There were also the *landes*, as dominant a physical feature as they were later, uncultivated though certainly not unutilized zones: in Caro in Transect N, just to the north of Ruffiac, rights to gather firewood and fruits from the *landes* were specified among ninth-century property rights.

Notwithstanding the end of Empire, the Roman road system must still have been recognizable in the area in the ninth century. Indeed, the main east–west Angers–Carhaix road is even nowadays a route along parts of the northern boundary of the core communes. A road called the "public" road ran through the village centre of Carentoir in the ninth century; and roads and bridges are mentioned in the *plebes* that surround Ruffiac and Carentoir – in Augan, Réminiac, Guer and Pipriac – differentiated in grades of footpath, road and public road. To the south and west of the communes lay the navigable River Oust; and the River Aff was navigable as far as Sixt (in Transect M), just beyond southeastern Carentoir.

The existence of a road and river network should not lead us to suppose that travel was swift and easy: it still took 12 hours to get from Redon to the coast in the eighteenth century; and people from the inland parishes demonstrably did not travel far (no more than a few kilometres) in the sixteenth and seventeenth centuries. However, it was possible for those who had the means to travel beyond the survey area if they wished, especially (for Carentoir and Ruffiac people) to north and south. Travel within the *plebes* must have been relatively easy: we hear of a plethora of small roads and crossroads as well as the main or "public" roads. A road ran between Lisbedu in Ruffiac and Liscelli in Guer; another ran past Lisnowid, for the machtiern Riwalt stopped there when he was sick and travelling from Augan; the latter road was certainly big enough to take a cart. Perhaps it was the Roman Le Yaudet–Nantes road, running on through Ruffiac as one of the two "public" roads that bounded several properties (see Fig. 4.8). Another public road, beside which were sited two landmark crosses, ran to Carentoir church, and a house lay on this or another public road within that *plebs*. A reference to the public road (?the Roman Angers–Carhaix road) that crossed the River Rau (in modern Tréal) mentions no bridge at the crossing (the river may have been forded) but two Ruffiac bridges are mentioned, including one across the Guidecourt near Lodineu.

There were clearly houses around the two focal churches in each village, forming two principal nucleations in the core area: one *ran* in Ruffiac is recorded as having its house beside the church; but there was equally clearly a scatter of hamlets across the whole area – as there is now – as well as the occasional aristocratic residence, like the machtiern's *lis*. These *lisiou* lay on roads and some almost seem to have functioned like stations of the imperial post, public reference points on the main routes, where public business was sometimes done. What were these machtiernly residences like? They cannot have been very grand, like the princely residences of the texts or the excavated ninth-/tenth-century site at Locronan in western Brittany, for these were men of much lower social scale (Guigon 1992). Our only excavation evidence of an early medieval structure of any kind comes from Field H132, beside La Ruée in Ruffiac; this suggests nothing very substantial, although there were pits and ditches, previous to the massive stone structure of the (?) twelfth century (Davies & Astill 1994: 143–51). It is also worth noting that the ninth-century *Gesta Sanctorum Rotonensium* records that a "powerful man (*potens uir*)", called Ronwallon, gave his house to the monks of Redon: since it was built of wood, they sent ox carts (plural) to collect it and bring it to the monastery (Brett 1989: 169). We can also note that the *lis* element occurs in the place-name Lezalain, in eastern Carentoir; sherds of the tenth-century ware, Fabric 10, were picked up in the area but there is no sign today of early structural features, nor suggestive banks or ditches. However, a ninth-century *lis* may have been located in this area; and Lisbedu or Lisnowid could perfectly well have been on the Angers–Carhaix Roman road.

Settlements of every kind must have been liberally scattered all over the worked area: we hear of isolated houses (*mansiones*) on property boundaries and of houses attached to and situated on the individual *ran*, as well as the *mansiunculi* ("little houses") where the serfs lived on the properties they worked. Properties were also identified as lying in hamlets in named areas of *plebes*, like Lodineu in Lerniac in Ruffiac or Botriwaloe in Réminiac in Caro.

This was a well-used landscape in the ninth century, a landscape worked by a group of small farmers who were careful of their rights, which they tenaciously fought to maintain. Most of the men in Ruffiac and Carentoir were used to labouring and supported their own families, and did so reasonably comfortably; there was clearly plenty of surplus generated. Although there was some coinage about, the denominations were high: money was for special not everyday use, and it is most unlikely that everyone used it. Just as a notable proportion of those with accumulations of properties were local priests and clerics (4 of 18 named in Ruffiac and 5 of 10 in Carentoir), so those with cash to use — typically by taking a pledge of property in return for their cash — were overwhelmingly priests. Unlikely, too, that most people went to market: some did, for there was plenty of market activity in the area of Redon, by the River Vilaine, but it was only a tiny proportion of the population that did so, the 10% or so of richer peasants, clerics, machtierns. Small wonder, then, that we find so little material of the early middle ages in the core survey area.

Fabric 10

Thinly scattered across the core survey area can be found sherds of the ware we have termed Fabric 10, a very hard grey ware with distinctive white quartz and feldspar inclusions, occurring in two main forms, jars and bowls. It is clearly not of local origin and, while it is in the tradition of the Roman wares found in the region, its fabric is so different from known Roman wares that it must be of post-Roman date. It is, in fact, similar to material coming from a tenth-century kiln site at Guipel, 20 km north of Rennes, with an archaeomagnetic date of 940±15 AD for the last firing; Guipel jars are similar in form to the jars from the survey area and there are bowls in the same fabric from Tinténiac, 10 km west of Guipel. The available evidence therefore suggests that Fabric 10 is a tenth-century fabric (Davies & Astill 1994: 188, 191).

This fabric occurs extremely rarely: fewer than 150 sherds were recovered in the core, with a total weight of 1,200g from transect-walking, total collection and excavations there. This is much rarer than Iron-Age material. None was recovered from sample transect P, negligible amounts from N and R (17g and 14g respectively) and not much more from Transect M (54g). The sherds are very small. Fabric 10 was found in only 29 of the 1,949 fields walked at 50m intervals in the core, comprising 0.39% of all fabrics found (356g), and in 15 of the 1,067 fields walked in the sample transects (85g), although it did occur in just over 50% of fields from which total collection was made. Despite this higher occurrence, the total collection finds were in very small quantities, often less than 1% of all medieval sherds recovered and only in the exceptional case of D61 more than 10% of medieval sherds (see Table 5.1). It is therefore reasonable to conclude from the relationship between the transect-walking and total collection recovery rates that the ware must have been more densely distributed across the core than present results suggest; however, it is not reasonable to conclude that relative quantities would have been much greater had total collection been made from more fields: it seems unlikely that Fabric 10 would have constituted much more than 1% of all pottery found. In one case (K445/446), it was picked up in transect-walking but not in total collection, although in two others (A116 and D61) it was picked up in both. While it occurred on the surface of seven excavated fields, it was not found in excavation.

Table 5.1 The occurrence of Fabric 10 in total collection fields

Field no.	Fabric 10 as % of medieval sherds	% of Roman pottery in field
A31/79	0.4	2.0
A91	6.0	6.0
A92	8.0	13.0
A116	0.7	0.2
A159	0.5	4.0
B283	1.0	2.0
B319	0.8	0.5
B324	4.0	10.0
B347	2.0	22.0
B409	0.7	3.0
C559	2.0	24.0
D61	58.0	80.0
D142	2.0	10.0
D221	8.0	15.0
D282	2.0	0.3
F187	0.5	0.4
F212	0.8	0.5
G60/61	0.3	0.6
G74	0.2	0.7
H132	0.3	0.4
J165	2.0	0.2
L26	0.1	0.2
L80	0.1	0.1

Fabric 10 as percentage of medieval pottery from each total collection assemblage, together with percentage of Roman pottery in each complete total collection assemblage

There are two areas within the core where Fabric 10 is more commonly found: on either side of the Guer–La Gacilly road in Carentoir and in the basin to the south of Ruffiac (overwhelmingly, that is, in the neighbourhood of the Roman roads from Corseul to Rieux and Le Yaudet to Nantes); relatively little has been found in the modern communes of Saint-Nicolas-du-Tertre and Tréal, that is in a broad band running from northeast to southwest across the centre of the core survey area (Fig. 5.3). Put another way, one might say that it occurs around the commune centres of Ruffiac and Carentoir and – beyond those – in relation to Roman roads and the principal Rivers Oust and Aff. Finds from sample transect M also concentrate near the rivers, both Aff and Vilaine.[4] Total collection finds do not distort the transect-walking distribution pattern, except that they supply findspots roughly in the middle of the core, in the "Roman" area of La Ruaudaie/Le Cleu (above, pp. 76, 84). It is not unreasonable to propose that more intensive fieldwalking coverage of the surface would not significantly change the spatial distribution pattern.

Like Roman sites and tile scatters, Fabric 10 appears relatively frequently on high land in the core, and rather more often than one might expect (see Table 5.2). It also occurs less often on north-facing slopes than do other fabrics. These are both features which differentiate the distribution of this ware from that of the standard twelfth- to sixteenth-century fabrics. It is

Table 5.2 The characteristics of Fabric 10 findspots in the core survey area

	Fabric 10	All fields mean	Roman pottery	Fabric 1
Contour				
‹20m	0	2	0	1.0
20–60m	61	65	69	71.0
›70m	28	14	17	11.0
Slope				
Flat	31	24	25	24.0
South	40	38	35	39.0
North	14	26	25	21.0
Distance from stream				
‹101m	49	33	39	36.0
Distance cadastral settlement				
‹51m	37	22	25	24.0
‹101m	60	45	53	42.0
Cadastral land-use				
Arable	70	62	80	76.0
Curtilage	9	2	3	1.5
Lande	9	24	13	11.0

Percentage of all fields with Fabric 10 by topographic and cadastral category; of transect-walked fields with a) Roman pottery and b) Fabric 1; and of all fields transect-walked

also the case that Fabric 10 occurs close (<101m) to cadastral settlements in a surprising proportion of cases (60%) and is very much more common in cadastral curtilage than are most other fabrics.

These basic statistics indicate that Fabric 10 tends to be found on or near Roman sites and closer than usual to early nineteenth-century cadastral sites in the core (this is less obviously so in sample transects – where in any case there is less Fabric 10 material). This suggests that the finds derive from assemblages that relate to settlement sites, of whatever period; if so, the distribution is extremely unlikely to denote tenth-century arable.

Of course, quantities of this ware are small and patterns may be skewed by the small number of finds. However, we can note that Roman material has a limited occurrence in the survey area: there are very small quantities of Roman pottery (only 4% of all pottery recovered in transect-walking in the core) and larger quantities of tile; they occur in clearly discrete zones and are not widely scattered across the entire area (above, p. 85). In view of this limited occurrence, it must be significant that 62% of Fabric 10 findspots in the core and 45% in Transect M have some kind of Roman association (Fig. 5.3).[5] Five of the 50 core findspots coincide with sites of Roman villas or other structures;[6] 13 of the findspots are within 350m of a Roman site; ten have small quantities of Roman pottery on the surface of the same field; and three have small quantities of Roman pottery on fields within 100m. Lest it be immediately concluded that Fabric 10 must therefore be a Roman fabric, it should also be noted that 96% of Fabric 10 findspots in the core (and 100% in the sample transects) have some sort of medieval association, that Fabric 10 was *not* found in two-thirds of assemblages with Roman material nor in half of the heavy tile scatters that are associated with a wide range of Roman fabrics, and that no Fabric 10 was found in excavation of Roman sites. The relationship with the Roman period and with Roman material cannot be a direct one.

Relationship with the medieval is more direct. There is vastly more medieval than Roman material on the surface of fields, although 40% of fields have none at all; one would therefore expect to find Fabric 10 in assemblages of medieval fabrics and the 96% and 100% with medieval associations are no surprise. This medieval material has both an earlier and a later dimension (eleventh- to fourteenth-century, fifteenth- and sixteenth-century). 11 of 50 Fabric 10 findspots in the core coincide with such high concentrations of the earlier group as to suggest that they are the locations of twelfth- to fourteenth-century settlements; a further two findspots are close to such sites. 31 of the Fabric 10 findspots are in fields with smaller quantities of this material, representing arable worked at that period. Ten of the Fabric 10 findspots coincide with high concentrations of the later medieval material, indicating settlements of that period, while 36 occur

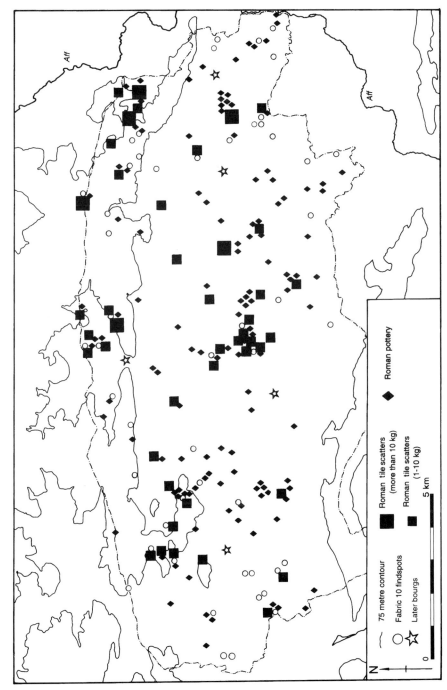

Figure 5.3 *Distribution of all finds of Fabric 10, together with Roman material*

Roman pottery

Roman tile scatters
(more than 10 kg)

Roman tile scatters
(1-10 kg)

75 metre contour

Fabric 10 findspots

Later bourgs

5 km

N

0

Aff

Aff

with the smaller quantities that represent fifteenth- and sixteenth-century arable.[7] All but one of the "later" concentrations are distinguished by high quantities of Fabric 8. This is a heavy ware that was used for storage vessels. It is therefore likely that the later medieval settlements with which Fabric 10 is associated were storage places rather than simple residences, and they almost certainly had lordly connotations at that time (see below, p. 144, n.17). Finds in Transect M have a broadly similar relationship, two of eleven coinciding with twelfth- to fourteenth-century settlement sites.

What does this mean? Two of the 50 Fabric 10 findspots had no medieval pottery at all when walked at 50m intervals, which is very unusual, and five had only very small quantities. These could of course be chance occurrences, but if they are significant the land cannot have been arable of the central and later middle ages: Fabric 10 must here have been dropped in areas that were not cultivated in the succeeding centuries.

It makes sense to suppose that the people who used pottery in the tenth century tended to live in and work from areas with a background of Roman use, whether residential or agricultural; they were much more likely to do this than to develop a completely new zone. The relationship of Fabric 10 to Roman roads and to high land reinforces this Roman association. The Roman background does not have to imply continuity of occupation nor of land-use from the mid or late Roman period: it could be that material from old and collapsing buildings was re-used, or that sites and land that were suitable for occupation or cultivation in the Roman period were just as suitable (and better than others) in the tenth century.

It also makes sense to suppose that the places where people were losing pottery in the tenth century were sometimes the precursors of noble settlements – or places appurtenant to those – of the later middle ages. This is demonstrably so at the later noble site H132, hard by the Château de la Ruée; and virtually all of the Fabric 10 findspots that coincide with medieval settlement sites have some sort of "noble" context in the thirteenth, fourteenth and fifteenth centuries, as well as accumulations of Fabric 8 (see below, pp. 126–7). In other words, people using Fabric 10 dropped it in places that were frequently to become noble residences in the future. It is therefore likely that these were richer people, whose descendants may have thrived to become the minor nobility of the fourteenth century; an association with the wealthy would in any case be suggested by the fact that Fabric 10 is rare, that it is an import and that no other wares have survived from that period in the survey area.

Given the limited horizons and limited market activity of most of the peasant population of the ninth century, this fits. The distribution of Fabric 10, therefore, is broadly – although obviously not entirely – an indication of the distribution of the properties of richer households of the tenth century and/or of households with external connections. Since it is impossible to locate ninth-century Redon properties precisely, we cannot argue that this non-local material arrived in the context of relationships with the monastery. It is, of course, likely that some did. There are three zones of Redon interest that can be approximately identified: the environs of Lodineu in Ruffiac, and of Quoiqueneuc and of Le Vieux Bourg in Tréal. All three certainly have a scatter of Fabric 10 but these scatters do not dominate the overall distribution pattern within the core. Similarly, the much more precise location of Redon properties in the fifteenth to eighteenth centuries shows some correlation with Fabric 10 distribution, but this is far from total:[8] fewer than half of Fabric 10 findspots are within 500m of Redon properties of that period. Hence, there is no strong correlation with known Redon properties of the ninth century or later and it must be unlikely that Redon was entirely responsible for the imports. It must in any case be significant that the imports come from the north, beyond Rennes, and not from the southwest from the (nearer) late eighth- to tenth-century Meudon potteries outside Vannes (Le Roux & Thollard 1990: 70–71; Fichet de Clairfontaine 1996: 76–7); nor does the survey area have pottery which matches the ninth-/tenth-century kiln debris from Langon to the southeast, 7½ km south of Transect M.[9]

It is worth noting that we have another glimpse of external contacts not dominated by Redon: round about 950 a man called Moysen gave a *tref* (a farm) in Carentoir to the monastery of Landévennec on the far west Breton coast. What is interesting about Moysen is not only that he made a pious donation to a distant monastery but he did the transaction 80 km away in Nantes, where it was witnessed by the bishop, a count and a viscount (La Borderie 1888: no. 40). Another text from the Landévennec collection suggests that Moysen was a *fidelis* (member of the retinue) of the Breton ruler Alan (who himself made a large grant of land, vineyards, fisheries and saltpans near Nantes (Batz-Guérande) to Landévennec, at about the same time (La Borderie 1888: no. 25)). By the mid tenth century, then, at least one Carentoir property owner had very wide interests and (probably) a place at the top of the Breton social scale. It is certainly credible to see such men bringing hard, serviceable pottery into the area; it is quite clear that some Ruffiac and Carentoir people were involved in networks other than, or in addition to, the very powerful religious network.

Three fields had disproportionately large quantities of Fabric 10 (11, 10 and 22 sherds respectively): A116 (Les Viviers), B409 (Le Bois Guillaume) and D61 (Les Cormiers).[10] A116 is a medieval settlement site, by deduction noble, not far from a Roman tile scatter (see below, pp. 125–6); B409 the same, but near a larger Roman tile scatter; D61 has a very large tile scatter, with Roman pottery associated and very little medieval material (though a

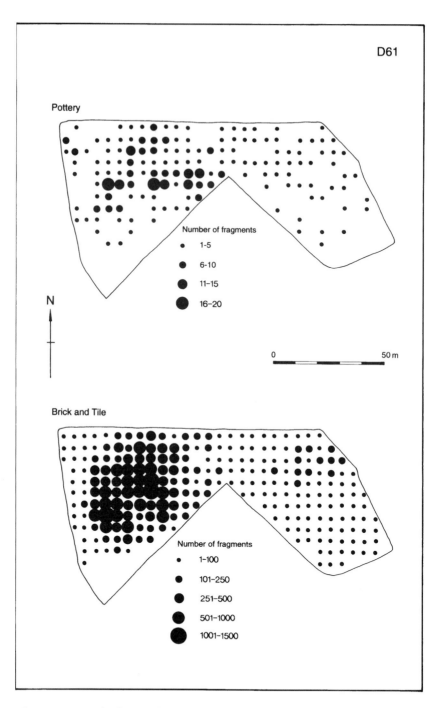

Figure 5.4 *Total collection plots for Field D61*

little Fabric 8) (Fig. 5.4). The three core accumulations reinforce the general point that Fabric 10 users often lived and worked near Roman sites, many of which foreshadowed medieval noble sites, especially of the eleventh to fourteenth centuries. All three may well be tenth-century settlement sites, given these accumulations of an otherwise rare fabric. We see no reason why the neighbourhood of D61 should not have had a *lis*, lying as it does on the main Angers–Carhaix Roman road, not far from Le Mur and with a probable background as a stopping place of the Roman period (see above, pp. 81–3 and Fig. 4.10); if this were so, it may suggest some continuity of special, route-related function for this zone from Roman through early medieval period.

The impact of Redon

Despite some disturbances from outside, the monastery of Redon became an established presence in Brittany and a powerful lord. During this period it suffered two major dislocations, both caused by Viking activity: such were the dangers of living near the coast that in the mid ninth century the bishop of Vannes was captured, the bishop of Nantes was forced to flee his city and the abbot of Redon asked the Breton ruler Salomon for a safer place to live; by 866 the community had been given an inland site at Plélan, 20 km north of Carentoir, and the relics of St Maxent were translated there, with great ceremony, in 869 (see Fig. 5.5). Although 40 km north of Redon, Plélan was still in the area of the monastery's property interests and the displacement of the community seems to have made little difference to its business in southeast Brittany (cf. Smith 1992: 200–01). Half a century later the problems were more severe and in the 920s the community left Redon, travelling east to Candé and Auxerre before turning south and settling at Poitiers, all at a time when Viking invasion had also forced Breton political leaders to England and other monastic communities to several parts of northern France (Guillotel 1982; Chédeville & Guillotel 1984: 363–8, 374–402). However, it looks as if some members of the community remained at Redon through all this disruption: many of the properties acquired in the ninth and early tenth centuries still belonged to Redon in later centuries.

The impact of the monastery on the region of southeast Brittany was considerable. Already by 900 it had amassed enormous wealth, from which it could expect a substantial annual income in goods and cash – the highest we know of after that of the Breton ruler and his family. The abbot and his agents moved throughout southeastern Brittany and did so as major lords: they had some property in every *plebs* for an area of 30 × 55 km around the monastery, and in clusters of *plebes* beyond that, especially in the saltpans of Guérande to the southeast and in Locmariaquer on the coast to the west (Davies 1988: 188–90). They also controlled whole *plebes*, including a core of five around Redon itself. Even the first abbot, Conwoion, was clearly involved in commercial activities, taking wax to sell in the markets of Tours, and by the 860s he was buying and otherwise acquiring considerable interests in the saltpans near the Loire mouth; by 870 Abbot Ritcant was renewing and renegotiating the terms of inland agricultural tenancies. Abbot and monks ran their property as a business and ran it for profit. They went to market, literally, and were also in the market in the wider sense. However, although all of Redon's properties were therefore touched by commerce – in that surplus was taken for commercial use – market activity was very much focussed in the area near Redon itself, whose accessibility by land and sea (and therefore suitability as market and port) was emphasized by the writer of the *Gesta Sanctorum Rotonensium* (Brett 1989: 119). Here the *plebes* were different in character from inland *plebes* like Ruffiac and Carentoir; further, where production was specialized it was in the lands east of the River Vilaine (and particularly near the Loire mouth), not in inland parts (Davies 1988: 192-9). The development before the twelfth century of a specialized pottery industry just outside Redon, at Saint-Jean-la-Poterie, though not necessarily connected with the monastery, is a further indicator of the commercial quality of that neighbourhood (Fig. 5.5).

The impact of Redon on Ruffiac and Carentoir was also major, although it may not have appeared to be so at the time. The monastery acquired many properties in each village, with at least 52 different units in Ruffiac and 21 in Carentoir by the end of the ninth century. These properties were still owned by Redon in the (well-documented) fourteenth to eighteenth centuries, many then being managed from the Priory at Ruffiac. We do not know why the numbers are so high, but it is likely that personal connections were responsible: according to the *Gesta Sanctorum Rotonensium*, the family of the first abbot, Conwoion, came from Comblessac (Brett 1989: 111). Comblessac is adjacent to Carentoir, lying to the northeast, in Transect R, and includes the major early settlement site of Le Mur (see above, pp. 81–3). Conwoion's companions in the new foundation may well have had Ruffiac and Carentoir family connections.

As a consequence of these property (and perhaps personal) interests, there was some coming and going between the survey area and Redon in the ninth century – by rich donors, priests, monastic agents – although this was not sufficient to bring Ruffiac and Carentoir into the commercial mainstream; the region must have been too far from the port. Priests took to retiring to the monastery of Redon at the end of their lives:

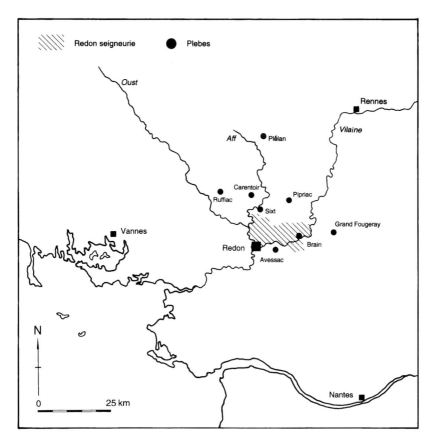

Figure 5.5 *Map to show Redon in context*

Maenwethen, priest of Ruffiac, retired there, taking with him a property that had been given him as village priest; this caused trouble in the locality, for the original donor had meant the gift to be to the benefit of Ruffiac church, not of some far-off monastery; only when Maenwethen made him a substantial cash payment, sometime after 866, did the donor agree to withdraw his objections (de Courson 1863: nos. 144, 143).

The most obvious effect of the impact of Redon on the survey area is not an increase in commercial contacts but a change in the patterns of proprietorship: not only was a major landlord introduced into the locality, but many former peasant proprietors became tenants. This change was particularly rapid during the decade of the 860s, when many peasants made gifts of land to the monks – which they immediately received back as tenancies. Life continued as before; they lived in their old homes and managed the daily round as they had done for decades. They kept their freedom, and they kept their lifestyle, but they were no longer property owners and a proportion of their produce now went away from the locality to the coast. This must have drained some wealth from the villages and it is likely to have affected the internal social structure of the communities.

Possibilities

We have virtually no evidence about what was going on in the survey area during the "great gap" of AD 400–800. However, in view of the intensity of use of this landscape in both the first and second centuries and the ninth century, the region cannot have been deserted. There is no hint of any post-Roman (or later) cataclysm. Indeed, the very fact that someone was buried with late Roman military equipment in Guer, to the north of Carentoir, may suggest some controlled immigration (Petit 1970); and the partial rebuilding at the Roman villa at La Démardais, also to the north, with its sherds of several early medieval fabrics, implies use of this Roman site from at least the eighth to twelfth centuries and probably before (Blin 1993: 21–2, 35–6).[11] The Roman road from Vannes still ran past Le Mur and northeast Carentoir in the seventh/eighth centuries, and Le Mur was still recognized as a *castrum* (fort, camp); this must suggest the continuity of some elements of the late Roman population. Indeed, Le Mur was known at that time by the Gallo-Roman name of "Marsac", a name nowadays restricted to a hamlet (where there is a heavy tile scatter) 1 km to the southwest (Krusch 1896: 373–4) (cf. Fig. 4.10); "Marsac" may have been a term for the whole zone of northeast Carentoir/south Comblessac, like "Lerniac" in the Ruffiac basin in the ninth century.

The likelihood is that the land continued to be worked throughout this period, in a largely self-sufficient way – a likelihood reinforced by the Gallo-Roman names of the *plebes* (Vallerie 1986: 90, 219–22). Indeed, Noel-Yves Tonnerre has even argued for demographic *growth* in the region, given immigration of some British into the Vannetais, and this proposal is certainly worth serious consideration (1994: 119–23). Recent commentators on the local toponymy would, however, see the survey area itself as predominantly Gallo-Roman, with rather less settlement by incoming British than parts to the north and west (Vallerie 1986: 90, 217–21); some gradual infiltration in the sixth and seventh centuries is postulated (Tonnerre 1994: 42–62). This is perfectly credible, provided we remember that personal and place-names were – by the ninth century –

overwhelmingly Breton; indeed, Anowareth, from Maur to the northeast of Carentoir, was a Breton speaker in the ninth century (Planiol 1893–4: 237); some social change clearly took place, even if that was essentially one of linguistic rather than population shift.[12]

Patterns of proprietorship and the shape and nature of aristocratic residences will have changed since the heyday of the Roman Empire; building in stone seems to have stopped and cereal production levels may well have dropped.[13] The structure of political authority will have changed too, although this cannot be expected to have had much impact on rural communities. Most obviously, tax will have stopped going to a very distant and high-level central authority and roads will have stopped being maintained. It is likely that a proportion of surplus continued to be creamed off the hamlets by local big men but that a proportion remained with the producers; peasants may even have become a little richer. Elsewhere in the southeast, in Plélan, Avessac, Brain, Grand Fougeray, a good case can be made that Roman imperial property was acquired by powerful men like counts, ultimately coming into the hands of the ninth-century Breton rulers; the same case cannot be made for the survey area, which was dominated by communities of small-scale proprietors until Redon established its interests.

The machtiern system was clearly in decline when evidenced in the ninth century, since by then it was common for a single individual to be machtiern of several *plebes* and for a few families to control several machtiernships; in the tenth and eleventh centuries the system petered out completely. If it was in decline in the ninth century it may well have been fully operational in the seventh and eighth centuries: in such circumstances we should expect there to have been one machtiern per *plebs*, a greater range of duties undertaken by machtierns, including overseeing the operation of the suretyship system, and less of a hereditary quality to the exercise of the office.

Another development of the period 400–800 must have been the establishment of rural Christianity, with "conversion" of the local population, setting up of local priests for each community, and the building of churches. There is no need to associate this directly with migration of British from Britain[14] but it is nevertheless reasonable to suppose that it was happening across the late fifth, sixth and early seventh centuries: bishops from eastern Armorica appeared regularly at northern Frankish councils in the century from 461 to 567, with, notably, bishops from Rennes *and* Vannes *and* Nantes appearing at the all-France council of 511 (de Clercq 1963: 13). These were councils concerned with definition of spheres of ecclesiastical authority and standards for the clergy, as well as proper respect for church property and the liturgy. British Christians were clearly not integrated into any Gallo-Roman pastoral machinery in 509–21, for the bishops of Rennes, Angers and Tours had to write to two local priests to protest about them carrying portable altars to their compatriots' cottages, celebrating mass with the assistance of women (La Borderie 1896–1914: II.526–7). The use of extremely archaic formulary material in local records in the ninth-century villages, especially in Ruffiac, must give this Christian impact a pre-seventh-century origin (for these are basically sixth-century formulas, picked up by the Christian clergy to record donations and then repeated for generations; Davies 1990a: 79–80).

Of the ninth and tenth centuries we can say that there was intensive use of the land, with plenty of settlements and plenty of arable; there may well have been some increase in cereal production and perhaps some introduction of buckwheat. Smallholdings were often discrete, with mixed land-use within their bounds, although sometimes there were larger expanses of arable, in which several peasants had shares, with meadow pasture and wood lying beyond; and in both types of case the *lande* lay beyond again. Many (perhaps most) people lived on the land they worked, although some lived in larger or smaller nucleations. Even the latter cannot have been far from the workplace: all would have walked to work easily; even where they had to cross 25 hectares, this is only 10 or 15 minutes' walk. Communities were largely self-sufficient, but there were religious and other networks with a very wide span, covering a lot of ground, and rather smaller networks – across two or three *plebes* – of the more influential local worthies who served as judges and took other leading community roles. A little tax went to the Breton ruler and some dues went to the local machtierns.

There is not a hint in these inland communes of any Viking, or other political, dislocation or disaster. The raids do not seem to have touched peasant life at all and there is no sign of anything that could be classified as a Viking or anti-Viking defence, like the two sets of earthworks at Trans in northeast Brittany (Langouet et al. 1977; Hamel-Simon et al. 1979). Nothing suggests that there were many durable material goods in the inland *plebes* and they were probably not worth raiding: there was both food and manpower on the coasts. Until the tenth century the inland culture may have been essentially aceramic, although it is equally possible that people used pottery of such poor quality that it has not survived. In the tenth century some individuals in the area started acquiring pottery that lasted. This can only have been the richer people, for it came from some distance away and there does not seem to have been much of it.

The fact that this pottery can be found on higher land, and never below 20m, suggests that climatic factors may have influenced the distribution of the residences of those who lost it. We should expect the weather to have been wetter in the ninth and tenth centuries than it is now, so it would have made sense to avoid valley bottoms. The fact that away to the south by Renac the surrounding basin was flooded enough to be called a port gives us some written evidence of wet lowlands.

The richer people of the tenth century often used old Roman sites. A few of the areas where they dropped pottery did not become arable or residences of the central and later middle ages, but most did; and a third are at sites that were later to become settlements that were associated with the nobility.

Notes

1. For a helpful survey of the evidence about the region as a whole in this period, see Chédeville & Guillotel 1984: 21–190.
2. For what follows in this section, in much greater detail, see Davies 1988.
3. It does not follow that the rents reflect overall product proportions (cf. below, pp. 138, 170), but the use of a *sowable* area as the standard measure must be a significant indicator of common land-use.
4. The two Transect N findspots (N161/162, N192) are in the north (Les Toulans and Les Tieulais); the two Transect R findspots are in the south (near the Angers–Carhaix road), La Hayette (R28) and La Cruyère (R62). Four of the Transect M finds were near the Aff (M12, M95, M103, M151) and four near the Vilaine (M499, M562, M564, M651); the other three (M284, M311, M405) were distributed across the transect. The Aff and Oust valleys clearly cannot have been deserted in the tenth century, as has been suggested for earlier centuries of the early middle ages (Tonnerre 1994: 120).
5. Also in the sample transects: R28 (Roman Fabric 50) and N161/162 (a large tile scatter).
6. Cf. Transect M, at one probable villa site, M12.
7. Half of the later medieval settlements are continuing earlier settlements.
8. AD Ille-et-Vilaine 3H187, 3H188 L4 & L5, 3H190, 3H191[2] L2, 3H193; AD Loire-Atlantique B1999.
9. Langon (La Chenac) kiln wasters were studied by GGA at the Direction des Antiquités in the 1980s; we understand that publication is forthcoming.
10. D190 (Le Château du Boschet) produced one extremely large sherd; it had a *little* of the medieval Fabrics 1, 4 and 6, but not much else.
11. Potentially an early medieval site of great importance: sherds of Merovingian, Meudon-, Trans- *and* Chartres-de-Bretagne-type were discovered, as well as extensive metalworking of the central middle ages.
12. There is an enormous literature on linguistic change in early medieval Brittany and the subject remains controversial (e.g. Fleuriot 1980: 79–97; Tanguy 1980). There has been a tendency to downplay the significance of the overwhelmingly Breton nomenclature of the Redon Cartulary west of the river Vilaine by arguing that because ninth-century Brittany was ruled by Bretons, the witnesses to transactions must have been high-status Bretons, and hence the mass of the peasant population could have had (unevidenced) Latin/Roman names. In view of the facts that: (i) the mass of the ninth-century Redon

Cartulary actors and witnesses west of the Vilaine are demonstrably peasants, (ii) the mass of names of property units and minor topographic features are Breton, (iii) a significant number of distinctive (and decaying) institutions have Breton names, it cannot rationally be maintained that the survey area was other than overwhelmingly Breton-speaking in the ninth century. The contrast with the Romance-speaking area east of the Vilaine is perfectly clear – where witnesses and actors have overwhelmingly Latin (or Germanic) names (Davies 1988: 13–16). It does not, of course, follow from this that the survey area was overrun by British from Britain prior to the ninth century; there could well have been a relatively small infiltration, as is indeed postulated by several scholars of the present generation, but by reason of processes that we do not fully understand a shift in the vernacular language took place. We know too little about language change, for all its crucial importance for social change, but it does happen.

13. A drop in cereal production levels might be expected given the displacement of the villa owners. Dated pollen diagrams from Brittany tend to indicate a decline in cereal pollens in the late Roman period (see above, pp. 86–7); cereal presence picks up round about the ninth century and some cores (e.g. near Melrand, to the west) show an increase in the central middle ages, as also the introduction of buckwheat (Chédeville & Guillotel 1984: 42; Marguerie & Langouet 1993; Marguerie 1992: 241–2; Visset 1994). It is therefore difficult to avoid the conclusion that, in general, cereal production declined in the late and/or post-Roman period and revived several centuries later; this must have been in part a consequence of the climatic change (colder and wetter weather) which is known to have occurred in the fifth/sixth century, whatever the local social and political changes. It is, however, impossible to be precise both about the absolute chronology of change in the historic period and about practice in every locality. Given the way that pollen moves in some soils, the significance of the precise location of the pollen core and the inevitably wide dating band (usually ± at least 50 years), we have some difficulty with interpretations of pollen cores that have been related to specific historical events (e.g. the brief period of Viking dislocation or the larger period of British colonization; Tonnerre 1994, 277–8, 152–3).

No dated cores have been taken from the survey area itself and the cores from near-by Beaumont, in Saint-Laurent, did not supply usable data for this period (see above, p. 69); those from Kerfontaine in Sérent (the next nearest, 10 km west of Ruffiac) are hard by one of the few areas of more extensive early medieval woodland; however, they demonstrate nicely that: (i) in this more marginal zone woodland clearance, and the consequent spread of heathland flora, is a development of the early historic period; (ii) the heathland was intermittently cultivated from about the eighth century until the twentieth (Visset 1994). Cf. the two corn-drying ovens discovered in post-Roman/pre-eleventh- and twelfth-century levels in excavations at Le Yaudet in 1995, where, interestingly, there seems to have been a shift from wheat to rye predominance after the Roman period (pers. comm. Patrick Galliou).

14. La Borderie (1896–1914: I.281–2, II.142–4), among others, argued that the *plebs/plou* was originally a lay group of immigrants from Britain, with its own secular and religious leaders; Largillière (1925: 197–219) argued that the *plou* was an autonomous ecclesiastical parish arising from the missionary activities of priests during social and political disorder in the fifth and sixth centuries; Bernier (1982: 51–2, 88, 92) refined Largillière's thesis. Other recent commentators emphasize this or that element of the original theses, although there is a tendency to prefer lay colonizing groups that quickly took on a

religious significance (Chédeville & Guillotel 1984: 89–97; Tonnerre 1994: 208–13). The point is equally, and reasonably, made that some Christian groupings *must* have had pre-Breton origins (cf. Vallerie 1986: 221).

In the absence of contemporary evidence, it is impossible to reach a firm view on any of these approaches; *plebes* were certainly not ecclesiastically independent in the ninth century and, though they had a religious aspect, their civil dimension is more strongly evidenced than the religious in ninth-century texts; see Davies 1983.

CHAPTER 6

Nobles and peasants

Castles and towns

Whether or not we believe in the Feudal Revolution and the very particular series of social changes that have been proposed for the eleventh century, it is not unreasonable to say that the year 1000 ushered in a new era.[1] In western Europe as a whole we are accustomed to view the succeeding eleventh and twelfth centuries as a period of economic growth, of the establishment of towns and of the construction of castles – at first relatively simple timber structures placed on a *motte* or artificial mound but by the later twelfth century much more substantial stone buildings.

The changes of this period were not purely material, for there were accompanying changes in the social order and in the nature of politics. New men came into the western European aristocracies, which – in France especially – had a heightened military character: these were fighting men who went crusading in the east and later in the south, and who had military obligations to their lords and leaders. While slavery and the personal unfreedom of the ninth century rapidly declined in northwest Europe, peasants became subject to new exactions from old and new landlords, taken as labour, as rent and as dues of various kinds. And beyond the world of agricultural labour, new kinds of community expressed new kinds of identity, as townspeople on the one hand and as members of reformed religious orders on the other.

There is very little direct evidence from the survey area, whether written or material, for these two centuries of change. Although one major development was the availability of pottery on a scale not experienced since the Roman period, if ever, the pottery most used in the survey area was made of a fabric that had a very long currency (Fabric 1). While it was probably used until the fifteenth century we cannot precisely date the moment when it appeared. The likelihood is that a few sherds survive from the late eleventh century, rather more from the twelfth, and the bulk of it from the thirteenth and fourteenth (Davies & Astill 1994: 189–94). We cannot therefore use pottery to date the start of new developments in the survey area.

Despite the small quantity of indisputably eleventh- and twelfth-century evidence, the paucity of material is itself significant in a world in which written text and material goods were multiplying daily. This very paucity, among other factors, allows us to sketch the place of the area within the developing framework.

The charters added to the Redon Cartulary in the eleventh and twelfth centuries show the presence of the new kind of fighting men (*milites*), castles (*castra* and *castella*), small towns (*burgi*), mills, grants of land for building, new forms of income – and an aristocratic grip on the latter – across the region. They make it clear that eastern Brittany as a whole shared in the general western European trends of urban development, castle-building and increased aristocratic control of the product of the land, even if town communities did not show the institutional development of northern Italy or the Low Countries, military obligations were slow to institutionalize and stone castle-building was late to develop (Galliou & Jones 1991: 210, 170; Chédeville & Tonnerre 1987: 184-9, 192). However, although there are charters that relate to Sérent (west of Transect P, beyond the Oust), to Guer to the north, and to Sixt and Guipry in and around Transect M, there is none that relates to the core of the survey area. *Milites* from Sérent gave lands and a proportion of rents to Redon in mid eleventh and early twelfth centuries; *milites* from Sixt gave lands, and an interest in mills, and places to build both houses and a mill in the early twelfth century; a viscount of the castle at La Nouée (Bieuzy) – himself the brother of the viscount of the major castle at Josselin – gave some rights in Guer church and a place beside the church to build a house and garden, among other gifts, in 1124–5; and the *miles nobilissimus* of Lohéac (just north of Guipry), *princeps* of the castle there, gave property, toll and mill rights, including several such rights in Guipry, in 1101 (de Courson 1863: nos. 322, 351, 382; 372, 349, 368; 391; 366).

While it could of course be chance that these gifts were made from places surrounding the core survey area rather than from within it, it is likely that the omission is significant – particularly when we remember the prominence of this core in the ninth-century Redon collection. There is no castle and no *mottes* have been identified there.[2] It is more than possible, indeed likely, that these parishes were *not* dominated by the new *milites*.

The absence of *milites* can in fact be explained: there was a strong lordly presence through the monastery of Redon's extensive properties in the three core parishes. This was such a major presence that the area cannot have suggested itself as an obvious target for any "upstart" *miles*. *Mottes* were certainly thrown up just beyond the core: there are five in Comblessac, at the southern end of Transect R, two being on the slopes of Le Mur, and there is another at the northern end of the transect, by Penhouet (SRAB Comblessac 6, 7, 9; SRAB Les Brûlais 1H; Brand' Honneur 1990: 56). Castles were constructed at Malestroit, beyond the western end of Transect P, by the late eleventh century, and at La Gacilly (at that time in the south of Carentoir parish but now south of the commune) in the twelfth. Each became the centre of a major *seigneurie*,[3] and in the mid fifteenth century the status of the lordship of Malestroit was raised to the ranks of the "nine great barons" (Leguay & Martin 1982: 27; Gallet 1983: 126–31; Jones 1988: 233). Both stimulated urban development in their immediate neighbourhoods, though the town of Malestroit grew earlier and much more rapidly than that of La Gacilly (still smaller than Carentoir *bourg* in the late middle ages); indeed, Malestroit was noted for fulling by the early thirteenth century (Chédeville & Tonnerre 1987: 394–5, 405).

Peasant tenants of Redon became subject to lordly and other dues: by the time that detailed documentation of these obligations becomes available in the fifteenth century they were well established and clearly ancient. They are best explained as a development of the twelfth century. Tenants owed "obedience", "corporal residence" (the obligation to keep the property occupied and the rent flowing) and harvest work, and were committed to return varying proportions of their produce – the tenth sheaf of cereals, for example.[4]

In the longrun other *sieurs* and *seigneurs* became established in the core – including powerful nobles like the *seigneurs* of Coëtion and La Boixière – but we do not have to suppose that they all took their origin from new men of the eleventh and/or twelfth centuries. Indeed Coëtion, like Le Bois Guillaume (Le Fossé in late medieval terms), may well have been a noble house of long slow growth, from at least tenth-century origins (see above, pp. 105, 107, and below, pp. 125–6).

Just as this was no arena for new *milites* to flex their muscles, so also the core of the survey area does not seem to have seen the establishment of any new religious house of the reformed orders of the late eleventh century – there were no Cistercians, for example. However, it is likely that the Redon outpost at Prieuré in Ruffiac took shape as a Priory at this period, a community from which the monastic lands in the core and beyond were managed. There was also one major new religious development in eastern Carentoir in the twelfth century, which had significant consequences for the future: a foundation of the military order of Knights Templar was established, at the site of the present hamlet of Le Temple. This important foundation (one of only six in Brittany) became the seat of a Commandery of the Hospitallers after 1312, following confiscation of the Templars' goods, one of only eight in Brittany (Leguay & Martin 1982: 67). The Commander had his own *château* till the late sixteenth century, and, consequently, with its large church and special sanctuary rights, Le Temple became a separate, very small, parish within Carentoir from 1387. The special settlement attracted development around it: its *bourg* was comparable in size to that of La Gacilly in the sixteenth century.

The importance of pottery

Land-use and settlement

The most widely occurring of pottery fabrics of all periods is our "Fabric 1", a soft brown coarseware of local origin used both for tableware and cooking vessels in the thirteenth and fourteenth centuries, perhaps beginning as early as the eleventh and continuing into the fifteenth century. So common is it that it was found on the surface of just over half (52%) of all fields walked in the initial fieldwalking programme in the core, on 69% of fields walked in Transect P to the west, on 49% in Transect N to the northwest, on 46% in Transect M to the east, and on a very low 33% in Transect R to the northeast. Its dominance of the surface collection record is therefore especially striking, and the very large quantities recovered allow some serious statistical analysis (22.719 kg came from the first phase of fieldwalking alone).

The surface distribution of this material has the following characteristics: it occurs throughout the survey area, though less densely in the centre of the core than in Carentoir and in western transects of Ruffiac, and less densely in the south than in the north (although it avoids the northern, Roman, boundary road) (Fig. 6.1). Although widespread in its occurrence, it is absent from some well-defined zones, like the areas north of Les Vignes and around Le Bois Faux (Car) and south of La Ville Robert (Ruff), and in and around the modern *bourg* of Tréal (Fig. 6.2). In the sample transects it was widespread in Transect P; widespread in Transect N, although rare in a zone across the Caro–Augan boundary; common in the north of Transect

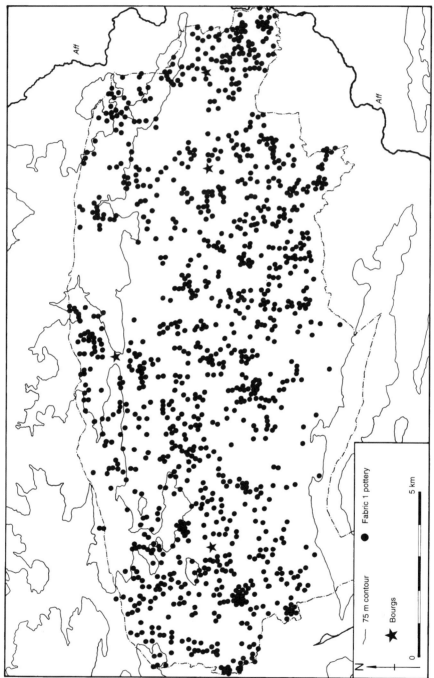

Figure 6.1 *Distribution of Fabric 1 in the core survey area*

120

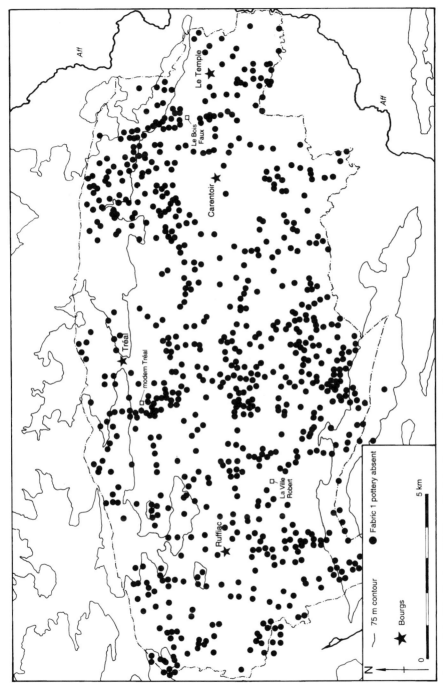

Figure 6.2 *Distribution of fields walked in the core where Fabric 1 was absent*

R but sporadic in the south, especially near Le Mur and the River Aff; and common in much of Transect M, although rare in the commune of Bruc. As in the core, it was absent from some well-defined zones of the sample transects, and had an essentially similar type of occurrence. Zones associated with modern French "wood" names, like *bois*, are notable in the gaps, although the earlier "wood" names like *touche* are often used of fields or settlements which do have Fabric 1, as are places with names denoting poor land, like *friches* and *roche*. Most of the material lies between 20m and 60m, but we find it across the whole contour range, and more frequently on south- than north-facing slopes, and within 250m of water. These topographical characteristics reflect the characteristics of all fields walked (percentages lie very close to the "all fields" mean), although Fabric 1 does occur more frequently than the norm on steep slopes and is rare in low wet valley bottoms and on high flat ridges (see Table 8.4). Its absence in low wet valley bottoms is particularly marked in Transect R and Transect M.

Apart from the local interest of zones with and without the pottery, there is little here that is remarkable. But, the distinctive, and significant, aspect of this fabric's distribution is that fields with Fabric 1 tend to occur in discrete groups, creating zones of the order of 50–60 ha. The definition of these groups of fields is not a chance consequence of the fieldwalking programme, since the zones are often surrounded by walked fields that lack fabrics of the central to late medieval period (Fig. 6.3); indeed, it is often the case that fields at the edge of the zone have very late or post-medieval fabrics (such as Fabric 4) but no Fabric 1. Further, most of the fields in each group have very small quantities of the fabric, evenly or haphazardly distributed – quantities of the order of 5g, 10g, 20g. Everything suggests that this material occurs as a consequence of agricultural activity, and has been distributed in the course of manuring: it does not derive from sub-surface features, and quantities decrease through the ploughsoil (see above, pp. 28–9). Hence, these groups of fields identify arable manured with farmyard waste of the thirteenth and fourteenth centuries.

It is striking that in virtually every group there is one field (and occasionally more than one field) with much larger quantities of pottery, quantities that range from 50g to more than 500g; in such cases the distribution of sherds within the field is neither even nor haphazard but clusters on the surface, covering areas from $1,250m^2$ to (exceptionally) $123,000m^2$. Other medieval fabrics (earlier: 10; 5, 7, 58; and later: 4, 6, 8, 23) usually occur in the cluster; indeed, the thin-walled tableware Fabric 7 hardly ever occurs except in or in association with such clusters of material (see Table 6.4, pp. 140–1). Where excavation has been carried out, the clusters can be seen to overlie sub-surface structural features or debris.[5] In other words, the clusters reflect the presence of settlements of the central to

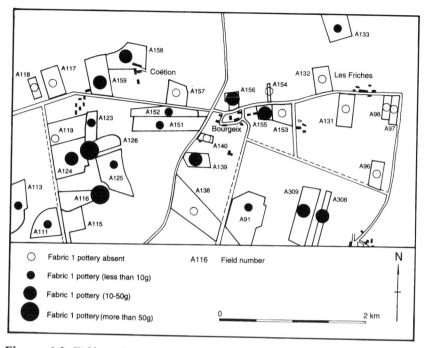

Figure 6.3 *Fields with and without Fabric 1 in the area of Coëtion/Bourgeix (Ruffiac)*

late middle ages. (They lie overwhelmingly between 20m and 60m (82%) and within 200m of water (66%), as one would expect of settlement locations.) A group of Fabric 1 fields therefore locates the area of a settlement, *together with* the fertilized arable worked from that settlement.

Where – as occasionally happens – a group lacks a field with a dense cluster, it is likely that the "settlement" field was not walked, since it lay under pasture or wood or existing buildings. There are also some isolated fields with Fabric 1 that have no obvious relationship with the discrete groups. These isolated fields must mark the location of additional arable and in some cases of considerably less substantial, less well furnished settlements or even farm buildings. Fields with Fabric 1 also surround three of the present commune centres in the core, Ruffiac, Saint-Nicolas and Carentoir, and could well reflect the presence of "open fields" in these locations, as later (see below, pp. 247–8).

Overall the distribution of Fabric 1 is an exceptionally important tool for defining the arable fertilized from the twelfth to the fifteenth century. The pattern is distinctive and period-specific. There are 56 clearly identifiable groups of Fabric 1 fields (each of the order of 50–60 ha). The occurrence of the pottery on steep slopes implies some pressure on land for cultivation in this period, as does its association with the stony land indicated by *friche/roche* names.

Settlement pattern

The above material is very useful for indicating the location and distribution of arable worked from the twelfth to the fifteenth century. But it also has settlement implications. What does it tell us of the overall settlement pattern at this period?

Everything suggests that the present commune centres of Ruffiac and Carentoir in the core, and Comblessac and Pipriac in the sample transects, were already residential centres at this period.[6] Carentoir and Ruffiac had Romanesque churches on the site of the present parish churches (the former replaced in the late nineteenth century, the latter enlarged and restored after the twelfth). We also know from elsewhere in the region (Guer just to the north) that houses were built by parish churches in the early twelfth century (de Courson 1863: no. 391). It is clear from the manuring scatters discussed above that there were arable fields near the *bourgs* that were not associated with large (settlement) clusters; they were doubtless worked by walking daily to the fields from the *bourgs*, as was still the case in the 1820s. Tréal's *bourg* was located at the present hamlet of Le Vieux Bourg by 1484, and is likely to have been ancient at that time since its Bourg*neuf*, 300m to the southwest, was also well established in 1484.[7]

It is also perfectly clear from archival material, from excavation and from surface scatters that habitation was not confined to the *bourgs*, and that settlement was dispersed across the area. The broad settlement pattern, then, is one both of nucleation and of dispersal: both things are characteristic, as they had been in the ninth century. In the later middle ages the dispersed settlements must have included seigneurial complexes as well as peasant hamlets, since we know that there was a large, and growing, nobility in Brittany at this time. Given the regional statistics, we should expect there to have been a substantial number of noble households in this area: we know, for example, that there were at least 25 noble households in the parish of Carentoir in the mid fifteenth century.[8]

"Nobility" was a legal category in northern France, from the late twelfth century, with distinctive rules of succession. "Nobles" had considerable privileges – especially greater control over their feudal tenures and exemption from payment of *fouages* (hearth taxes) – but they also had special responsibilities and were obliged to do military service. The period from the thirteenth to the mid fifteenth century is one in which many families sought to acquire, and succeeded in acquiring, noble status in

Brittany, such that there were about 10,000 noble families in the region by c.1450 (something near 5% of the estimated population and more than twice the proportion in France as a whole) (Galliou & Jones 1991: 257; cf. Gallet 1983: 81–93, on the Vannetais). Although this nobility included *grands seigneurs* like the Rohans and the baron of Malestroit, many were people of exceptionally modest means and small properties: the latter could even be smaller than 20 ha; 90% of *seigneuries* and *sieuries* in the fifteenth-century Vannetais were of small scale, that is of 30–40 ha (Gallet 1983: 92–3).

Can we say that noble settlements are archaeologically distinguishable at this period within the pattern of dispersed settlements? The surface material patterns are neither clear enough nor consistent enough to produce a water-tight model for the "noble" surface scatter. However, one or two aspects are distinctive and there is enough consistency to make some credible suggestions. Firstly, Fabric 1 clusters which are quite exceptionally dense and also include some quantity of Fabrics 5 and 7, and of the later 6 and 8, all lie in the neighbourhood of known major grand houses of the sixteenth and seventeenth centuries. There are four of these in the core: A116, 300m from the *château* of Coëtion, L96, hard by the substantial house La Charmille on the outskirts of Ruffiac *bourg*, H132, 150m from the Château de la Ruée (all in Ruffiac), and C292/293, hard by the *château* of Peccadeuc (in Carentoir) (Table 6.1).

Even though quantities of Fabrics 5, 7 and 6 are small (and H132 lacked Fabric 7 in transect-walking, though it was present in small proportions in total collection and excavation), this is so distinctive a pattern that there must be a very strong presumption that these are the sites of noble settlements in the thirteenth and fourteenth centuries: in terms of the material culture of the area, they are "high status" sites. In three of these cases, there are exceptional quantities of Fabric 8, a fabric characteristically used for storage vessels, implying the presence of storage places within the noble complexes.

A116 and H132 were subject to total collection and excavation as well as transect-walking. Results from this more detailed investigation support the

Table 6.1 The densest clusters of Fabric 1 in the core survey area

Field	Fabric 1	Fabric 5	Fabric 6	Fabric 7	Fabric 8
A116	454.5	1.0	22	4	221.5
L96	174.0	6.0	65	30	174.0
H132	329.0	27.5	23	0	391.5
C292/293	107.5	11.0	6	44	26.0

Quantities of surface material per dense cluster, by fabric, in grams

implication of settlement by the thirteenth and fourteenth centuries: each produced structural evidence, the massive stone foundations of H132 being considerably more substantial than the other; and each produced five spindle whorls. Quantities and proportions of Fabric 1 were overwhelming in total collection and excavation (2,749 and 1,305 sherds respectively, 95% and 91% of fabrics of this period) but Fabrics 5 and 7 were present at both. The implication that the residents were wealthy is supported by the presence of a few sherds of the very rare imported ware *céramique onctueuse* (Fabric 308) from H132 excavations and of the Rennes jug or pitcher (Fabric 172) from A116 excavations, as also by the marked presence of tableware in the forms of both.[9]

The second clear point about "noble" scatters is this: Fabric 1 clusters which are in the neighbourhood of recorded noble sites of the fifteenth century tend to have some quantity of Fabrics 6 and 8 as well, and often of the earlier Fabric 5, and tend to have relatively large quantities of these wares (de Laigue 1902 for the records).[10] In these cases, 17 in all, it is reasonable to presume that the Fabric 1 cluster represents at least a "pre-noble", if not a noble, nucleus in the thirteenth and fourteenth centuries that continued through to the fifteenth century. Occasionally a sherd of the few imported fabrics also features in these assemblages: Saintonge ware (Fabric 309) at A116 and B409, as well as the *céramique onctueuse* at H132 and Rennes ware at A116, but these imports are exceptionally rare, too rare to allow general regional comments.

By analogy – that is by identifying clusters with more than 50g of Fabric 1, with Fabrics 6 and 8 present (totally ›95g) – we can identify a further 28 "pre-noble" nuclei in the core, with a further 1 in Transect P (in the present outskirts of Malestroit) and 3 in Transect M (one on the outskirts of Pipriac and two near the River Vilaine).[11] This gives a total of 45 "pre-noble" clusters for the core survey area; given that we know of at least 25 noble households in Carentoir parish in the mid fifteenth century, and that the period from the thirteenth to the fifteenth century was one of rapid ennoblement for many families, 45 for the whole of the core is a number of the right order. One cannot, of course, go further than "pre-noble *or* noble".

There remain 32 Fabric 1 clusters in the core, which lack the presence of Fabrics 5, 6, 7 or 8, or have them in really negligible quantities.[12] They are less materially rich and presumably represent peasant hamlets, outside the parish *bourgs*. It is also notable that there is very little of Fabrics 5, 6, 7 or 8 in fields walked in and around the *bourgs*.

It is evident from the numbers cited above that there are more fields with a dense cluster of Fabric 1 than there are groups of Fabric 1 fields: in fact, 13 of the groups in the core are polyfocal, having several areas of sherd concentration.[13] Seven of these have noble or "pre-noble" characteristics, and the rest do not. There is a tri-focal cluster at La Cossais in Carentoir, for example, a place which is certainly recorded as a noble settlement in the fifteenth century. And several fields by the present hamlet of Béculeu have both enormous quantities of pottery and the range of the above fabrics; K450, in particular, is extremely like H132 in its surface characteristics.[14] If the analogies have any value, then this looks like a polyfocal site of some significance. It therefore looks as if these polyfocal groups represent both noble and peasant settlements with several structures (cf. below, pp. 132, 135).

We clearly cannot recover the totality of this medieval settlement pattern: we cannot know, for example, how many isolated, meagre settlements there may have been or if any early settlements lie precisely beneath standing structures. However, later evidence demonstrates that settlement locations tended to become fixed in the sixteenth and seventeenth centuries (below, pp. 204–5) and it must therefore be likely that relatively few lie beneath current buildings. The Fabric 1 clusters therefore sketch out a credible pattern of principal settlements (see Fig. 6.7).

Opening up new lands

Land-use and settlement

We can apply the same approach to the distribution of other widely occurring fabrics and we find comparable results from analysis of Fabric 4, a fifteenth- to early seventeenth-century fabric used initially for bowls and latterly for cooking ware that could be brought to table (Davies & Astill 1994: 199–200). Fields with Fabric 4 have very similar topographical characteristics to those with Fabric 1, and are therefore similarly very close to the mean for all fields walked. This fabric occurs on the surface of fewer than half of fields walked in the core (38%), and is rather more common in Carentoir than in Ruffiac; it is about as common in Transects M, N and P as it is in the core, and much less common in Transect R (25% of fields). Like Fabric 1 it occurs across the whole study area and is frequently found in discrete groups of fields; it is absent from some well-defined areas (Fig. 6.4). Like the pattern of occurrence of Fabric 1, most fields in a discrete group of Fabric 4 fields have small quantities of the material and one field has a cluster of it.

Although common, this fabric is much less common than Fabric 1, and it is quite clear that some other fabrics were in use when it was current. Its distribution does not therefore *define* the land-use/settlement pattern in the same way as the earlier fabric does. Take Fabrics 6 and 23, fifteenth-/sixteenth-century tablewares (Davies & Astill 1994: 200–02): Fabric 6

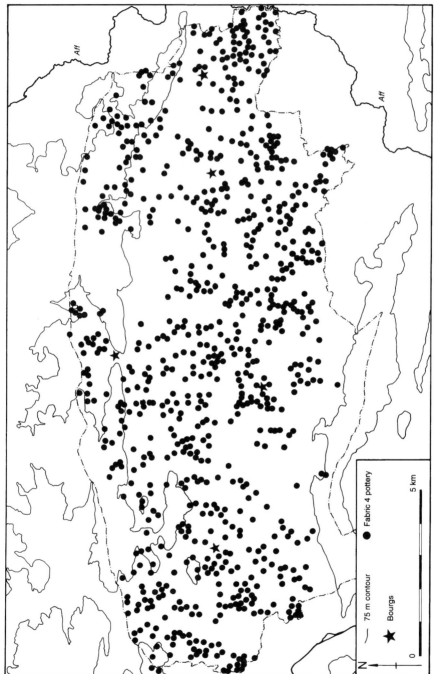

Figure 6.4 *Distribution of Fabric 4 in the core survey area*

occurs in 30% of fields walked in the core, and is more common in Ruffiac than in Carentoir (Fig. 6.5); it is as common in Transect N to the northwest, slightly more common in Transect P to the west, and much less common in Transects R and M to the northeast and east (12% and 17% of fields respectively); it therefore has a pronounced western distribution. The regional import Fabric 23 occurs in 37% of fields walked in the core; like Fabric 6, it is as common in Transect N, more common in Transect P, and less common in Transects R and M (30% and 22% of fields respectively), also showing a tendency to western distribution. Like Fabrics 1 and 4 these two fabrics also occur in discrete groups of fields, with clusters in some, although quantities per field are very much smaller than those of Fabric 1. Taken together, fields with Fabrics 4, 6 or 23 have very similar topographical characteristics to those with Fabric 1, although they are rarer above 70m and Fabrics 6 and 23 tend to be closer to water.

The distribution of Fabrics 4, 6 and 23 is very similar to that of Fabric 1, and occurs in similar types of location. However, it is not identical. Many fields with small quantities of Fabric 1 also have small quantities of Fabrics 4, 6 and/or 23; many fields with clusters of Fabric 1 also have clusters of Fabrics 4, 6 and/or 23. The implication is clear: arable of the thirteenth century was still being cultivated in the sixteenth; settlements inhabited in the thirteenth were still occupied in the sixteenth. However, there are cases of fields with Fabric 1 that lack any Fabrics 4, 6 or 23 (22% of Fabric 1 fields), and correspondingly cases of fields with Fabrics 4, 6 or 23 that lack any Fabric 1 (32% of Fabric 4/6/23 fields). Again, the implication is clear: some fields went out of cultivation between the thirteenth and sixteenth centuries, probably in response to demographic decline (see below, pp. 134–5), and some came in afresh; the overall increase on the thirteenth-/fourteenth-century arable by the late sixteenth century was 15%. Likewise, some settlements went out of occupation (or shifted) and some new ones were established (Table 6.2).

Table 6.2 Fields with clusters of ›50g Fabric 1, with no Fabrics 4 or 6 or 23 in the field

Field number	Fabric 1	Fabric 4	Fabric 6	Fabric 23	Name modern settlement
A027	69	0	0	0	Les Éclaiches
C579	69	0	0	0	La Brocherie
D215	52	0	0	0	Les Vignes
F264	114	0	0	0	La Cossais

Quantities of sherds in selected Fabric 1 clusters, by fabric, in grams

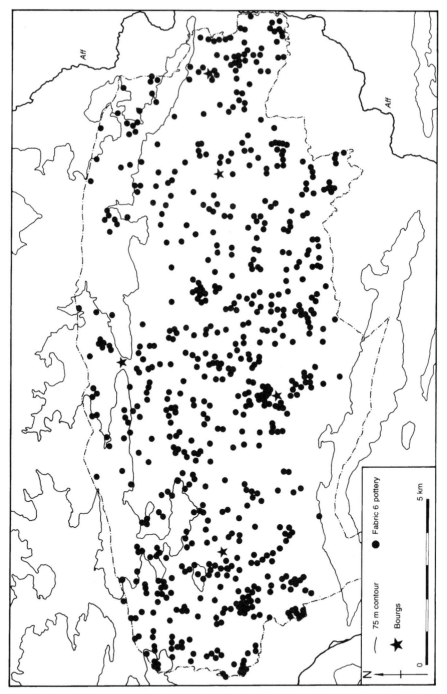

Figure 6.5 *Distribution of Fabric 6 in the core survey area*

There is only one part of the survey area where there are extensive contrasts between fields with earlier and those with later medieval fabrics and that is in Transect M. Here low-lying, wet areas – especially by the River Aff and south of Pipriac – frequently lacked Fabric 1 and did have Fabrics 4, 6 or 23; the same is also true of the western, southern and eastern edges of the extensive Bruc *lande*. (The same may be implied by pollen evidence indicating pre-nineteenth-century cultivation from the edge of the *lande* in the core survey area (Davies & Astill 1994: 267).) In Transect M there is therefore a strong indication that substantial new lands were cultivated in the later fifteenth and sixteenth centuries; some of those lands had reverted to *lande* by 1831, as had isolated spots in the core (Fig. 6.6). This suggests some demographic pressure and may well reflect the increasing population of the sixteenth century (see further below, p. 177).

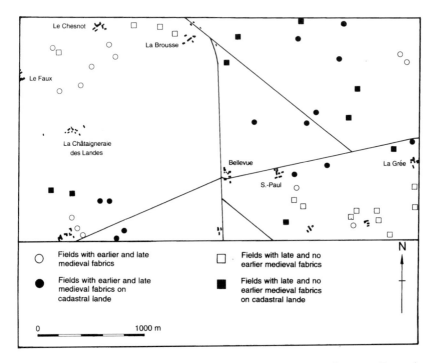

Figure 6.6 *Medieval fabrics in the centre of Transect M: southwestern Bruc; the blank area in the middle of the figure contains fields which were walked but yielded no medieval pottery*

Settlement pattern

If we compare the number and location of the Fabric 1 clusters (the fields with more than 50g of Fabric 1) with the number and location of Fabric 4/6/23 clusters, we get the following results. There are 77 Fabric 1 clusters in the core and 34 in the sample transects (Fig. 6.7). In 53 cases in the core, these same sites also have accumulations of later medieval and/or post-medieval wares – most strikingly of Fabric 4, but sometimes of Fabrics 6 or 23. Quantities of these later wares are not so great, reflecting the lower amounts found overall; nevertheless quantities of Fabrics 4, 6 and 23 are often relatively high – relative, that is, to surface finds on purely "arable" fields. Hence, for example, the site at B10, by La Touche in Tréal, has 70g of Fabric 4, 41g of Fabric 6 and 31g of Fabric 23 to add to its 212g of Fabric 1; the site at M637, near Malon in Guipry, has 154g of Fabric 4 and 3g of Fabric 6 to add to its 214g of Fabric 1 (though it should be noted that clusters in sample transects P, N and R do not normally have the sheer quantities found in the core at this period). These features combine to suggest that two-thirds of settlement sites of the central middle ages continued to be used in the early modern period. The remaining third of Fabric 1 settlement sites does not appear to have been used after the fifteenth century.

One or two of the sites are unusual in having more Fabric 4 than Fabric 1: D241, in the outskirts of Carentoir, for example, which has a good range of later fabrics too; or J229, near Le Plessis in Tréal, again with some later fabrics.[15] In these cases, given the overall preponderance of Fabric 1 in the survey area, it looks as if minor sites of the thirteenth and fourteenth centuries continued and grew rapidly in later centuries.

We can undertake a comparable exercise with the Fabric 4/6/23 clusters. There are 28 fields in the core with clusters of more than 50g of Fabric 4, eight with clusters of more than 50g of Fabric 6 (of which four are included in the 28 above), twelve with more than 50g of Fabric 23 (of which five are already included above), and 35 further fields with clusters of more than 50g of some combination of Fabrics 4, 6 and 23 – three relate to a single area north of Triguého.[16] 16 of these clusters are on the site of Fabric 1 clusters, making a total of 58 new sites. With the remaining 37 continuing Fabric 1 settlements detailed above, there is a potential minimum of 111 distinctive settlement sites in the core. Some of the Fabric 4/6/23 discrete groups are polyfocal, like Triguého and Bot Colin.[17] Emphasizing the point, written records imply that hamlets in Carentoir ranged from large to small, from one with more than 14 households, through several with more than seven or eight, to the many with one, two or three.[18]

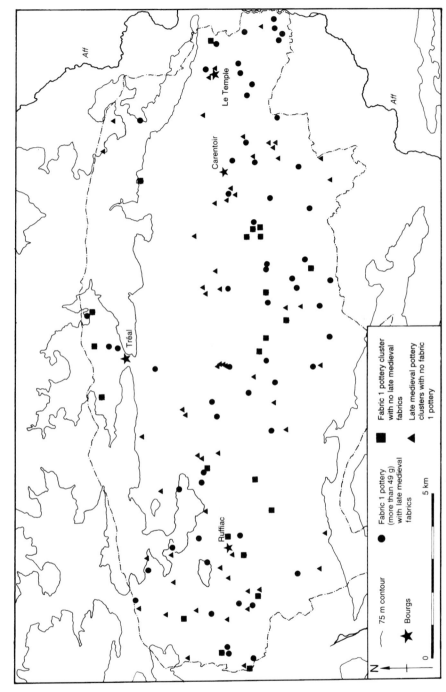

Figure 6.7 *Distribution of Fabric 1 clusters, >=50g, and of Fabric 4, 6 and/or 23 clusters, >=50g*

Le Temple

Carentoir

Tréal

Ruffiac

Aff

Aff

N

5 km

0

■ Fabric 1 pottery cluster with no late medieval fabrics

● Fabric 1 pottery (more than 49 g) with late medieval fabrics

▲ Late medieval pottery clusters with no fabric 1 pottery

— 75 m contour

★ Bourgs

Nobles and peasants

Population size

For the fifteenth and sixteenth centuries we have a series of records listing households liable to pay the hearth tax – the *fouages*. There survive records for 1426–30, 1427, 1440, 1447, 1513, 1536 and beyond. They note the number of households liable to pay the tax, sometimes by hamlet, and also frequently note exempted households, that is those of nobles and their *métayers*, the dead, and – occasionally – the poor (de Laigue 1902: 130–48, 670–77, 827–32). The sixteenth-century texts relate to the whole of the core survey area, as does that of 1426–30 (which gives global totals for each parish and does not specify individual hamlets); those of 1427 and 1447 relate to Carentoir only (see above, p. 14). Even the Carentoir *fouages* do not provide us with a comprehensive and systematic record of all settlements: there are gaps and inconsistencies, and a tendency sometimes to include nobles and sometimes to ignore them. Nevertheless, they do provide a mass of data which can be systematically compared with the field evidence, and this is valuable.

At this period we can also begin to make some viable suggestions about household and population size, given the existence of the *fouages* and some detailed local surveys from farther west (Gallet 1981; Minois 1976).

The present consensus is that population in Brittany was high in 1300 relative to the land's productive capacity – given that there was migration out of the region, enrolment in the army, and intense parcellation of peasant tenures (Leguay & Martin 1982: 54). Although the Black Death of the mid fourteenth century may not have had quite such dramatic effects on population levels as it did in some other parts of Europe, nevertheless there were recurrent epidemics across the late fourteenth and fifteenth centuries, and by 1430 there were clear population reductions. This is demonstrated by the several *réformations* of the *fouage*, adjusting the number of fiscal units down to the reduced population size. On the basis of the *réformation* of 1426–30 it is estimated that there was at least a 25% drop in the Breton population between 1395–1410 and 1426 (Kerhervé 1987: 551); and Gallet cites abandoned tenures in a few specific parishes of the Vannetais, just to the southwest of the survey area, of 40% and more (1983: 69–75). Population levels did not recover till the end of the fifteenth century.

With a Breton average of 4.3 *feux* (fiscal units) per km^2 and 2.8 households per *feu*, one might expect the core of the survey area to have had in the order of 1,540 households. However, inland parishes were much less densely populated than those of the coast: it is suggested that the parishes of the core were relatively weakly populated at the time of the

1426-30 enquiry, at just under half the Breton average (except for the much denser 4km ^{2} of Le Temple)[19] (Kerhervé 1987: 547).

Though the recorded counts of the fifteenth century for the core survey area are not consistent with each other,[20] four points are clear. The 1426–30 data specify the numbers of "old" *feux* (the fiscal units used in the late fourteenth century) for Ruffiac, Carentoir, Tréal and Le Temple parishes, 110, 312, 29 and 12 respectively. These total 463, which at 2.8 households per *feu* and 5 persons per household would suggest a population *c*.1400 for the whole parishes (excluding nobles, *métayers* and poor) of 6,482, i.e. about 5,000 for the area now defined by the four core communes; with exemptees added one might expect the total for the core communes to be about 5,900.[21] Secondly, the 1426–30 data specify a reduction of 175 *feux* *c*.1430, a 38% reduction, and in addition specify numbers of nobles, *métayers* and poor (132 households in total) at that date. This would suggest an overall population for the whole parishes of 4,700 and for the area of the present communes of about 3,600 at that date. Thirdly, in the nucleations of Carentoir and La Gacilly we can estimate a total population of over 300 and 100 respectively (the *bourg* of Carentoir had 57 non-noble households and La Gacilly 14 before 1447). Fourthly, using the detailed data available for Carentoir in 1447, and taking note of dead householders enumerated in the latter, Carentoir's 40% drop in population (modern commune area only) can be seen to be very unevenly distributed: a drop of 50% in the *bourg*, nothing in some hamlets, and total in others like Villeneuve and Calny.[22] None of this is good enough for any sort of certainty, but it may not be unreasonable to suggest a mid-fifteenth-century population of over 3,000 for the core survey area.

Noble and non-noble settlement

Of the 145 settlements recorded in miscellaneous sources in the fifteenth and sixteenth centuries in the core outside the centres, 69 are purely peasant, 57 distinctively noble, and the rest mixed; in other words, 52% of recorded settlements have some kind of noble association. Comparison of the surface record with this written data produces consistent and credible results.

Firstly, it is notable that surface pottery tends to cluster in the neighbourhood of documented fifteenth-century settlements with nobles.[23] There are 68 recorded noble houses located in the core, of which at least 27 had absentee nobles and were run by *métayers*; with their properties managed by (peasant) *métayers*, the material culture of these properties may not have been distinguishable. Of the remaining noble settlements 28 have concentrations of late medieval pottery (large quantities) in their neighbourhoods, and a further two have noticeably high quantities of sherds near by. The assemblage of fabrics on these fields is not consistent: no fabric is invariable (although both Fabrics 4 and 23 are very common), and the combinations present no obvious pattern. What is striking at this period is the relative quantity of pottery – sometimes very large – and the clustering, rather than the assemblage: in particular, the imported Rhineland and Beauvaisis stonewares and Beauvaisis earthenwares (Fabrics 51 and 19) do *not* necessarily feature in these "noble" assemblages and do feature in non-noble contexts (see Table 6.5, pp. 142–3).

There is, then, a close correlation between recorded noble properties and large surface clusters, usually surrounded by fields with small quantities of late medieval wares. It is therefore the case that arable fields surrounded noble settlements as they did peasant settlements; there was no surrounding woodland or meadow at this period. And we should remember that the areas associated with some nobles in the records can be very small indeed: 4 ha for the *sieur* of La Boixière Launay (Car) in 1444; but 11 ha plus further land in Réminiac in demesne for the *sieur* of La Guichardais (Tr) in 1578, with three times as much in fief.[24] Some noble properties were tightly packed together, like La Tronchaie and Daranlo in Carentoir.

Secondly, in the case of a small number of *métairies* that are not recorded before the sixteenth century (e.g. La Ville Régent, La Ville Marie), the surface pattern is quite different.[25] Quantities in the neighbourhood of these places are nearly always very small (none is greater than 50g total), and sherds do not cluster on the field surface. They have no, or very small quantities of Fabric 1, and not much of later medieval fabrics – except for small accumulations of Fabric 8. Given the large quantities from the neighbourhood of La Boutinais (Saint-Nicolas), it seems unreasonable to expect *métairies* to leave little trace. It therefore seems unlikely that the small quantities from the sixteenth-century *métairies* arise from different methods of rubbish disposal. The best explanation for the low surface record is that we did not walk the right fields. There must therefore be a strong chance that the sixteenth-century sites lie beneath present settlements; hence greater continuity from the sixteenth century is implied for these *métairie* sites. It is also noticeable that none of these sixteenth-century *métairies* has surface traces which suggest previous settlements in their neighbourhoods – in contrast to the known noble residences of fifteenth and sixteenth centuries, where this is often so. This suggests that the *métairies* were often on new sites (Table 6.3, and see below, pp. 147–8).

Thirdly, there are 88 recorded non-noble settlements of the fifteenth and sixteenth centuries in the core survey area, of which 19 included nobles or *métayers* in the same settlement. 104 fields were walked in the neighbourhood of these settlements, providing some element of survey for all but 12 of them. Although nearly half of these fields were initially

Table 6.3 Noble, non-noble and *métayer* fifteenth- and sixteenth-century documented settlements with medieval fabrics near by

	Fabric 1	Fabric 5	Fabric 7	Fabric 8	Fabric 4	Fabric 6	Fabric 23
Noble	83	37	10	55	70	66	72
Métairies	44	25	6	50	56	50	69
Non–noble	71	35	6	56	71	62	65

Percentage of noble, non–noble and *métayer* recorded settlements with medieval fabrics in their neighbourhood, by fabric

classified as "sites" (i.e. they had clusters of surface material), it is striking that absolute quantities of surface material were usually small: only 16 fields had more than 100g of pottery on the surface, of *any* sort of fabric, let alone accumulations of a single fabric or period, and only five had more than 50g of Fabrics 4 or 23. Although, then, there is a tendency for surface pottery to cluster in the neighbourhood of recorded non–noble settlements of this period, it is rare for crude quantities to be large. Further, the range of fabrics occurring is initially surprising: Fabrics 5 and 8 occur as often in the neighbourhood of fifteenth-/sixteenth-century peasant settlements as they do in the neighbourhood of fifteenth-century noble settlements (though not necessarily as densely). These wares are clearly not exclusively associated with noble properties. Moreover, the assemblages are not distinctive; and no one fabric occurs consistently. The most frequently occurring assemblage (found in the neighbourhood of a third of non–noble settlements) is in fact of Fabrics 1, 4, 6, 8 and 23; this is no different from the assemblage one might find in the neighbourhood of a noble settlement. Hence, non–noble settlements do not appear to be differentiated from noble in their fabric range at this later period, particularly with regard to imports, in contrast to the situation in the thirteenth and fourteenth centuries. On the other hand, non–noble settlements tend to be differentiated by the *quantity* of material on the surface, particularly in respect of Fabrics 7, 4, 6 and 23 (largely tablewares).

A different world

By the sixteenth century much had changed in the survey area since the year 1000. The road from Redon to Ploermel, a major road (*grand chemin*), ran past the Priory in eastern Ruffiac, with some of the Prior's tenancies ranged along its course. Another major road ran north from La Gacilly, through Carentoir and on to Guer, and there was a plethora of lesser roads and paths leading to the *bourgs* of Ruffiac, Tréal and Carentoir.[26] There were in fact at least four and probably five *bourgs* in the core by the late sixteenth century – with Saint-Nicolas and Le Temple to add to the earlier parish centres. Carentoir was by far the largest. There was a sizable minor nobility (*sieurs* and *petits seigneurs*), with properties scattered across the whole of the core, whose status was publicly recognized in the periodic calls to military service. There were also some *grands seigneurs* – like the de la Bourdonnayes at La Basse Boixière, La Boixière Launay, Fanhouet, La Ruée and Coëtion – among whom the Prior had an influential position, not least by virtue of his (wind) mills at Prieuré and Saint-Nicolas.[27] And some even grander *seigneurs* held some properties within the core although their bases were outside it: the Rohans at La Haute Boixière (and La Gacilly), and the barony of Malestroit with its large scatter of dependent fiefs. The town of Malestroit was thriving close by to the west, the vigour and strong identity of its townspeople demonstrated by its role in the Wars of Religion (see above, pp. 44–5); it was by far the largest town in the neighbourhood of the core (cf. Leguay & Martin 1982: 39). While the major *seigneurie* of La Gacilly continued influential till the late sixteenth century, its small *bourg* grew slowly and its notaries performed services for many in Carentoir.[28]

There had also been significant changes in material culture: for the first time since the Roman period, in the later middle ages quantities of imported pottery became noticeable – both regional imports like Fabric 23 and those from farther afield in the Beauvaisis and Rhineland. Neither was confined to noble sites and they appear to have been available to and used by the peasant population, in marked contrast to the (rare) imports of the thirteenth and fourteenth centuries.

What the peasant population was doing was growing things, and some were also probably making linen and canvas cloth – given the range of cloth available at Malestroit. We have no way of estimating the total product of the land but we can see from the many surviving rentals what was valued by landlords in the late fifteenth and sixteenth centuries. Apart from the vineyards at La Châtaigneraie, the standard elements in rents are wheat, oats, hens (in small numbers) and money (as well as "obedience"); the occasional references to rye and buckwheat remind us that wheat and oats are unlikely to have been the predominant cereal and that buckwheat became common from the sixteenth century (it starts to bulge dramatically in pollen cores at about this period, as do wheat, rye and hemp (Marguerie 1992: 104, 113, 242)). There must have been animals in addition to poultry: roughly a third of the small tenure at L'Abbaye aux Alines (Car) was meadow in 1540; while 50% of the demesne of La Guichardais in Tréal, and 50% of its fief at Couedic, were *lande* or *friches* in 1578. Flax and hemp were grown in the tenancies of the Priory (hemp appears suddenly in pollen cores from Manéantoux en Bubry during the central middle ages

(Marguerie 1992: 104)), a hint of significance to come in the next few centuries.[29]

The core of our survey area may have changed since the twelfth century but it was still distinctive. It is in this period that it becomes clearly distinguishable from the sample transects for the first time, particularly in its material culture; sample transects (apart from P, towards Malestroit) have significantly less pottery, fewer settlements and fewer nobles (cf. Kerhervé 1987: 559). The core was very productive: it supported an active peasant population over most of its surface and on top of them a host of nobles, greater and smaller. That there were so many, even by Breton standards, may have something to do with the background of strong, active, free peasant proprietors: some of the descendants of the vociferous peasantry of the ninth century must have thrived and risen into the nobility, particularly given the absence of new *milites* in the eleventh and twelfth centuries.

By the sixteenth century there were plenty of signs of recovery from the demographic crises of the early fifteenth century: new lands were taken in, new settlements established. And the world was poised for more change – in land-use, land management and housing.

Table 6.4 Clusters of ›50g Fabric 1, with other medieval fabrics associated with the cluster

Field number	Fabric 1	Fabric 10	Fabric 5	Fabric 7	Fabric 8	Fabric 4	Fabric 23	Fabric 6	Fabric 58
A027	69	0	0	0	0	0	0	0	0
A047	86	0	1	0	18	31	161	7	0
A055/62/63/64	138	0	0	0	39	2	0	0	0
A112	76	0	0	0	13	18	50	0	0
A116	455	35	1	4	222	13	34	22	0
A201	120	0	0	8	0	0	44	10	0
A211	51	0	1	0	0	0	6	17	0
A382	54	0	0	0	24	11	5	8	0
A450	558	0	5	115	0	135	81	108	0
B010	212	0	11	4	18	70	31	41	0
B051	70	0	5	0	20	15	18	14	0
B191	56	0	0	0	36	16	10	26	0
B232/233/234	180	0	0	0	24	17	21	12	0
B242	69	0	0	0	0	0	2	8	0
B269	120	0	0	0	0	12	0	1	0
B279	57	0	3	4	13	8	0	15	0
B282/283	75	0	0	17	89	41	7	6	0
B313	60	0	0	0	25	48	35	16	9
B318	62	0	0	0	0	5	8	1	0
B409	125	0	6	0	3	15	12	0	0
C219	98	0	0	0	16	0	11	5	0
C291	99	0	12	0	24	46	31	22	0
C292/293	108	0	11	44	26	13	8	6	0
C324	99	0	0	0	5	21	0	24	0
C402	101	0	0	0	28	15	0	11	0
C403	73	0	0	0	0	9	6	23	0
C411	60	0	0	3	0	4	2	0	0
C533	55	0	0	0	86	48	0	12	0
C541	76	0	0	0	0	0	0	20	0
C573	112	0	2	0	64	26	12	67	0
C579	69	0	0	0	0	0	0	0	0
D143	65	0	0	0	17	28	1	0	0
D202	81	0	5	0	18	64	4	11	0
D215	52	0	0	0	11	0	0	0	0
D224/225	61	0	0	0	0	21	0	34	0
D241	79	0	0	13	78	116	7	34	0
E003	55	0	0	0	0	27	0	2	0
E044	143	0	4	0	10	1	5	30	5
E089	57	0	1	0	150	17	37	1	0
E091	61	0	0	0	19	17	12	22	0
E095	147	0	0	0	12	53	1	13	3
E097	123	0	11	0	0	62	10	16	0
F252	76	0	0	0	0	20	0	0	0
F264	114	0	0	0	0	0	0	0	0
F264/270/271	61	0	10	0	44	1	10	7	0

continued

Table 6.4 Clusters of ›50g Fabric 1, with other medieval fabrics associated with the cluster (*contd.*)

Field number	Fabric 1	Fabric 10	Fabric 5	Fabric 7	Fabric 8	Fabric 4	Fabric 23	Fabric 6	Fabric 58
F264	125	0	1	0	80	14	3	0	0
F267	58	0	0	0	0	1	0	2	0
F355	51	0	2	0	0	0	0	6	0
F524/526	60	2	0	0	5	4	1	17	0
G060/61	72	0	2	0	18	8	0	45	0
G074	85	0	3	0	20	40	5	45	0
G101	63	0	2	0	0	40	2	10	0
G102	55	0	0	0	30	20	0	5	0
G217	114	0	28	0	2	93	3	20	0
G220	145	0	2	0	3	25	2	3	0
H015	130	0	2	0	0	4	24	0	0
H056	52	0	0	0	35	6	13	1	0
H074	61	0	3	0	0	0	0	2	0
H132	329	0	28	0	392	142	38	23	0
J098	182	0	0	0	0	10	9	13	0
J229	72	0	0	0	68	77	26	27	0
J237	58	0	0	0	2	5	6	30	0
J277	59	0	15	0	30	22	14	0	0
J321	62	0	0	0	0	36	2	0	0
J357	52	0	27	0	0	0	14	2	0
K422	71	0	0	0	5	4	0	0	0
K427	54	0	0	0	107	6	28	50	0
K445/446	171	6	13	0	0	18	9	17	0
K447/448	96	0	2	0	13	40	78	9	0
K450	508	0	31	0	252	147	44	93	17
L021	77	0	7	0	14	6	38	27	0
L023	67	4	0	0	29	12	9	19	0
L070	98	0	0	0	6	21	20	25	0
L096	174	0	6	30	174	69	168	65	0
L107	83	0	0	0	7	17	57	34	0
L119	100	0	0	0	0	6	0	5	0
L124	119	0	0	0	0	12	31	3	0

Quantities of sherds in all Fabric 1 clusters, by fabric, in grams

Table 6.5 Medieval fabrics in the neighbourhood of recorded fifteenth- and sixteenth-century noble houses

	Fabric 1	Fabric 5	Fabric 7	Fabric 8	Fabric 4	Fabric 6	Fabric 19	Fabric 23	Fabric 51
Bérais	Y	Y		Y				Y	
Bois Guillaume	Y	Y		Y	Y			Y	
Bois Brassu									
Boisby	Y					Y			
Bois Brun									
Boixière (Basse)								Y	
Balangeart	Y								
Bodel	Y		Y		Y	Y		Y	
Bot	Y	Y							
Boutinais	Y			Y	Y			Y	
Buardais	Y			Y	Y	Y		Y	
Carentoir	Y			Y		Y			
Châtaigneraie	Y								
Chênais	Y				Y	Y		Y	
Chauvelaye	Y				Y	Y			
Charmille	Y	Y	Y	Y	Y	Y		Y	Y
Clazeul				Y	Y	Y		Y	
Coëtion	Y			Y	Y	Y		Y	
Cossais	Y	Y		Y	Y	Y		Y	
Couedic									
Couetu	Y	Y			Y	Y		Y	
Danais	Y			Y	Y			Y	
Daranlo									
Fanhouet	Y			Y	Y	Y		Y	
Feuges	Y			Y					
Gaincru	Y			Y	Y	Y		Y	
Gélinais						Y		Y	
Gras									
Gravaud					Y	Y		Y	
Greffins									
Grée Michel	Y				Y			Y	
Grée Orlay	Y	Y		Y	Y	Y		Y	
Guichardais (C)	Y				Y	Y			
Guichardais (C)	Y	Y		Y	Y	Y			
Guichardais (T)	Y			Y	Y	Y		Y	
Haute Boixière	Y	Y				Y			
Herblinaye	Y	Y	Y	Y	Y	Y		Y	
Hunelaye		Y							
Landes du Houssa				Y	Y			Y	
Launay	Y			Y	Y	Y		Y	
Lorgerais	Y				Y				
Mur	Y				Y	Y		Y	
Nouan	Y	Y		Y	Y	Y		Y	
Peccadeuc	Y	Y	Y	Y	Y	Y	Y	Y	
Plessis	Y			Y	Y	Y		Y	Y
Porte	Y				Y				

continued

Table 6.5 Medieval fabrics in the neighbourhood of recorded fifteenth- and sixteenth-century noble houses (*contd.*)

	Fabric 1	Fabric 5	Fabric 7	Fabric 8	Fabric 4	Fabric 6	Fabric 19	Fabric 23	Fabric 51
Préclos	Y					Y		Y	Y
Prieuré	Y			Y	Y	Y		Y	
Provotaye									
Rangera					Y	Y		Y	
Ruée	Y	Y		Y	Y	Y		Y	
St-Donat								Y	
Salle									
Temple	Y	Y		Y	Y	Y		Y	
Thiolais	Y			Y	Y	Y		Y	
Touche	Y	Y	Y	Y	Y	Y		Y	
Touche aux Roux	Y				Y				
Touche Peschard	Y	Y			Y	Y		Y	
Trélo	Y			Y	Y				
Trécouet	Y						Y		
Tronchaie	Y						Y	Y	
Vallée	Y	Y			Y			Y	
Vallée du Grais				Y			Y		
Vignes	Y			Y	Y	Y		Y	
Ville Robert				Y				Y	

Y indicates presence of fabric, however little, within 150m of the later residence

Notes

1. For the Feudal Revolution see, for example, Bois 1992, Bonnassie 1991, and the kernel of the model in Duby 1968; for some problems associated with the model see Davies 1996.
2. The mound known as "La motte" near Le Gras in Ruffiac appears to be a natural formation.
3. A *seigneurie* is best described as a sphere of political power exercised by a noble, involving a degree of control of the peasant population residing there, with dues and obligations expected in addition to simple rent (e.g. the obligation to have grain milled at the *seigneur*'s mill). Although in fact the terms have an overlapping range of reference in late medieval and early modern texts, Gallet adopts the helpful convention of using the words *seigneur* and *sieur* to distinguish between those with greater and those with lesser powers, reserving *seigneur* for those with rights of jurisdiction over different classes of legal case (*basse*, *moyenne* and *haute justice*) in addition to rights to obligations and dues (1983: 595–7, for a useful discussion of the terms). Early medievalists are accustomed to use the term "seigneurial" for all who exercised powers of control, whether or not these included justice, but we have followed Gallet's usage.
4. AD Ille-et-Vilaine 3H187 L5; 3H188 L5, L10, for example.
5. A116, H132, H145: Davies & Astill 1994: 78–80, 143–51, 89–94.

6. The sample transects did not cross the *bourgs* of the other communes.

7. AD Loire-Atlantique B1991 L3.

8. The figure of 25 is a minimum and the total may well have been higher. Attempts to count noble households (as opposed to noble properties) are bedevilled by (i) inconsistencies in the mode of recording *fouages* and *montres*; (ii) discrepancies between records of noble residents and of noble properties. A noble property worked by a *métayer* was sometimes explicitly recorded as the property of an absentee landlord; later in the fifteenth century the same properties sometimes had a resident noble as well as a *métayer*. It is not safe to assume noble presence or absence unless specified.

9. Fabric 5 includes glazed jugs and Fabric 7 tableware; H132 has both table and kitchen vessels in Fabric 1; A116 has mostly cooking pots in Fabric 1, but with some table wares too.

10. All but two cases have more than 95g of Fabrics 1, 6 and 8 together. A116 (+ Fabric 5), A201 (+ Fabric 7, no Fabric 8), B10 (+5, +7), B191, B409 (+5, no 6), C292/293 (+5), C541 (no 8), D215 (no 6, 62g only), E44 (+5), F264 (+5), G220 (+5), H56 (88g only), H132 (+5), J98 (no 8), J229, L96 (+5, +7), L124 (no 8).

11. A47, A450, B51, B232/233, B282/283, B313, C219, C291, C324, C402, C533, C573, D202, D241, E89, E91, E95, G60/61, G74, G217, K427, K445/446 (no Fabric 8), K447/448, K450, L21, L23, L70, L107 (see Table 6.4); P54, M384, M562, M637. Although A450, La Nouette, not far from H132, produced no Fabric 8, it had quite exceptional surface quantities of material: 557.5g Fabric 1, 5g Fabric 5, 108g Fabric 6, 114.5g Fabric 7 (the largest quantity found on the surface of any field); although this field was walked at 25m intervals, even if quantities are quartered they are still enormous.

12. In sample transects, P: 2; N: 4; R: 1; M: 19 (two-thirds are in the eastern part of the transect).

13. In sample transects, 1 group has 2 foci in Transect N, and 2 have 2 foci each in Transect M.

14. 508g Fabric 1, 31g Fab 5, 93g Fab 6, 251g Fab 8. The records of the Commission régionale de l'Inventaire de Bretagne note a seventeenth-century house of some grandeur, including rear stair turret.

15. See below, pp. 192–3, for later dumping on some of these sites.

16. In sample transects, ›50g Fabric 4: 8 in M, 1 in N; ›50g Fabric 6: 1 in N; ›50g Fabric 23: 2 in M, 2 in N; ›50g Fabrics 4, 6 and/or 23: 2 in R, 6 in N, 3 in P, 3 in M.

17. In some places there are clusters of ›50g of other late medieval fabrics, that is of Fabrics 8, 19 and 51 (representing 23%, ‹1% and 2% respectively of surface finds in transect-walking in the core; in Transect P: 16%, 0 and 5%; Transect N: 12%, 0 and ‹1%; Transect R: 11%, ‹1% and ‹1%; Transect M: 14%, ‹1% and 3%).
There are 33 clusters of ›50g Fabric 8 in the core in addition to clusters already identified; of these 16 are ›100g; there are also 1 in Transect R, 7 in Transect M and 1 in Transect P. There are no separate large clusters of Fabric 19.
There are an additional 4 clusters of ›50g Fabric 51 in the core, 3 in Transect M, 1 in Transect P, 1 in Transect N.
Fabric 51 occurs so rarely that it is impossible to make the systematic density contrasts possible for other fabrics; we do not therefore include these clusters as settlement indicators. Since Fabric 8 is a very heavy storage ware, accumulations greater than 50g do not have the same significance as those in other fabrics. However, the large quantities are notable and where they occur without large quantities of table and/or cooking wares

they may well indicate the former presence of a building of storage capacity, like a barn or shieling.

18. AD Loire-Atlantique B2986 lists taxable households; these figures therefore indicate minimum household numbers; see below, p. 135.

19. Le Temple lies in the east of the parish; cf. the fact that Carentoir population concentrated in the south of the parish and on its present eastern border; AD Loire-Atlantique B2986.

20. AD Loire-Atlantique B2988 gives global totals of *feux* for the parishes in 1426–30, sometimes with numbers of households contributing, and numbers of poor/beggars and *métayers*; AD Loire-Atlantique B2986 gives precise detail of *feux* for nearly every contributing hamlet in Carentoir in 1447 (though some are totalled in *frairies*), plus numbers of dead, some nobles and some *métayers*.

21. Pace Tonnerre 1994: 448, where it is maintained that there had been little growth in Ruffiac and Carentoir since the ninth century.

22. The "dead" households in the 1447 text appear to refer back to the old units of the late fourteenth century rather than represent a new, post-1430, decline; while one cannot be absolutely sure that this is the correct interpretation of the text, on balance it is more likely. If the dead noted in 1447 were to represent a new drop, it would imply a further reduction by about 1,400 to 2,500 total population for the core survey area *c*.1450.

23. In this, and what follows, we have taken "neighbourhood" to mean fields within 150m of the present settlement bearing the fifteenth-century name.

24. AD Loire-Atlantique B1957; AD Loire-Atlantique B1991 L3.

25. Note that these places with *ville* names – classically regarded as an indicator of new twelfth-century settlement – lie in lands that were *not* exploited until the very late middle ages. As always, while a given type of place-name may begin to be used at a datable period, it does not follow – unless there is very precise textual evidence – that all such forms should be dated to that period.

26. AD Ille-et-Vilaine 3H188 L8; AD Morbihan G1066 ff. 40–1, 123. Lesser roads, for example: AD Loire-Atlantique B1991 L3 (Tréal); AD Ille-et-Vilaine 3H187 L5, 3H188 L8, L10 (Ruffiac); *ibid*. 3H188 L9 (Carentoir).

27. AD Ille-et-Vilaine 3H193 (1556).

28. AD Morbihan G1066 (e.g. 1582, 1583, 1584).

29. AD Ille-et-Vilaine 3H190 L2 (vines); 3H188 L9 (L'Abbaye aux Alines) – but this should not be taken as *typical*: other *tenues* give quite different proportions; AD Loire-Atlantique B1991 L3 (La Guichardais); AD Ille-et-Vilaine 3H187 L5 (flax and hemp).

A note on *métairies*

Although in some parts of Brittany the *métayer* had a share-cropping arrangement with his landlord, the late medieval *métayer* in this area was a person, usually a peasant, who had contracted to work a noble's home farm for a specified, usually high, return (often grain), especially in his absence on military and other duties (see Gallet 1983: 210). He was exempted from payment of *fouages*, like the noble. The Duke's decree of 1426 allowed one *métayer* per noble (and per *manoir*) to be exempt from *fouage* (thereby indicating an assumption that any noble might have a *métayer* living and working in close association with the noble household). In fact there were rather more *métayers* recorded than nobles in the subsequent enquiries (Kerhervé 1987: 564–7); Carentoir in 1426–30 had 18 nobles and 25 *métayers* and Ruffiac 6 nobles and 11 *métayers* (AD Loire-Atlantique B2988).

The recorder of the 1447 *fouages* for this area clearly expected that every noble would have a *métayer* installed in his property in or by the noble residence; this usually seems to have been the case, but often the noble lived there too alongside the farmer, and sometimes the noble lived there alone, with or without a *métayer* living at some distance from the noble house, at a *métairie*. A couple of entries make the explicit point that, as a noble was living there, he had no need of a *métayer*. (Cf. the large quantities of Fabric 8 (storage vessels) at the same location as many tablewares at some sites – implying storage places and farm buildings within the noble complex; see above, p. 125.)

From the late fifteenth century there are more and more references to the existence of separate establishments for *métayers*, and it looks as if the earlier arrangements gave way to a new one in which the noble lived in one residence and the *métayer* at a distinct other, often at some distance. By the mid sixteenth century a thriving *sieur* could have two, three or more *métairies* associated with his *manoir*, and in the seventeenth century *métairies* tended to get larger. However, at the same time the increasing tenurial complexities meant that *métairies* could be let to one or more tenants (and/ or the *sieur* might have *valets* to run them for him), who would *not* necessarily be called *métayers* (cf. the two households at La Hunelaye in Ruffiac in 1559); hence, the meaning of "*métayer*" in the old sense was changing by the late sixteenth century. Nevertheless, *métayers* with contractual relationships with landlords continue to be evidenced until the late eighteenth century. By that time, however, the basis of tenure had so changed that the term almost entirely dropped out of use in this area – to be replaced by *fermier* for those with leasing contracts. The change in terms begins to be consistently reflected in the records of this area *c.* 1760–80 (see below, pp. 166–7). Despite the change in terminology (it is no more than this in this area), government enquiries continued to differentiate between *métayer* and *fermier* throughout the nineteenth century, expecting them to refer respectively to those who returned produce and those who returned cash.

The *métairie* (the *métayer's* house and workbase) in the sixteenth-century sense also often disappeared, although the word tended to continue to be used, whether or not there was a change in the occupier's function and relationships: the Métairie de la Marche of 1540 was simply a house name in Le Vieux Bourg (Tr) in the 1820s. La Métairie au Joly (Car) must once have been a functioning *métairie* but it is not recorded as such; it had taxable (i.e. peasant) households in the fifteenth century, and was already a relatively large hamlet then. By the 1820s it was an extremely large village.

From the number of references to *métairies* in local texts, especially parish registers, it appears that *métairies* continued to be established in the seventeenth and eighteenth centuries. A number of these disappeared between the mid eighteenth century and the 1820s (e.g. in Tréal the *métairies* of Meriennes, Le Verger, La Vigne, Les Landiers, Renecheuc) and others disappeared between the 1820s and the twentieth century, e.g. Le Tayat.

It helps to see associations between nobles and *métayers* as part of a continuing process: from at least the thirteenth century the noble would negotiate with a *métayer* to ensure that he received a healthy return on the produce from his land; as generations passed, the close association would dissolve and the *métairie* would become lettable, just like any other piece of property; but as new nobles became established or acquired larger properties the need for a *métayer* would again arise and the process begin again.

CHAPTER 7

Landscaping

Changing land-use and settlement shift

New lands

If we compare the thirteenth-/fourteenth- with the fifteenth-/sixteenth-century patterns of land-use and settlement, we immediately become aware of both continuities and discontinuities. Most of the arable worked in the central middle ages was still worked in the late middle ages; but some went out of cultivation and some new land was taken in. Noticeably, the land that went out of cultivation was sometimes high (a fifth of these fields were above 70m, as against the Fabric 1 mean of 11%), and sometimes on north-facing slopes (29%, as against a mean of 23%). The land that came into cultivation anew was more likely to lie at 200–400m from water than the norm and, in Transect M especially, included land that subsequently reverted to *lande* (see Fig. 6.6). When changes came, they were slight: some retreat from exposed high land, then later some 15% expansion of the earlier arable maximum; and some tendency to choose new land to exploit, especially land farther from water (see above, p. 129).[1]

Although slight relative to the overall pattern of exploitation, these changes must reflect responses to two major phases of social change: firstly, as epidemics took their toll and population dropped by over 30%, retreat in the fifteenth century from the unkind lands exploited during the period of high demographic pressure *c.*1300; and then the piecemeal extension of the arable, in new zones (including some small stands of woodland), as demographic pressures began to increase again in the sixteenth century and nobles looked for economic opportunity.

Some of the new land taken in at this period was in the neighbourhood of noble settlements, and represents an extension of land already being worked. Such are the fields north of the Château de La Ruée, H122 and H123 (Ruff); south of Trélo Château (Car), D266; by Gayon, a *métairie* associated with Coëtion, L161 and L162 (Ruff); and southwest of Bodel Château, L166 and L167 (in Ruff). These small extensions are represented by fields with small quantities of later medieval pottery, but none of the earlier Fabric 1 (that is, manuring scatters of the late but not of the central middle ages), although they are close to fields that do have Fabric 1.

Other cases of new arable are associated with recorded fifteenth-century noble sites that look comparatively recent, that is new establishments in new zones. Such are the fields west of Gravaud (E140, E285); fields by Le Bois Brassu (E283); fields by Gélinais (D191, D192, D193) (all Car); fields by Les Landes du Houssa (A4, A6) (Ruff); and, most strikingly, fields in and around the present commune centre of Tréal, the location of La Ville Lio, a *métairie* first mentioned in 1427, which stands in lands devoid of Fabric 1 but with plenty of fabrics of the later middle ages (J179, J195 and so on) (Fig. 7.1). It is of particular interest to note that this exploitation of new areas had begun already in the early fifteenth century, although of course there is no reason to suppose that it was confined to that period and every reason to suppose that it continued through much of the sixteenth century.

It is also striking that recorded noble properties of the fifteenth century have a distinctive distribution: most lie in the centre of the survey area; 71% in eastern Ruffiac, Tréal, Saint-Nicolas and western Carentoir (Transects A, H, J, B, C). In fact, a third lie in the small communes of Tréal and Saint-Nicolas. In other words, they tend to be sited away from the old-established parish centres of Ruffiac and Carentoir (cf. Fig. 7.5). The same point is made in a different way by the fact that two-thirds lie near large areas of nineteenth-century uncultivated *lande* or on a north–south or east–west commune boundary (and at least nine lie within 300m of Roman villa sites, perhaps drawn by the availability of building materials in otherwise unworked areas).[2]

A significant proportion of the noble farms of the fifteenth and sixteenth centuries were lands of new exploitation. A good 40% of them had no, or negligible, Fabric 1 on the surface of surrounding fields, and no central medieval exploitation in the neighbourhood (17 with none and 10 with <10g); nearly all of these fields also have no or negligible Fabric 8. While, on the whole, therefore, there were strong continuities from the thirteenth to the sixteenth century in land-use and settlement patterns, there were new developments; these lie overwhelmingly in association with noble properties.

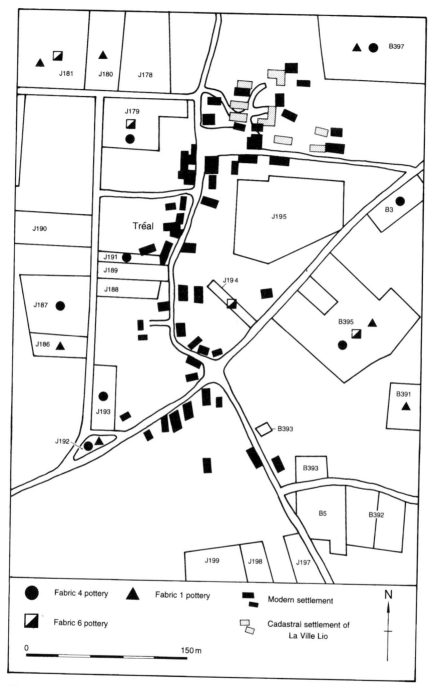

Figure 7.1 *Fields walked round La Ville Lio (Tréal modern bourg)*

Settlement shift

Some noble settlements of the late middle ages appear to have been located on or very near an earlier site. Fields by grand houses like Launay, La Ruée and La Charmille have large quantities of Fabric 1, but also very significant quantities of the later wares. Others look like new developments in new areas: in the case of Les Landes du Houssa, the cluster of pottery at A4 may well indicate the site of the new establishment; so too the clusters at Clazeul (Car) in F224, and at La Buardais (Tr), with its two linked concentrations at J214/215. All of these cases are striking for the combination of a cluster of late medieval pottery and the total absence of Fabric 1, a fabric which, as we have seen, is extremely common (see Fig. 6.1). Distinctive Fabric 4/6/23 clusters with no known noble associations may well reflect expanding or new peasant settlements: the cluster at E49, near La Roche Pélerin (Car); and those at B88 (Triguého, Tr), C439 (La Provotaie), D151 (Bot Colin), and F247 (La Madeleine; all Car).

Some established noble settlements can be clearly shown to have shifted site. Near La Guichardais, in northern Tréal, there is a cluster of Fabric 1 at J98, and of Fabric 8 at J97, and then the sixteenth-century *château* near by; it looks as if there was a shift of settlement from J98 to the present site, with J97 perhaps marking a late medieval storage site. So too the successive clusters at Gaincru in Ruffiac, L124 (Fabric 1), L127 (Fabric 8), and the present site; and perhaps at Rangera not far away (A55/62/362 to L76). At H132, beside the Château de la Ruée, there were two distinct clusters: the medieval cluster above the stone structure of that period and to the east an equally large cluster of late medieval fabrics (see above, pp. 125–6); the implication is that the medieval structure was abandoned in favour of a new structure to the east, itself abandoned when the field was laid down to meadow and the present *château* built in the seventeenth century (see below, p. 158).

In a complex of fields in northern Ruffiac there are at least five distinct clusters, which appear to locate the forerunners of the important seventeenth-century *château* of Coëtion and two of its associated *métairies* (Le Bas Coëtion and La Touche Gourelle): Fabric 1 and Fabric 8 together at A116; two smaller clusters of Fabric 1 at A123/124/126 and A124; Fabric 5 at A119, not far from the present buildings of La Touche Gourelle; and Fabric 8 at A159 to the north; the *château* of Coëtion itself lies slightly to the east of this (Fig. 7.2). There were in fact two noble houses at Coëtion in the fifteenth century and this complex of clusters, covering 35 ha, suggests a lengthy pre-fifteenth-century background of special settlement in the area. The cluster of central medieval tableware, including 13 sherds from a single early jug, is suggestive of a dump at the eastern end of A119, close to a

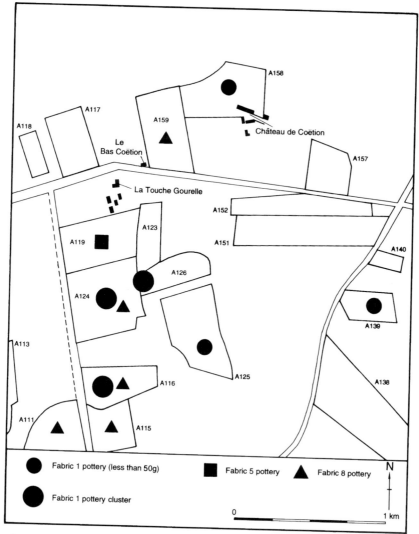

Figure 7.2 *Clusters of medieval fabrics in the neighbourhood of Coëtion (Ruffiac)*

residence; the field has no Fabric 1 and is most unlikely to have been worked at the time that the tableware was dumped.

At Le Bois Guillaume, in field B409, itself an Iron-Age settlement site (see above, pp. 63–4), there were large quantities of Fabric 1 in two separate clusters, with notable quantities of foreign stone (i.e. building debris) in the ploughsoil. Fields B411/412 to the west, with greater quantities of Fabric 8, may be near a settlement which succeeded the building(s) on B409, particularly since they are adjacent to a field called Le Fossé, which was the name of this noble house in 1427; the present house lies between the two. Late medieval fabrics were evenly distributed on B409 itself, suggesting manuring by *c*.1500. Both A116 and B409 are also notable for their finds of the tenth-century Fabric 10 (see above, pp. 105, 107); it seems likely that these "pre-noble" settlements of the thirteenth century had their origins in the tenth century (or before).

In considering the thirteenth and fourteenth centuries, we suggested that a number of clusters (by analogy with those in the vicinity of noble houses recorded in the fifteenth and sixteenth centuries) reflected pre-noble nuclei. Many of these analogous cases did not develop to become noble sites (or do not appear to have done so, for they do not have sufficient later pottery to suggest later settlement of any sort). The failure to develop implies that the sites shifted considerably (like J277 to Le Pont Bily (S-N), or C573 to La Touche Peschart (Car)); or that the properties were acquired by absentee nobles; or that the residents failed to maintain the momentum towards noble status, perhaps damaged by the demographic pressures of the late fourteenth and fifteenth centuries. All three alternatives are possible, and entirely appropriate to the real and changing world of the fifteenth century.

Sixteenth-century transformations

Our texts suggest that the nobility of this area continued to grow through the later fifteenth and early sixteenth centuries, but at a much reduced rate: the number of nobles named in Carentoir in 1426 had increased slightly by the 1536 enumeration, although those of Ruffiac and Tréal remained about the same. Incidental references suggest some general increase in population in the survey area by the mid sixteenth century, in accordance with regional trends: while only two taxable households were recorded at L'Abbaye aux Alines (Car) in 1447, there were more than ten households answering for the *tenue* (tenure) to the Priory in 1540.[3] This certainly does not have to constitute a five-fold increase, since the *fouages* will have exempted some, but it does suggest an upward tendency.

What is most striking, however, is the change in the *composition* not the number of the nobility in the early sixteenth century. A series of fifteenth-century muster-rolls names nobles, in addition to the listings of nobles and *métayers* of the *fouages*. Over the course of this series, there were some additions and some changes in the holders of noble seats, although many of the early fifteenth century were still there in 1481: the

Gueno family was at Trélo in 1427 and still there in 1481, like the Bouxel family at La Basse Boixière and the Sorel family at Clazeul. However, the first *fouage* of the sixteenth century records a striking number of new names; and by 1536, of the 51 noble families named in Carentoir parish no more than 17 appear to have held the properties in the fifteenth century – a 66% replacement (in Ruffiac 62%, and Tréal 64%). While this must in part have been a consequence of the death of male heirs – a common problem in an era of epidemic – some new men clearly appeared in the area. We can see families like the de la Bourdonnayes acquiring noble properties in the late fifteenth century; by the early sixteenth they held at least Couedic and Fanhouet in Tréal, where they did not live, as well as La Ruée and Coëtion (de Laigue 1902: 675, 677, 830–2). The Robitels appeared at La Herblinaie, La Tronchaie and Carentoir *bourg* in 1536; as did *sieurs* from other parishes with a hand on core properties (*sieurs* from Maure, La Morlaye, Kerbiguet, Villeder, La Chaussée, Monbeille, for example). Other new men, like Le Berruyer at La Touche aux Roux, with interests on a much smaller scale, appeared at the same time (de Laigue 1902: 145–7).

These changes in noble personnel were not unique. They echo a process that has been very well documented for the Vannetais, just to the southwest of the survey area. Here Gallet has shown that many families which became established in the late fifteenth century remained in place for 150 or 200 years or more; how, in the early sixteenth century especially, the petty nobility cleared new lands, created new *manoirs*, built *métairies*, bought *tenues*; how the *sieuries* grew (a little) bigger and rents taken by the *sieurs* increased, especially in grain (Gallet 1983: 311–76 especially). The *sieurs* of Ruffiac, Tréal and Carentoir clearly began to thrive in the sixteenth century, sharing in the flurry of petty noble activity that characterized the wider region.

Château landscaping

Whether associated with new or long established families, it is quite clear that there were new ideas in the air in the sixteenth century and new approaches to the exploitation of land in the survey area. There was building and rebuilding of noble houses – sixteenth-century fabric still survives today in some cases (Couedic, for example, where the fifteenth-century structure was first extended and then a ceiling inserted in the open hall; see Figs 11.2, 11.3). But more than that, there was construction of parks and gardens and – in some cases – a complete remodelling of the noble landscape. References to the meadows and gardens associated with noble properties begin in this area in the early sixteenth century – like the

155

two meadows, garden, and arable held by the tenant of part of La Ville Marie in 1542.[4] They are common enough to make it clear that these were characteristic of noble properties here, as they were elsewhere. But there is more than the haphazard creation of woods and gardens, orchards and vineyards: in some cases, the meadows, gardens and arable were laid out in a planned way, for striking aesthetic effect (Fig. 7.3).

The cadastral record of the 1820s records in detail the existence of these planned landscapes, landscapes which by the 1820s were evidently no longer maintained as initially intended. Where they remain clear, the *cadastre* reveals what we may term "château landscapes" (see above, pp. 14–15): discrete areas, with large rectangular arable fields, in striking contrast to the irregular divided *bandes* of peasant agriculture; with substantial amounts of meadow, again often in rectangular fields, and again in striking contrast to the narrow zones of peasant water meadow; with planted woodland, often as a backdrop to the noble house; with diversion of streams to fill ponds or lakes in front of the house, creating a pleasing outlook; with long straight avenues of trees leading up to the main entrance of the residence; with enclosed gardens to rear and side of it, and orchards and vineyards near it. These were integrated landscapes, covering up to 60–70 ha. Sometimes a farm lay beside the noble house, but in other cases one or more *métairies* lay at some distance from it – we know there were two for Le Bois Brassu by 1568 and three for Clazeul by 1606 (both Car). None of this is confined to the parishes of the core survey area: there is château landscaping round La Fresnaye in Transect N (Réminiac); very elaborate landscaping at La Morlaye in Transect P (Missiriac), with two formal woods as well as a formal garden, and at the Château de la Boulaye in Transect M (Bruc), with no fewer than four avenues; and an exceptionally large area of landscaping round the *château* of Bodel in Transect N (Caro, noted under Ruffiac in 1426).

Now it happens that items in the corpus of sixteenth- and seventeenth-century records often refer to individual fields, and nearly always refer to the land-use of such fields; some are described in a very precise way and are localizable; and many of these localizable fields belong to the planned landscapes of the survey area. It is therefore often demonstrable that the features recorded in the 1820s cadastral record were *already* present in the sixteenth or seventeenth centuries: the rectangular meadows, the avenues, the planted woodland were already laid out in the immediate post-medieval period. The earliest precisely localizable reference to planned features in this area comes in 1542 (near La Gicquelaye, Ruff), while it is perfectly clear that descriptions of properties in fifteenth-century *aveux* do not indicate the same carefully modelled features.[5] A change happened between the fifteenth and sixteenth (sometimes seventeenth) centuries. It

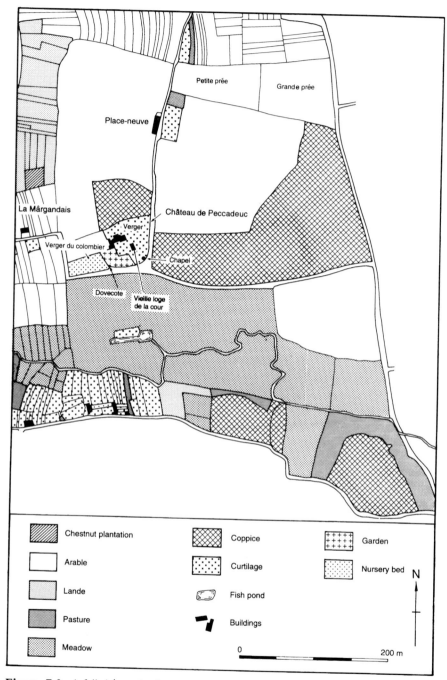

Petite prée

Grande prée

Place-neuve

La Mârgandais

Verger

Château de Peccadeuc

Verger du colombier

Chapel

Dovecote

Vieille loge
de la cour

Chestnut plantation	Coppice	Garden
Arable	Curtilage	Nursery bed
Lande	Fish pond	N
Pasture	Buildings	
Meadow		

0   200 m

Figure 7.3 *A full château landscape: Peccadeuc (Carentoir)*

therefore looks as if the laying-out of these château landscapes was a process which began in the sixteenth century and largely belonged to the later sixteenth and early seventeenth centuries, although the grandest clearly continued to be refined and improved through the seventeenth and eighteenth centuries; the grandest of all – that surrounding the large *château* of La Bourdonnaye – is a creation of the early eighteenth century, and is on a totally different scale.

The very fact that by the 1820s the characteristic features of the landscapes are sometimes barely detectable in the cadastral record emphasizes that the landscapes were at that time ancient: that surrounding La Danais in Carentoir, which the Coetdor family held continuously from the early fifteenth century till the mid sixteenth, had only some angular arable fields, some stream diversion, and a block of former woodland in the 1820s; that surrounding Le Plessis (Tr) has gardens used as arable, and rectangular arable fields whose shape is barely discernible given the mixture of nineteenth-century land-use within them (Fig. 7.4). The antiquity of these distinctive landscapes is also demonstrated in a more general way by the large quantities and proportions of pasture and meadow associated with noble properties in the sixteenth- and seventeenth-century texts, by contrast with the largely arable peasant holdings (cf. Figs 7.3, 7.4).

Confirmation of this dating is also provided by surface finds on château-landscaped fields, particularly on meadow. Many of the landscaped meadows were newly established in focal positions, replacing earlier arable (and in some cases former settlements). Surface finds on these meadows invariably lack (or have single sherds of) the salt-glazed and other regional imports of the seventeenth and eighteenth centuries; they nearly always have plenty of Fabric 1, and often have Fabrics 4, 8 and 23. In other words, while these fields had been fertilized for arable use in the middle ages, manure-spreading stopped sometime in the sixteenth or very early seventeenth century, as the use turned from arable to meadow; broken pottery therefore no longer found its way on to the fields. So, the field by La Ruée, H132, site of the substantial building of the central middle ages and notable for the large quantities of Fabrics 1, 4 and 8 on its surface, was put down to meadow by 1609 (see above, pp. 125–6).[6] In this case, laying out of fields, avenue, pond, and perhaps the beginning of the new house, seem to have taken place in the late sixteenth century, after Yvon de la Ruée took on new *tenues* in that area and other members of his family went to live at the near-by *métairie* of La Ville Marie.[7] H132 and La Ruée provide a strikingly good example (as do the cadastral meadows A116 and B409, in relation to Coëtion and Le Bois Guillaume/Le Fossé) because excavation has demonstrated the sequence from arable to meadow; however, fieldwalking of cadastral meadow beside noble houses sends the

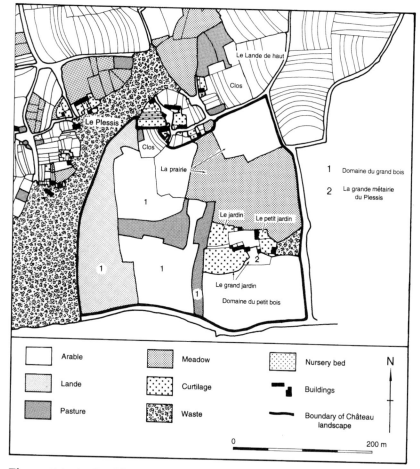

Figure 7.4 *A relict château landscape in the 1820s: Le Plessis (Tréal)*

same message again and again: medieval fabrics (denoting medieval arable) occur on the meadows C292/293 by the noble house at Peccadeuc, on C305 by Les Feuges, on C565 by La Touche Peschart (all Car), on J97/98/206 by La Guichardais, on J264 by Lorgerais (both Tr), on L166/168 by Bodel (Davies & Astill 1994: 215–16, for further detail). The date range of the pottery scatters emphasizes both the change of use from arable to meadow and the date of so doing.

The full château landscapes recorded in the 1820s number 24 in the core survey area; there are some six additional relict château landscapes, as well as 11 small-scale or partial landscapes of this type.[8] Although it is

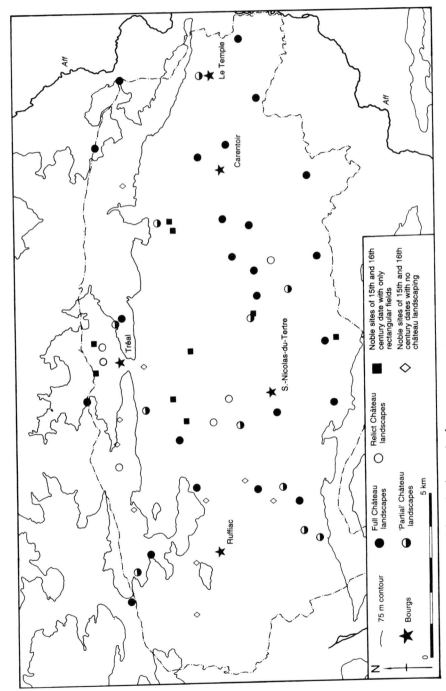

Figure 7.5 *Distribution of château landscapes in the core survey area*

Noble sites of 15th and 16th century date with only rectangular fields

Noble sites of 15th and 16th century dates with no château landscaping

Relict Château landscapes

Full Château landscapes

'Partial' Château landscapes

75 m contour

Bourgs

Le Temple

Carentoir

S.-Nicolas-du-Tertre

Tréal

Ruffiac

Aff

N

5 km

conceivable that there were many more such landscapes that have completely disappeared, it seems likely that the total number in the late sixteenth/early seventeenth century would have fallen short of the 68 sixteenth-century recorded noble houses of the survey core: not every noble went to these lengths. Not surprisingly, it is the properties associated with established local noble families present and living in the parishes that have the landscaping, not the properties associated with absentee nobles. Hence, although the distribution of château landscapes broadly reflects that of fifteenth-/sixteenth-century noble properties, it does not completely mirror it; indeed, château-landscaping occurs near the ancient *bourgs* of Ruffiac and Carentoir (for example, at Clazeul and La Guichardais in Carentoir) as much as in the "new" lands peripheral to those *bourgs* (Fig. 7.5). Occasionally the landscaping occurs on a small scale in association with an isolated *métairie*, like La Ville Lio (Fig. 7.6).

By the end of the sixteenth century noble owners treated their lands in different ways: many of those who lived in the parishes began to construct grand houses, set in planned landscapes (see Fig. 7.8); but some constructed the house without the landscape (La Charmille, Balangeart (Ruff)), and a few constructed the landscape with a less ambitious residence (La Cossais (Car)), while several – including some *métayers* – merely adopted a few features of the château landscapes (the rectangular fields, perhaps the meadow, without the avenues, ponds, gardens and woodland), and considerably less pretentious houses (La Porte (S-N)); a few made the barest nod by establishing rectangular fields, but no more – like La Boixière Launay (Car), one of the oldest recorded noble houses, or La Buardais (Tr) (Fig. 7.7); and some do not appear to have opted for grandeur at all (Gaincru (Ruff), La Chênais (Tr)). There are therefore clear manifestations in the landscape of differentiation within the early modern nobility, a differentiation which may have been as much conditioned by regular presence in the locality as by crude wealth.

The practice of creating parks and gardens is well known in western Europe, an effect of the spread of Renaissance culture through the noble courts of Italy, France and England especially (cf. Johnson 1996: 146–7). What is particularly interesting in this small locality is both the finesse and intricacy of the planning of the landscapes and also the very limited social scale of the *sieurs* who created them. These were not *grands seigneurs*; their landscapes were small. But they were intrinsically distinctive as well as quite distinct from the peasant *tenues* surrounding them (see Figs 2.1, 7.3, 7.4). It was doubtless the increased rents from the *tenues* – and particularly the grain to sell – that provided the means to turn idea into vista.

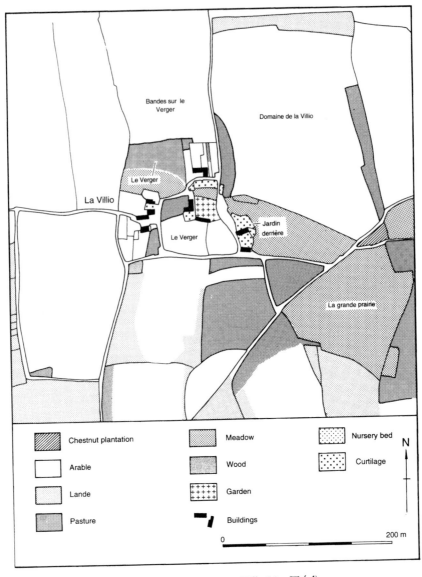

Figure 7.6 *A partial château landscape at La Ville Lio (Tréal)*

La Villio

Bandes sur le Verger

Domaine de la Villio

Le Verger

Le Verger

Jardin derrière

La grande prairie

Chestnut plantation

Arable

Lande

Pasture

Meadow

Wood

Garden

Buildings

Nursery bed

Curtilage

N

0   200 m

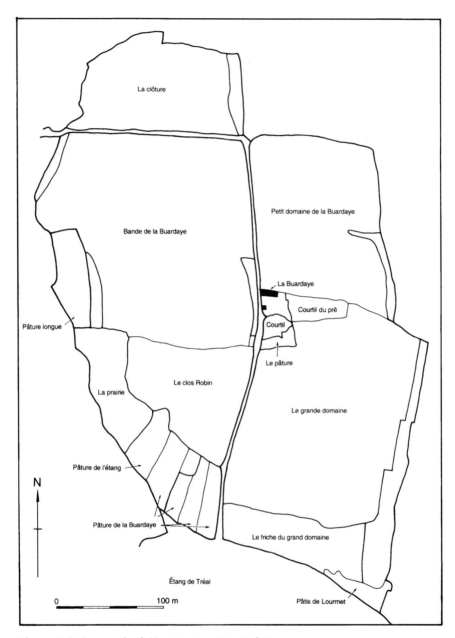

Figure 7.7 *Rectangular fields at La Buardais (Tréal)*

Figure 7.8 *The petit château at La Châtaigneraie (Saint-Nicolas)*

Notes

1. Whereas a higher proportion of *newly* worked land (i.e. that with no fabrics of the central middle ages) was farther from water than the "all fields" mean, it is nevertheless also the case that new fields with Fabrics 6 and 23 are in some parts found in wet valley bottoms (especially Transect M, see above, p. 131). Different processes are at work here: whereas people were walking farther to some fields, in order to increase the available arable, it also looks as if areas that were previously too wet for arable cultivation became workable, almost certainly for reasons of climatic change.

2. For example, La Herblinaie, La Touche aux Roux, Le Mur, La Grée Michel, La Guichardais (all in Carentoir); and La Boulaye in Bruc.

3. AD Loire-Atlantique B2986; AD Ille-et-Vilaine 3H188 L9.

4. AD Ille-et-Vilaine 3H188 L5.

5. AD Ille-et-Vilaine 3H188 L5.

6. AD Ille-et-Vilaine 3H188 L5.

7. AD Ille-et-Vilaine 3H188 L5 (1542), 3H193 (1556), 3H187 L2 (1576). Yvon de la Ruée was holding land in the neighbourhood of La Gicquelaye and La Ville Marie in 1542 and was called *sieur* in the Priory *aveu* of 1556; the *sieur de la Ruée* is thereafter commonly noted. Yvon held the *tenue* of La Ville Marie from the Priory in 1556, and the *métairie* of La Ville Marie continued to be associated with Ruée holdings through the seventeenth century (though the Priory questioned its noble status in 1715, in a dispute with Louis de la Ruée (3H192 L6)).

   The house La Ruée is not noted in the fifteenth-century *fouage* records but was held in the early sixteenth century (listed at that time under Tréal parish) by the de la

Bourdonnayes, who had acquired it in the late fifteenth (de Laigue 1902: 831–2). In view of the very close connection between Ruée family properties and the Priory in the later sixteenth and seventeenth centuries, and the present location of the Château de la Ruée 150m from the Priory, it is likely that the forerunner of the present *château* (on field H132) was one of the noble houses listed under the "Abbaye Prior" in 1426 and again separately (unlocated) in 1440 (de Laigue 1902: 671, 674).

8. Sample transects: 2 full in P, 4 in N and 6 in M; however, since these transects are thin slices through whole parishes they cannot give a representative indication of the density of château landscaping in the parishes surrounding the core.

CHAPTER 8

Rising population

The noble imprint on the landscape remained through much of the seventeenth and eighteenth centuries; nobles continued to expect a range of obligations from their peasant tenants; and dozens of *sieurs* continue to be evidenced. Nevertheless one cannot escape a sense that by 1750 the nobility was not quite what it had been in 1550. Seventeenth-century records continue to note the obligations of obedience, corporal residence and using the *seigneur's* mill; if anything, there is even more emphasis on the lordly monopoly of milling than there had been in the sixteenth century. They also note days of harvest work due from tenants. However, while harvest days continue, obedience, corporal residence and milling fade from the records in the eighteenth century: the ancient bases of tenancy were shifting.

At a higher level, the introduction of new arrangements for noble landholding is striking by the mid eighteenth century: shorter- and longer-term leases were concluded on parts of ancient fiefs or of the demesne, for largely commercial considerations. So, while Trotereau of Lorgerais (Tr) had the Ruffiac Priory lands in farm beforehand, in June 1735 Julien Blanchard (officer of the Marquis of La Bourdonnaye) took a seven-year lease on the Priory and its lands, soon to sell on rights in the lease to a Caro man for six and a half years. [1]

Some properties which had previously been described as noble lost the designation: such are Le Bot (S-N), an ancient noble house of the fifteenth century, or La Hiarnaie (Ruff) and La Ville Jeanne (Tr), both of which had had *sieurs* in the seventeenth century. The earlier links between title and residence often dissolved: in 1697 the *sieur* of Préclos (Tr) lived at Peccadeuc (Car) and in 1715 the *sieur* of Lorgerais lived at Préclos. *Sieuries* (and *seigneuries*) became united, in name as well as in practice: the most powerful was the *seigneurie* of the Marquis de la Bourdonnaye, combining the lands of the *seigneurs* of La Gacilly, La Haute and La Basse Boixière and Coëtion from 1717; but there are lesser examples too, like the combining of Le Bois Brassu, Peccadeuc and Boisby in 1761 or of Préclos, La Provotaye, Lorgerais and La Touche aux Roux in 1771. Members of the surviving families, of course, might live at several houses – like the de la Ruée de la Bourdonnayes at La Ruée and Préclos as well as at La Bourdonnaye, nine of them witnessing a wedding in Tréal in 1788.

The word *métayer* gradually disappeared as *fermier* (farmer) took its place (see above, pp. 147–8). By the late eighteenth century some of the most ancient noble places had *fermiers* living in the buildings and managing the lands – like Couedic (Tr), with a *sieur* in sixteenth and seventeenth centuries but a *fermier* from 1785; or La Guichardais (Tr), from 1773; or Le Bois Brun and Bostubois, from 1782 and 1762 respectively. This was in part simply a change in terminology, for nobles had contracted with others to manage their lands for centuries; but the change in language went down to the day-to-day level of the parish records and reflects the declining presence of active nobility.[2]

It is not surprising, therefore, that the taxation lists of the later eighteenth century note fewer noble households than do those of the sixteenth – fewer than 25 in the 1762 *vingtième* for the area of modern Carentoir – and that the value of noble goods is often not high.[3] This was a regional trend: estimates of the proportion of nobles in eighteenth-century Brittany are much lower than those for the fifteenth or sixteenth – not much more than 1% of the population; indeed, the poverty of the petty nobility has been noted in many parts of the region (Nassiet 1993: 375–6).

Archives and land-use

In the seventeenth century there are plenty of written texts that tell us about land-use; *aveux*, rent-rolls, leases, dispute proceedings all give information about areas of arable, meadow, wood, and so on. These are not of course comprehensive records, like the cadastral surveys of the early nineteenth century, and they do not therefore allow us to reconstruct the entire picture of land-use. However, they let us make some suggestions about trends and some direct comparisons with the cadastral evidence.

There is much more localizable material from these sources for the seventeenth century than there is for the eighteenth, with 43 different usable texts, as against ten for the later period. In both centuries, texts make much more reference to the hedges and ditches surrounding arable and pasture than they had in the previous 200 years. By the second half of the seventeenth century texts relating to noble properties refer to hedges in such a way that they imply that it was common for noble crop fields to have them. By the eighteenth century maintenance of hedges and ditches is a frequent theme of leasing arrangements (specifically to keep cattle out of crops and woods), with dry ditches differentiated from wet. The latter were in some cases elaborate, carrying water for mills.[4] We hear once of complaints against the de la Bourdonnayes for enclosing common land near La Nouette (Ruff), not far from the Château de la Ruée, where people had been accustomed to let their animals run free, but this classic problem of the early modern period does not feature as a constant source of trouble.[5] Most texts in fact localize arable in a way that suggests that open fields, with portions lying side by side (as was the norm in the nineteenth century), were extremely common. During the seventeenth century about 45% of specified land-use was arable (slightly increasing towards the end of the century), about 20% was meadow, and another significant proportion *landes*, 20% in the early seventeenth century, declining towards the end of the century. Other common uses were as garden, woodland and pasture (always a small proportion). Vineyards are mentioned at the holdings of Le Cleu (Tr) and La Châtaigneraie (S-N) in 1649 and 1680 respectively; and a coppice at La Châtaigneraie was recorded as planted with chestnuts in 1680, while some land at La Basse Boixière was under seed with oak and chestnuts in 1708[6] (chestnut starts to appear in pollen cores in the sixteenth and seventeenth centuries (Marguerie 1992: 114)). In a few cases there are comments such as "meadow used as arable" or "*lande* as meadow", or field names indicate a recent change of use (where a field called "The Meadow" is arable, for example). While one would expect more references to arable, given the nature of these texts, the trends are interesting; the drift is that some meadow was losing its dedicated use; in most cases the change was to arable, but it was occasionally to *lande*. Overall, however, the seventeenth-century material consistently suggests a tendency to increase in arable usage and a decrease in the *landes* (Table 8.1).

It is interesting that there are few references to pasture. Inland areas of central Brittany, round Ploermel for example, have a long history of cattle-rearing (Collins 1994: 37–9). Cattle there certainly were in the survey area (as there were also a few sheep and pigs), and nobles paid some attention to stock-raising, as they undoubtedly did to woodland management. The overwhelming implication of the written evidence, however, is that these were areas of *mixed* farming, with cereals grown for sale as well as local consumption. Slate-roofed granges are a feature of noble properties at this period, and bread and grain concoctions were a major aspect of peasant diet

Table 8.1 Written references to land-use in localizable fields in the seventeenth and eighteenth centuries

	1600–30	1631–60	1661–1700	1701–30	1731–60	1761–1800
Arable	42	15	30	16	5	1
Arable/friche	0	1	0	0	0	0
Arable/lande	4	1	0	0	0	0
Arable/meadow	0	4	1	0	0	0
Arable/pasture	0	0	2	0	0	0
Coppice	0	0	2	5	0	0
Friche	1	3	0	2	0	0
Garden	5	1	3	9	3	1
Lande	16	2	4	9	4	1
Meadow	20	4	11	9	0	1
Meadow/friche	1	1	0	0	0	0
Meadow/lande	1	0	0	0	0	0
Meadow/pasture	0	0	1	0	0	0
Pasture	3	0	5	9	3	1
Pasture/lande	2	0	0	0	0	0
Vines	0	1	1	0	0	0
Wood	2	1	2	1	0	0
Wood/lande	1	0	0	0	0	0

By number of references; AD I-et-V 3H188, 3H189, 3H190, 3H192, 3H193, 3H194(1); ADM E1604, G981, G1066; AD L-A B1957b, B1991

(Croix 1981: 813–14; Thévenin 1993: 265–7). Indeed, letters from Ruffiac to the subdelegation of Malestroit asking for help in 1766 state that buckwheat was the staple food of the local inhabitants.[7]

Documentation of this type is not so plentiful for the eighteenth century, and most of it relates to the first two or three decades of the century. However, broadly, the proportions of arable, meadow and *lande* are the same as those mentioned at the end of the seventeeth century, although pasture is more evident (14% of specified land-use in the period 1700–30). There is no material that suggests later changes. The *landes*, of course, had a significant role in the agrarian economy; rights to cut fern and wood from the *lande*, for example, are sometimes specified in rentals.

Both seventeenth- and eighteenth-century evidence can be compared with the cadastral pattern of land-use, sometimes precisely, since documents of this period often localize fields by referring to roads and rivers, and by name; the field names are virtually always the same as the names of the cadastral record (true also of the sixteenth century). 72 seventeenth-century and 60 eighteenth-century fields can be precisely related to the maps of the core survey area of the 1820s. Of these, in each case 83% of usage remained the same in the early nineteenth century; in other words, the broad picture is one of very little change in the basic pattern of land-use over 250 years. Where there were changes between seventeenth or eighteenth centuries and the 1820s, they were *never* changes away from arable use, although there were changes from seventeenth-century meadow and pasture, in particular; and one of the vineyards was pasture by the 1820s and several of the gardens were ploughed or just backyard curtilage by then. The same is true of the surrounding communes: in sample transect N, in Réminiac, the château landscape around La Fresnaye indicates that some, though not all, of the *grand pré* round the house was used as arable in 1829.

All of this is consonant with a picture of increasing arable land-use, and perhaps a modest shift in balance in the agrarian economy. What was the product of this arable area? Rent-rolls continue to mention wheat, oats, rye, and buckwheat, through the seventeenth and eighteenth centuries (and occasionally millet); other texts indicate, as above, that buckwheat was the subsistence crop for the mass of the population. However, Ramponnet *métairie* (in Ruffiac *bourg*) planted twice as much rye as any other cereal (buckwheat, wheat, oats) in 1661. Hemp and flax are much more evident than they are in fifteenth- and sixteenth-century texts, especially in the eighteenth century, and payment of labourers to sow flax is mentioned in 1745. That there was an increased emphasis on hemp and flax is impressionistic but some precise evidence supports the impression: the 1669 *aveu* for La Ville Marie and La Gicquelaye is unusual in indicating that new rents were required;[8] the new elements of the rent involved a portion of the hemp crop, apparently for the first time, some poultry and an increase in grain return. Fibres were acquiring a new significance and, since landlords sold their revenues, there was an active local grain market. By 1785 even small farmers were agitated about any hindrance to the passage of grain to the markets of Malestroit, La Gacilly and Bruc. When crops failed, as they did frequently in the late eighteenth century, it must have been to these markets that poor farmers went with their government subsidy to buy seedcorn – although there was also a weekly market, and two annual fairs, in Ruffiac.[9]

Population

There is a wealth of demographic material extant for the core survey area, with parish registers surviving for most parishes from the sixteenth century, with few breaks in the series.[10] These registers are especially rich in locational and social detail for the sixteenth, seventeenth and eighteenth centuries, usually locating principal actors by hamlet within a given parish, and giving their ages, and often providing information about their occupations and social status. Copies of the material remain, in some cases, in the local *mairies* – as they do in Ruffiac – and these copies occasionally provide alternative detail to that filed in the Departmental Archives.[11]

As we have seen, the early parish of Carentoir included the area of the modern communes of La Gacilly, Quelneuc and La Chapelle Gaceline (see Fig. 3.10). Carentoir was therefore an extremely large parish, although the three later communes were *trèves* from the late middle ages, with their own churches and their own (incomplete) series of registers;[12] despite the latter, events concerning parishioners from the three *trèves* sometimes feature in the Carentoir registers in the sixteenth, seventeenth and eighteenth centuries. The small zone of Le Temple in eastern Carentoir (400 ha) was excluded, being a separate parish from sometime in the late middle ages (above, p. 119), and it had separate parish registers until July 1792.[13] Le Temple figures, as also La Haute Boixière (within Carentoir too), are totalled with Carentoir at Figures 8.1 and 8.4, for ease of comparison.

Ruffiac was also originally a larger parish, including Tréal and Saint-Nicolas-du-Tertre, and Saint-Laurent to the southwest. Both Tréal and Saint-Laurent became separate parishes in the middle ages (above, pp. 55–6). Saint-Nicolas was a *trève* of Ruffiac until it acquired separate parish status in 1802; in the sixteenth century its parishioners petitioned for their church to have baptismal rights, which it acquired in 1576; hence it has a separate series of registers. Ruffiac, Tréal and Saint-Nicolas baptism figures and baptism/burial ratios have been kept separate and relate in the sixteenth to eighteenth centuries to the approximate areas of the separate modern communes.

Mortality

The core communes share some major demographic trends from the late sixteenth century, but at some points there are surprising differences. Although, as indicated above, baptism records often survive from the sixteenth century, burial records do not: hence, although we can comment on sixteenth-century baptism trends, we cannot calculate baptism/burial ratios until the seventeenth century; once we can do that, we can comment with more confidence on overall population trends.

It is of exceptional interest that we can identify different demographic patterns in these four adjacent communes. Carentoir was by far the largest (now 5,902 ha and in the seventeenth and eighteenth centuries a parish of about 9,500 ha; Ruffiac now 3,647 ha and approximately the same then, as were Tréal and Saint-Nicolas, now 1,928 ha and 1,293 ha respectively). To give us some sense of the comparative size of the parish populations in the eighteenth century note the vital events of the year 1750: in Carentoir there were 129 baptisms, 20 marriages, 118 burials; in Ruffiac 61 baptisms, 13 marriages, 36 burials; in Tréal 38 baptisms, 10 marriages, 30 burials; in Saint-Nicolas 19 baptisms, 3 marriages, 9 burials (see below, pp. 177, 179, for the high level of burial in Carentoir).

The different parishes often experienced severe mortality in the same decades, especially in the late eighteenth century, with exceptional mortality in Tréal in 1775 (75 burials), Carentoir and La Haute Boixière in 1776 (233 and 42 burials respectively) and Ruffiac in 1777 (119 burials) – respectively 1.6, 1.9, 2.9 and 1.7 times the mean number of burials across ten years; Saint-Nicolas also had relatively high mortality in 1774 (30 burials). These were years of poor harvests and famine across northern France and the survey area clearly shared in a general crisis. Mortality was nearly as severe in 1803/4, in Tréal, Carentoir and Ruffiac, a year when it was high in the region as a whole. However, mortality in earlier years peaked at different places at different times. The highest recorded mortality for Tréal was in 1627 (82 burials).[14] There was high mortality in Ruffiac in 1643 (97 burials) – a year of high prices, famine and "tumults" in Brittany (Croix 1981: 324, 367); in Carentoir in 1694 (179 burials) – the year following an exceptionally severe winter in northern France – and 1743 (266 burials; also 43 in Le Temple); and in Ruffiac in 1782 (140 burials) (Fig. 8.1). The 1740s are well-known as crisis years and 1782 had high mortality in the region (Post 1985; Blayo & Henry 1975: 62).

We know, following many detailed studies, that there was a complex interplay between famine and disease in provoking crises (Dupâquier 1989; cf. Weir 1989). The close relationship between epidemic and food supply is sometimes made explicit in local texts: in 1765 Malestroit and Missiriac lost a tenth of their parishioners in an epidemic; the request for help refers to the additional misery caused by the shortage of grain (created by freak weather conditions); ten years later 14 groups of "poor farmers" received money to buy seed to plant.[15]

Sometimes whole families were struck in a crisis year, as is notable in 1804: in Carentoir in January three children at La Bourdonnaye (aged 7, 5 and $2\frac{1}{4}$) and two at La Porte Juhel (aged 2 and 4); in May, on two consecutive days, a 52-year-old father and his 18-year-old teenager at La Villeneuve; and in August and September a brother (20), his sister (26) and their father (62), at Les Vignes; in Tréal a whole family is described as "sick", with mother, father and two children dying.[16] The occasional notes of "sudden" death – in Saint-Nicolas through the 1780s, in Tréal in 1775, and in Ruffiac in 1782 – reflect the impact of disease, as does the passage of death from hamlet to hamlet: in Le Temple in 1743, from La Gilardais to Le Bourgneuf de Haut to Le Bois Faux to Le Haut du Bourg and Chauffaut;

and in Tréal in 1775: in Le Plessis in January–April, La Ville Hatte in May–June–July, and Quoiqueneuc in September–October–November.

Mortality in the crisis years struck nobles and peasants alike, and all age-ranges (as it struck a 27-year-old noble at Les Greffins in August 1782). In fact, despite a life-expectancy at birth that was relatively short, there is often reference to the very old; people could live to a considerable old age: 82, 84 and 87 noted in Ruffiac in 1777; 85 and 93 in Carentoir in 1804; 80 and 90 in Le Temple in 1743; 84 or 85, 84 and 86½ (*sic*) in Saint-Nicolas in 1777, 1776 and 1780 respectively; and a lady aged 95 died at La Vieille Abbaye (Car) on 28 August 1743. In many of the crisis years death particularly struck the very young: 56% of burials were of children aged under 11 in the *trève* of La Haute Boixière in 1776, 58% in Ruffiac in 1777 and 52% in Ruffiac in 1782; whereas the over-60s accounted for, respectively, only 7%, 18% and 13% of burials in these years. The strongest group, the 11–20-year-olds, rarely accounted for more than 5% of burials in any year, crisis year or not. That group apart, the pattern for Carentoir in 1803–4 is strikingly different, for this mortality struck at the old rather than the young: only 24% of burials were of the under-11s, and 52% were of the over-50s, including 36% over 60 (Table 8.2).

In fact, the incidence of mortality in "non-crisis" years provides a useful contrast: looking at the age distribution of all Saint-Nicolas burials for the 25 years 1767–91, the mean for burial of under-11s is 29%, while that for 21–50-year-olds is a surprising 30%, with 35% over 50 and 21% over 60. The Saint-Nicolas figures emphasize the unusual character of the 1804

Table 8.2 Comparison of mortality by age-group in selected crisis years in Carentoir, Ruffiac, Le Temple and Tréal and non-crisis years in Saint-Nicolas

	Crisis Years							Non-Crisis
	1743	1743	1775	1776	1777	1782	an.xii	Mean 1767–91
	Le Temple	Carentoir	Tréal	Haute Boix	Ruffiac	Ruffiac	Carentoir	Saint-Nicolas
‹11	33	34	41	56	58	52	24	29
11–20	11	8	3	0	4	5	5	5
21–50	30	25	26	28	12	20	19	30
51–70	14	24	23	12	15	18	36	24
›70	9	5	6	5	7	4	16	11
???	4	3	1	0	4	1	0	2
›60	19	15	20	7	18	13	36	21

Percentage of deaths by age-group, per annum and averaged across non-crisis years 1767–91 in Saint-Nicolas-du-Tertre

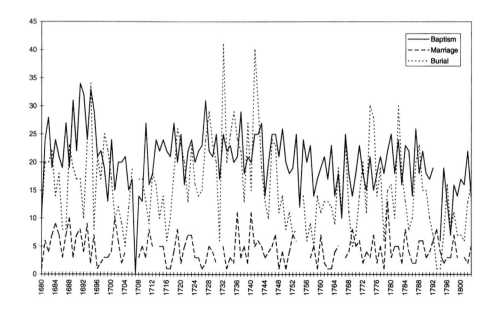

Figure 8.1a *Baptism, marriage and burial in Saint-Nicolas, 1680–1803*

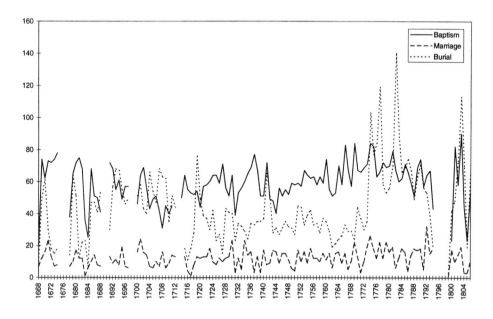

Figure 8.1b *Baptism, marriage and burial in Ruffiac, 1668–1806*

174

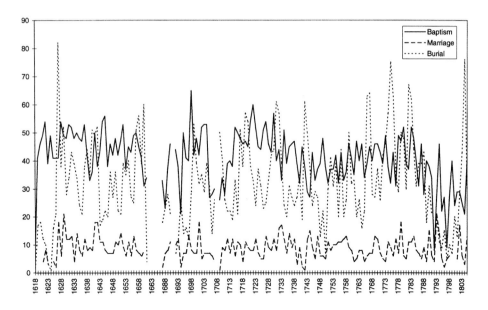

Figure 8.1c *Baptism, marriage and burial in Tréal, 1618–61, 1687–1805*

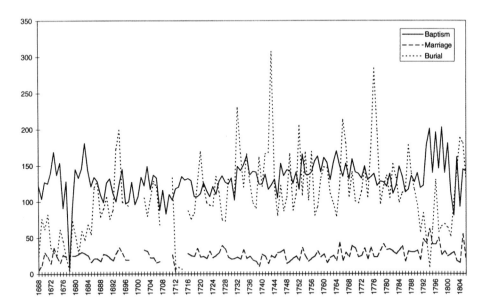

Figure 8.1d *Baptism, marriage and burial in Carentoir, with Le Temple and La Haute Boixière, 1668–1806*

mortality, with its attack on the older population, and at the same time emphasize the tendency for younger children to bear the brunt – even if not always at the level of Ruffiac in 1777.[17]

The core survey area was not alone in suffering great mortalities and sample transects were hit in similar ways: Bruc, Comblessac, Sixt and Pipriac in the 1770s (Transects R and M), for example, Guipry, Augan and Campénéac in the 1780s (Transects M and N), Malestroit and Missiriac in the 1760s (Transect P). Although many were struck by the great epidemics, by no means all died; indeed, in the late eighteenth century – for which there is massive documentation for the survey area – we have dozens of descriptions of surgeons' visits and treatments, lists of those affected and enumerations of those cured; in Carentoir, for example, 82 people were attacked in 1785 and 78 cured. The surgeons used several treatments, some preferring mixed herbal remedies, some focussing on basic nourishment of bread, meat and soup.

Payment of surgeons' bills for the poor normally came from government, via the subdelegation at Malestroit and the Intendant. However, in 1776, there is an interesting set of papers relating to the intervention of the Marquis de la Bourdonnaye: the Marquis's agent and the *curé* wrote to the Intendant on 30 May, noting the numbers of sick, by hamlet, in many parts of Carentoir and asking for help; two days later the Marquis wrote himself, analyzing the problems and proposing different solutions for different parts of the parish; these involved hire of a new surgeon (since his own was near death), for whom he volunteered to share costs and provide accommodation, at the same time continuing to pay for bread, soup and meat from his own resources as he had already been doing. Two days later we have the new surgeon's report of his visit, relating how he received details of the sick from the Marquis himself and then made his own visits, noting how the disease spread to those who handled the corpses as well as those who cared for the sick, and recommending a vigorous programme of hygiene.[18]

Changes in population over time

Given that exceptional mortality did not always strike all the parishes together, it is not surprising that demographic trends across the four core parishes are not identical. Although we have no ratios, we can comment for the sixteenth century on comparative numbers of baptisms (Fig. 8.2). In Le Temple the average annual number of baptisms shows some rise in the 1580s but was close to that of the eighteenth century. In Saint-Nicolas the annual number was comparable to that of the second half of the seventeenth century, although it experienced a sudden drop in the 1590s; both sixteenth-

and seventeenth-century annual averages, however, were noticeably higher than eighteenth-century numbers. In the much larger parish of Carentoir the rate of baptism was rising in the mid and very late sixteenth century, but sixteenth-century levels were noticeably less than those of seventeenth and eighteenth centuries (by a factor of two: annual baptisms of 60–80 in the sixteenth century were replaced by figures of 100-130 in the later seventeenth and eighteenth centuries). In Ruffiac there was a rise in the baptism rate in the early seventeenth century and overall a continuing very gradual rise thereafter.

All of this suggests that there is likely to have been some consistent rise in crude birth-rate through the sixteenth century, with a check late in the century, prior to a resumed rise after 1600. Although there is some local variation, the patterns looks broadly consistent with the trends suggested for Brittany as a whole, as they do for the succeeding two centuries: population growth through the sixteenth and seventeenth centuries (despite a regional blip in the rate of growth in the late sixteenth century), with high levels of fertility; another check in the last third of the seventeenth century, picking up again in the eighteenth century, although not at as high a rate as earlier (Croix 1981: 154–76, especially). By the late eighteenth century population density in Brittany was high relative to that of the rest of France (Dupâquier 1988: II.78).

All available evidence suggests that population levels, in all the parishes of the core survey area, continued to rise from 1600 until the 1690s. If we compute the ratio of baptisms to burials, and plot the outcome, using a ten-year moving average to establish the underlying trends, we can see that – until the 1690s – there was an increasing number of baptisms per year and a consistent surplus of births over deaths (Fig. 8.3). All the parishes saw a steep drop in the ratio of baptisms to burials in the late seventeenth century.

Then patterns diverged: Carentoir, having suffered the great mortality of 1694, entered a long phase (until 1748) when baptisms barely outnumbered burials and burials sometimes outnumbered baptisms. While this might look as if the population of Carentoir were declining in the 50 years till the mid eighteenth century, it is notable that the baptism *rates* drop only for 20 years or so and do so by much less than the average rise in burials (Fig. 8.4). Since the long-term outcome was a population of unusually high density (see below, p. 182), the best explanation is that, for a good half century, Carentoir experienced in-migration: more people were dying in Carentoir than were born there; people were coming – perhaps crowding – into the parish (see below, pp. 208–10).

Ruffiac also experienced a mean surplus of burials over baptisms, for ten years or so *c.*1700–1710, but only for that short period. Saint-Nicolas and Tréal both saw a sharp decline in the size of the surplus of baptisms but did

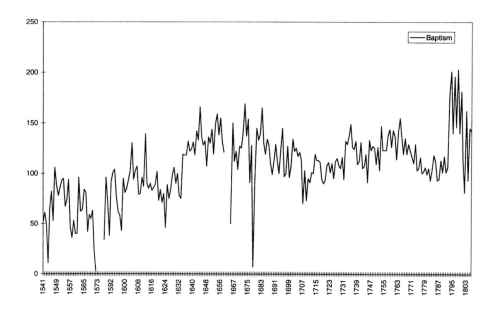

Figure 8.2a *Baptisms in Carentoir (excluding Le Temple), 1541–72, 1588–1658, 1665–1806*

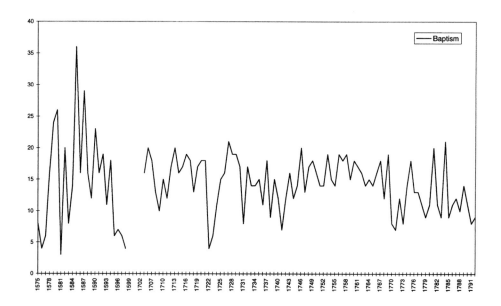

Figure 8.2b *Baptisms in Le Temple, 1575–98, 1703–92*

178

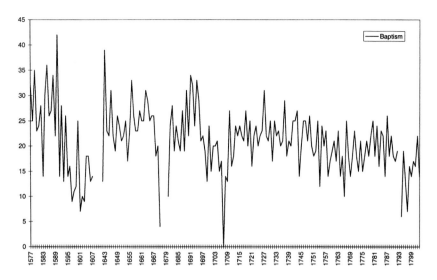

Figure 8.2c *Baptisms in Saint-Nicolas, 1577–1607, 1642–72, 1680–1803*

not at that stage move into a surplus of burials; both did however do so briefly in the period *c.*1730–40. The early eighteenth-century experience was therefore mixed, Ruffiac and Tréal continuing to increase naturally, albeit increasing less rapidly than in the seventeenth century, while Carentoir population levels were supplemented by incomers.[19]

In the second half of the eighteenth century it looks as if populations of all the parishes rose, but the severe mortality of the 1770s halted the rise. There was some recovery in the 1790s, with that of Carentoir dramatic (baptisms reached a peak of 160, from the 1775 low of 102, in 1793), with a subsequent levelling-off. The peaking of "births" in the 1790s reflects national trends (Dupâquier 1988: III.67).

The overall trend in the core survey area is therefore one of rapidly rising population during the seventeenth century; the crises of the late seventeenth century checked growth for a time, with Ruffiac and Tréal recovering to more modest levels during the eighteenth century and Carentoir getting a boost from incomers. Saint-Nicolas may have remained stable or declined slightly. By 1836 (the first census year to include all four communes) the population of Carentoir (including Quelneuc, La Haute Boixière, Le Temple and La Chapelle Gaceline but without La Gacilly), an area of approximately 8,066 ha, stood at 5,462 (6,864 including La Gacilly); Ruffiac was 1,756, Tréal 965 and Saint-Nicolas 541.

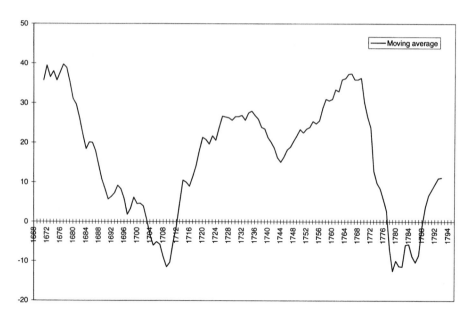

Figure 8.3a *Baptism/burial ratios (ten-year moving averages) for Ruffiac, 1668–1794, where + signifies a surplus of baptisms and − a surplus of burials*

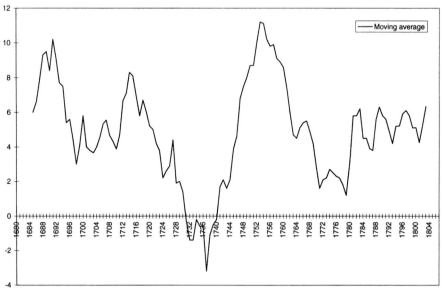

Figure 8.3b *Baptism/burial ratios (ten-year moving averages) for Saint-Nicolas, 1680–1803*

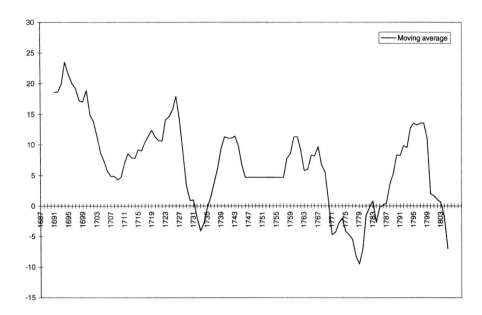

Figure 8.3c *Baptism/burial ratios (ten-year moving averages) for Tréal, 1687–1805*

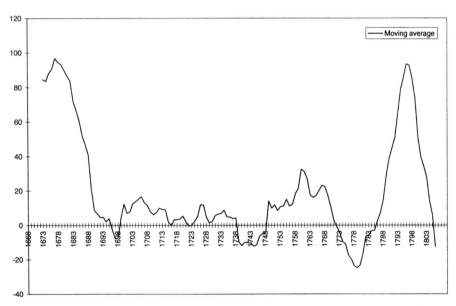

Figure 8.3d *Baptism/burial ratios (ten-year moving averages) for Carentoir (excluding Le Temple and La Haute Boixère) 1668–1806 (estimates supplied for missing years)*

181

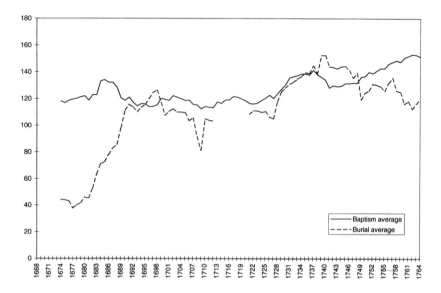

Figure 8.4 *Carentoir (including Le Temple and La Haute Boixière) baptisms and burials 1668–1765 (ten-year moving averages, with missing years omitted)*

Using the events detailed in the registers to work back from 1801 (when Carentoir and La Gacilly had a combined population of 7,012) we can calculate that the population of the two in 1700 was something under 5,650. (Ogée's estimate of 6,300 for the whole parish in the late eighteenth century is probably a little high (Croix 1981: 140).)

In 1801 Carentoir was not only by far the largest parish of the group but it was also by far the most densely populated: its density was 68 inhabitants per km^2 in 1836, as against Ruffiac's 48, Tréal's 50 and Saint-Nicolas's 42 (and it had been 70 in 1801). Carentoir's density is notable: while the other three communes do not sit uncomfortably with Alain Croix's estimate for (seventeenth-century) Brittany as a whole of 53 inhab/km^2, the entire commune of Carentoir has a density which starts to approach that of the small town of La Gacilly in 1836 (85 inhab/km^2). There is no reason to question the Carentoir figures: the count for 1801 was 5,681 and quinquennial counts till 1866 were comparable, though declining. And, judging from the number of households listed in 1784, Le Temple had an even higher density of population (see below, p. 200).

While noting the difference, we should not get this out of proportion: Carentoir was much less densely populated than many parts of southeast

England at the time (cf. Dobson 1997), although interestingly it *is* directly comparable with some mid Devon parishes in 1801 (Bradninch 67, Silverton 65, Thorverton 70) – themselves, like Carentoir, much more densely populated than the surrounding parishes.[20] However, the contrast between Carentoir and the rest remains striking and – since the parish was very large – it must raise the possibility of a dense (proto-urban) nucleation at the *bourg*, as also at the *bourg* of Le Temple. After 1801 the density of population in the commune declined, while that of the other three increased. By 1990 the four communes had little differentiation (though Carentoir was highest and Tréal lowest; see above, p. 52).

Post-medieval pottery

Can we see any reflection of this increasing population in the material culture of the survey area? A glance at the distribution of post-medieval fabrics across the surface of the survey area is initially very puzzling: far fewer fields have post-medieval than medieval fabrics (except in the case of sample transect R); and quantities are noticeably smaller. Post-medieval sherds clearly do not occur on the surface in the manner of medieval – nor for that matter of prehistoric or Roman – sherds. However, in the core the distribution is certainly weighted towards Carentoir and away from Ruffiac (Fig. 8.5).

"Post-medieval" fabrics are the sixteenth-, seventeenth- and eighteenth-century wares that can be found in the survey area (Davies & Astill 1994: 203–8). Many of the fine wares occur widely throughout northern France and sometimes beyond: the Normandy stonewares (Fabrics 56 and 21), glazed white pottery from Saintonge (Fabrics 18 and 42), tin-glazed wares from Rennes (Fabrics 25 and 28), and quartz- and stone-tempered wares from Rennes (Fabrics 22 and 38); there is also quartz-tempered tableware from Quimper (Fabric 36). Others may be more local in origin: the very rare quartz-tempered tablewares Fabrics 176, 44 and 77 (fine ware), and the rather more common Fabrics 24, 32 (wide-mouthed bowls) and 17 (thin-walled tableware). Of all these, Fabrics 17, 21 and 42 are by far the most common in the core survey area, occurring in (respectively) 6%, 16% and 14% of all fields walked; each of Fabrics 22, 24, 25, 28, 32, 36 and 56 occurs in from 2% to 4% of all fields walked; and the rest are even more rare (Davies & Astill 1994: 212).[21] The high proportion of imported material in the surface scatters is very striking, in complete contrast to medieval assemblages (see above, p. 126). In particular, it is the imported wares from Normandy and Saintonge that form the bulk of *all* finds (Table 8.3). Total

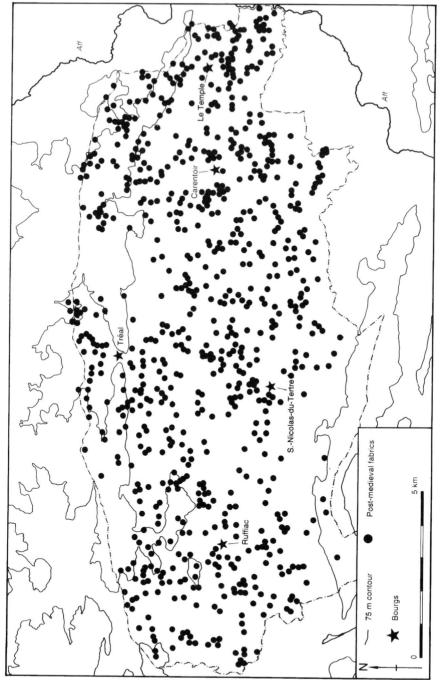

Figure 8.5 *Distribution of all post-medieval fabrics in the core survey area*

184

collection results supported those of transect-walking: respectively 94%, 92% and 96% of the post-medieval assemblages from A92, A159 and H132 were imports.

Overall, one or more post-medieval fabrics occur on the surface of 38% of all fields walked in the core – about as often as the single late medieval fabric, Fabric 4, and noticeably less often than the earlier medieval fabric, Fabric 1 (see above, pp. 119, 127).[22] The material lies overwhelmingly in central and eastern Carentoir, with occurrences in about half of all fields walked (but three-quarters in the case of Transect G, on the eastern edge of the present commune); although there are similar quantities in central Ruffiac, other transects in the rest of Ruffiac, Tréal and Saint-Nicolas have much less. The distribution contrasts with that of widely occurring medieval fabrics, which are much more evenly distributed across the whole area (see Figs. 6.1, 6.4, 6.5); and with the distribution of modern fabrics, which though a little less common are much more evident in eastern Ruffiac and the borders of Tréal and Saint-Nicolas (see below, p. 228 and Fig. 10.3). The contrast with the medieval distribution in itself suggests that the increase in population density in Carentoir was a post-medieval development, quite apart from the demographic evidence; the change

Table 8.3 Proportions of each post-medieval fabric in the core survey area

	All fields	K	L	A	H	J	B	C	F	D	E	G
All post-med.	38.0	32	51	31	30	34	37	49	49	55	52	78
F176	0.4	0	0	1	0	0	2	0	1	0	0	0
F44	0.8	1	1	0	0	‹1	1	1	3	2	2	0
F77	0.6	0	0	1	0	0	2	0	4	0	0	0
F36	4.0	2	5	2	1	4	7	7	12	4	3	2
F22	3.0	1	2	0	3	3	2	2	10	7	6	16
F24	2.0	1	5	1	2	4	1	3	1	4	1	0
F32	2.0	1	5	2	1	2	3	3	0	4	2	4
F17	6.0	0	5	3	7	3	4	7	11	12	7	22
F56	2.0	0	2	3	1	2	2	1	3	2	2	2
F21	14.0	12	17	11	12	10	16	26	15	31	30	39
F38	0.4	0	0	1	0	0	‹1	1	3	0	0	0
F25	3.0	3	3	3	6	2	3	2	5	6	2	0
F28	4.0	2	5	1	0	3	2	7	7	10	5	6
F42	13.0	19	25	10	12	9	8	18	7	20	23	41
F18	0.6	0	1	2	0	2	‹1	1	0	1	1	0
F1	52.0	56	53	52	50	50	50	70	68	55	57	100

Percentage of fields walked in which each post-medieval fabric occurs, by transect and for all fields (K the westernmost and G the easternmost transects); with Fabric 1 distribution for comparison

must have been happening from the late sixteenth and early seventeenth centuries.

Fabric 1 and/or other medieval fabrics usually occur in the same fields as do post-medieval fabrics, fields whose topographical and locational characteristics, taken together, are very similar to those of Fabric 1 fields. However, post-medieval fabrics are less likely to occur in fields with small quantities of surface pottery than does Fabric 1 (and less than the "all fields" mean (see Table 8.4)); this means that they tend to occur where there are *accumulations* of surface pottery, of whatever period. Post-medieval fabrics are also more likely to be found within 50m of cadastral settlements than are Fabric 1 or the mean; and are more likely to be found on south-facing slopes; and some (but not all) of the fabrics are much *less* likely to occur on high land than is Fabric 1 or the mean. These latter points indicate that, overall, post-medieval fabrics tend to occur in the neighbourhood of settlements – although of course they do occur in other locations: except in sample transect P, they are more likely to occur on cadastral *lande* than is Fabric 1.

The above comments refer to the totality of post-medieval sherd distribution, but individual post-medieval fabrics vary from this overall pattern. Most of them are more frequently found in Carentoir, declining across Tréal, Saint-Nicolas and Ruffiac, although Fabrics 24, 25 and 42 do occur widely in Ruffiac (see Table 8.3). On top of the weighting towards Carentoir, there are some east–west distinctions: in sample transects P and N, which run west and northwest from the Ruffiac boundary, while Fabrics 17 and 21 occur only half as often as they do in the core, Fabrics 25 and 42 occur about twice as often; and in sample transect M, to the east, Fabrics 17 and 21 occur more often than they do in the core, and Fabric 42 about as often. In other words, the Saintonge ware Fabric 42 is very widely distributed but local Fabric 17 and Normandy Fabric 21 are commoner in the east than in the west. Some fabrics, for example Fabrics 24 and 25, have distribution patterns that relate closely to the major roads – as if local people bought their pottery from travelling salesmen on those roads.[23]

Land-use and pottery distribution

How, then, do we explain the occurrence of post-medieval fabrics on the surface?

With some notable exceptions, they occur in the same general zones of the core survey area as medieval and late medieval fabrics, but in fewer fields and in smaller quantities – particularly in the west. Since we know that the population of the area was rising through the sixteenth and seventeenth

Table 8.4 Topographical and cadastral characteristics of post-medieval fabrics

	All post-medieval fabrics	F176	F44	F77	F36	F22	F24	F32	F17	All fields	F1
Arable	74	90	78	86	76	63	75	77	79	64	78
Lande	16		17	7	17	22	16	16	10	25	12
Meadow	5	10	6	7	4	6	6		7	5	5
Pasture	2				1	1	2	6	3	2	2
Château landscape	13	30	28	29	14	13	14	17	13	7	14
South slope	40	40	33	64	45	35	32	35	35	37	39
North slope	22	20	11	7	16	15	27	31	20	25	23
Contour:											
‹20m	1				2		2		1	2	1
20–60m	68	80	94	79	66	63	66	77	75	65	71
›70m	15		6		14	20	9	8	10	14	11
Stream:											
‹101m	31	70	28	57	35	24	30	35	27	33	36
‹201m	51	70	44	64	63	39	57	52	48	58	58
›400m	19		17	7	14	31	20	17	24	18	14
Settlement:											
‹51m	28	30	33	21	37	23	25	33	30	22	26
‹101m	41	40	33	43	51	33	34	46	50	35	42
‹201m	71	60	72	57	77	65	75	69	71	63	72
›400m	6		6	7	5	7	4	4	4	7	4

	All post-medieval fabrics	F56	F21	F38	F25	F28	F42	F18	All fields	F1
Arable	74	80	80	66	69	72	71	54	64	78
Lande	16	17	10	33	15	12	17	15	25	12
Meadow	5	3	5		9	5	6	15	5	5
Pasture	2		1		3	1	2		2	2
Château landscape	13	17	15	11	16	12	11	31	7	14
South slope	40	34	37	56	40	38	41	46	37	39
North slope	22	23	26		9	26	20	23	25	23
Contour:										
‹20m	1	3	1		1	2	2		2	1
20–60m	68	57	66	67	69	62	67	77	65	71
›70m	15	11	17	22	22	15	16	8	14	11
Stream:										
‹101m	31	37	32	22	35	27	30	38	33	36
‹201m	51	54	50	44	60	48	46	62	58	58
›400m	19	14	21	33	13	18	20	8	18	14
Settlement:										
‹51m	28	26	31	56	24	30	25	23	22	26
‹101m	41	31	47	56	32	40	35	38	35	42
‹201m	71	66	75	67	68	61	68	77	63	72
›400m	6	3	4	22	7	5	6	8	7	4

Percentage of each post-medieval fabric, by cadastral land-use, château landscape, contour, distance from water, slope and distance from nearest cadastral settlement; with all post-medieval fabrics, Fabric 1 and all fields for comparison

centuries, the relatively small quantity of post-medieval material suggests that household waste was not normally spread on the arable that that population worked. The point is reinforced by written evidence of land-use at that time: medieval but no post-medieval sherds were collected from the surface of a high proportion of the fields that we *know* were worked as arable in the seventeenth and eighteenth centuries (Davies & Astill 1994: 215-16). Take, for example, the arable at J318, J319 and J320, arable in 1568: these are fields immediately north of the *bourg* of Saint-Nicolas, still arable in the nineteenth century and indeed today. Or, even more strikingly, fields like A137, arable in 1551, 1646, the 1820s and today; B266, arable in 1577, 1739, the 1820s and today; L119, arable in 1621, 1739, the 1820s and today; all have large quantities of medieval sherds on the surface but no post-medieval fabrics at all.

Excavation evidence from T1, near Coëtion, makes the same point (Davies & Astill 1994: 60–5): this lynchet, with its large (1.8m) build-up of soil from many centuries of arable cultivation, did not include post-medieval fabrics. So too the sherd count from total collection fields: with one exception, the count is very consistent and uniformly very low (0.1–0.4 sherds per square).[24] Unless we are to believe that very few people used pottery in the seventeenth and eighteenth centuries, the implication must be that fertilization practices changed after the sixteenth century: post-medieval fabrics were much more likely to be left near settlements than to be spread on arable.

There are exceptions to the above statements. Firstly, one fabric in particular, the Saintonge Fabric 42, occurs across the arable fields associated with medieval settlements and on lands at some distance from settlements. The best explanation for this discrepancy is that the fabric was in relatively early use and household waste containing its sherds was spread on arable before manuring practice changed.

Secondly, most fields with post-medieval fabrics on the surface have medieval fabrics too; only 10% lack the medieval. Written evidence of land-use in effect makes the same point: some known arable of the seventeenth and eighteenth centuries had only post-medieval sherds on the surface – fields like A47 and A381 (both on the outskirts of Ruffiac), C329 within the Bourdonnaye forest, H121 and H122 a little north of La Ruée. The proportion of post-medieval fields without medieval sherds is small but it is significant. Most (88%) of these fields have small quantities of surface pottery, whatever the period; they are twice as likely to lie at high altitudes, over 70m, and at some distance from water, than the norms; and they are four times as likely to lie on cadastral *lande* as are fields with Fabric 1 (Table 8.5).

Table 8.5 Fields with post-medieval but no medieval fabrics

	Post-medieval & no medieval	All post-medieval	Fabric 1	All fields
›70m	27	15	11	14
›400m from stream	29	19	15	18
Lande	39	14	10	22

Attributes of fields with post-medieval but no medieval fabrics, by percentage of each category; with all fields with post-medieval fabrics, all fields and Fabric 1 fields for comparison

The absence of medieval fabrics means that these fields were not cultivated during the medieval period; and nearly half of them were not cultivated in the early nineteenth century. They look like new land that was taken in for arable use in the post-medieval centuries (*terres froides*), given the increase in population in most of the parishes: this amounted to an increase of some 6% on the late medieval arable; just under half (the cadastral *lande* fields, lying overwhelmingly on the large expanses of *lande* on northern and southern boundaries of the core) was taken in on a short-term basis, and just over half came permanently into the arable (Fig. 8.6). Not surprisingly, the new arable lands were often in less favourable positions although they are not noticeably farther from settlements. Atypically for the period, these lands must have been fertilized with household waste.

Fields with post-medieval pottery virtually always also have slate distributed on the surface, a practice which seems to have developed over the course of the sixteenth century (Davies & Astill 1994: 246–52). Slate fragments clearly *did* get into fertilizing material (whether intentionally or unintentionally). Fields with black slate and *no* sherds (11% of the sample) must therefore also reflect new post-medieval arable; they represent a further 13% or so added to the late medieval arable core. Again just over half became permanent arable and half had reverted to *lande* by the 1820s.

Accumulations of sherds

In by far the majority of fields, quantities of post-medieval fabrics are small and the range of fabrics is limited. No post-medieval fabric consistently occurs together with another: the strongest correlations are those of Fabric 17 with Fabrics 21 and 42, Fabric 22 with Fabrics 21 and 42, and Fabric 28 with Fabrics 21 and 42, but the correlations are not high (see Table 8.6). Correlation with Fabric 1 is very much stronger: for example, 65% of fields with Fabric 42 also have Fabric 1. The occurrence of post-medieval fabrics is therefore very variable.

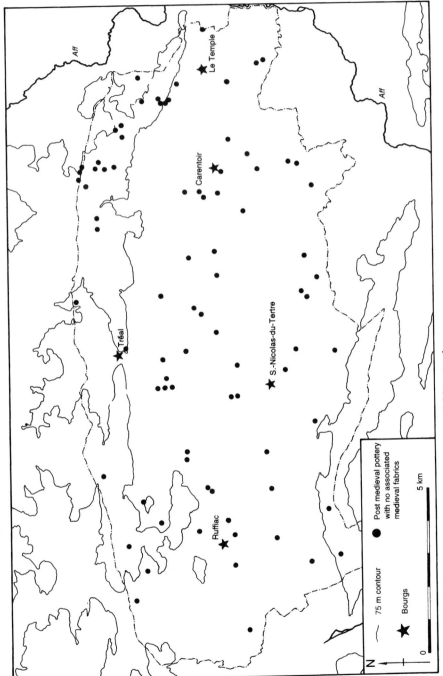

Figure 8.6 *Fields with post-medieval but no medieval fabrics in the core survey area*

Table 8.6 Post-medieval associations of the commonest post-medieval fabrics

	F17	F21	F22	F28	F36	F42
F17		43	5	13	8	30
F21	12		8	7	4	21
F22	8	48		17	17	35
F25	10	31	4	4	12	24
F28	16	32	10		11	32
F36	11	24	8	9		25
F42	11	24	8	15	8	

Percentage of records of common post-medieval fabrics with presence of other post-medieval fabrics

Ten grams or less was collected in the vast majority of fields walked; and accumulations over 50g are exceptionally rare, occurring in only 7% of records with post-medieval fabrics. As one might expect, however, the heavier fabric of Fabric 32 has more weighty accumulations (Table 8.7).

There are exceptions to the general rule and there is a body of fields with accumulations of different post-medieval fabrics, 38 in all; though the number is small (2% of all records, 5% of records with post-medieval fabrics), the assemblages are strikingly different because of their range of material. Were this material from an earlier age, one might be tempted to suggest that such accumulations denote the location of "high-status" settlement sites. But, these accumulations occur in a period from which we still have many standing buildings, and plentiful written evidence of settlement location. It is therefore intrinsically unlikely that they indicate settlement locations, not least because there are not nearly enough to

Table 8.7 Quantities of common post-medieval fabrics

	<11g	11–50g	>50g
F17	84	16	0
F21	53	42	5
F22	75	25	0
F24	75	25	0
F25	81	18	1
F28	80	20	0
F32	48	42	10
F36	88	11	1
F42	74	25	1
F56	54	46	0

Percentage of records of post-medieval fabrics with each fabric, by weight range, in grams

account for the households that lived here in this period (of the order of 2,000 or more in the core).

What, then, do they signify? No single post-medieval fabric dominates these collections, although Fabrics 21 and 42 occur in nearly half of the cases; by contrast, virtually all the fields (83% and 78%) have both Fabric 1 and Fabric 4 (Table 8.8). The fields are rarely steep; they are much more likely to be south-facing and less likely to be north-facing than the norms; and they are more likely to be within 50m (and less likely to be beyond 400m) of cadastral settlements than the norms. In other words, these accumulations tend to occur on fields used in the medieval period, in the neighbourhood of settlements of the early nineteenth century. In most cases the accumulations did not spread beyond two or three runs in transect-walking: they were in limited parts of each field; and they occur at 10m, 25m, 40m, 100m, 150m from cadastral buildings. Hence the clusters in B10 at the back of La Touche (Tr) and K450 at the back of Béculeu (Ruff), both very close to buildings; in F224, 25m from the *château* of Clazeul; in H132, north of the destroyed medieval structure but 100m east of the Château de la Ruée; in F524/526, 100m from buildings at Coetmorel; in D241 and D148, 150m from buildings in the *bourg* of Carentoir and the hamlet of Bot Colin respectively.

These accumulations must derive from dumps made in the neighbourhood of buildings, noble and otherwise, occurring as close as 10m and as far as 150m from structures. Their primary significance is

Table 8.8 Incidence of post-medieval fabrics in fields with clusters of post-medieval sherds

	% occurrence	<11g	11–100g	>100g
F17	40	84	16	0
F21	68	44	56	0
F22	36	71	29	0
F24	15	86	14	0
F25	17	75	25	0
F28	26	83	17	0
F32	9	50	50	0
F36	23	82	18	0
F42	55	50	50	0
F44	11	80	20	0
F1	83	11	71	18
F4	78	67	22	11

Percentage occurrence of each fabric in the 38 clusters, with percentage of each of these occurrences by weight; Fabric 1 and Fabric 4 for comparison, in the same clusters therefore as evidence of refuse disposal practice – much more than of settlement location, with which they clearly do not have a consistent spatial relationship. In a few cases, like D5 and D148, they are near *remembrement* mounds and relate to twentieth-century clearance processes, which themselves sometimes use a collapsed structure as focus. In a few other cases, they lie on the site of structures that have disappeared; the early nineteenth-century hamlet, La Nouette (Ruff), at A450, is a good case in point; the house platform at F321 near La Madeleine (Car) (not indicated on the *ancien cadastre*) is another; and there are local stories of former buildings, which do not feature on the cadastral plan, in the neighbourhood of similar dumps on H80 and L107 (known locally as "the casino" and "tunnels"). So, sometimes these dumps do in fact point to the neighbourhood of *earlier* settlement sites, although this is demonstrably so in only a small number of cases; we would not wish to argue from this small number to a general proposition – particularly given the fact that dumps could be hard by buildings, as at Béculeu, and given the more usual *absence* of written, structural, field and stone indications. The excavated L26, for example, was a late and post-medieval midden site 150m from a house, with no structural evidence associated, on a piece of land that was previously and subsequently cultivated (Davies & Astill 1994: 154–7).

Refuse disposal

Analysis of the occurrence of post-medieval fabrics across the surface leads to these conclusions: in the seventeenth and eighteenth centuries it was not normal for household refuse (containing sherds and other material) to be distributed on arable fields as a method of fertilizing the land. This means that there were significant differences in refuse disposal practice from medieval norms. The change may well be related to a change in housing arrangements, involving greater separation of domestic and animal quarters (see above, p. 31, below, pp. 204–5). Household waste seems to have been dumped, and left, outside buildings – at greater or nearer distance.[25] (By contrast, slate dumps, which must have been differentiated from domestic refuse, *did* get into the manure.) We cannot date this change precisely but it looks as if it was happening in the years on either side of 1600, that is when the Saintonge ware Fabric 42 was dropping out of currency.

As befits a period of social mobility, in which the poverty of the petty nobility is often striking, one cannot differentiate noble and peasant material culture in any tidy way. Certainly, rare fabrics are much more likely to occur on château landscapes than the norm or than Fabric 1; and Fabrics 32 and 56 are a little more likely to do so (see Table 8.4). Fabrics 32 and 56 are likely to have had landlordly associations. Fabric 32, quite a heavy ware, more often occurs on cadastral pasture and on north-facing slopes than the mean for all fields, for Fabric 1 and for post-medieval fabrics; it may well have been a fabric used for some agricultural purpose, for example dairy vessels. Unlike most fabrics, the finer Fabric 56 is much more likely to occur in fields with small quantities of pottery, in low-lying sites, and on steep land; its use could have been connected with some industrial purpose like, for example, milling.

Some of the dumps are near noble properties, but most are not. Hence, it is not unreasonable to suggest that people of all kinds had dumps near their houses. It may be that the appearance of household waste on new arable, in marginal situations, reflects the activities of people who still had older housing arrangements, with animals near humans, mixing domestic refuse and animal manure (see below, p. 204). If so, we may be seeing in these temporary extensions of the arable – in great contrast to the "permanent" expansion of the sixteenth century – the piecemeal extensions of small-scale enterprise, not the grand entrepreneurial initiatives of before. The new land denoted by black slate and an absence of ceramic need *not* have been linked to these types of householder (although that activity also looks piecemeal).

★★★★★★★

The seventeenth and eighteenth centuries define a period when the large-scale importation of ceramics gave the basic material culture of the survey area a new character. In this period too, for the first time, there were divergent material patterns in different parts of the area: crude quantities of pottery increased significantly in Transect R to the northeast, while there are differences between ceramic assemblages in Transects R/M to the east and those in Transects N/P to the west. The addition of 20% or so of arable to the late medieval fields is consonant with a drive to produce more cereals, in the context of population growth, in the seventeenth century especially. The drive is complemented by the diversification into chestnut plantations in the late seventeenth century. Reversion of about half of this new arable to *lande* by the nineteenth century probably reflects the very intermittent cultivation of these *terres froides*.

Increasing numbers, more mouths to feed, more imports and more exports are changes which all raise basic questions about the local economy, and therefore about work and housing. Where and how were these people living in the seventeenth and eighteenth centuries? There is a mass of relevant evidence, and the next chapter will pursue some of the emerging issues about this period.

Notes

1. Harvest days: AD Loire-Atlantique B1988 (1699); AD Morbihan E1604 (1775). Leasing: AD Ille-et-Vilaine 3H191^2 L1, L2.
2. See Tréal parish registers, *passim*, for the occurrence of *métairies*, *sieurs*, *fermiers* and nobles living in the parish.
3. AD Morbihan 21C513.
4. Hedges and ditches: AD Ille-et-Vilaine 3H188 L6 (1681), 3H189 L5 (1661), 3H190 L1 (1757).
   Maintenance: AD Morbihan E1604 (1775); AD I-et-V 3H187 L12 (1748), 3H191^2 L2 (1735, 1748).
   Waterworks: AD Loire-Atlantique B1999 (1677); AD I-et-V 3H194^2 (1743).
5. AD Ille-et-Vilaine 3H189 L9 (1669).
6. AD Ille-et-Vilaine 3H188 L6; 3H194^1; AD Loire-Atlantique B1957bis L2.
7. AD Ille-et-Vilaine C3909.
8. Crops: AD Loire-Atlantique B1957 (1694, 1708, 1712); AD Morbihan E1604 (1638, 1727); AD Ille-et-Vilaine 3H187 L12 (1748), 3H188 L4 (1609/1617), 3H188 L6, 3H189 L2 (1662), 3H192 L6 (1707/15).
   Ramponnet: AD I-et-V 3H189 L5.
   Millet: *ibid.* 3H191^2 L2 (1735).
   Sowing flax: *ibid.* 3H191^2 L1 (1745).
   La Ville Marie: *ibid.* 3H188 L5.
9. Malestroit etc. markets: AD Ille-et-Vilaine C4993.
   Subsidies: *ibid.* C1734, C3909.
   Ruffiac markets: AD Morbihan E1604 (1727).
10. We are indebted to Lesley Ritchie for her analysis of the parish registers. She collected all the sixteenth- to eighteenth-century records of baptism, marriage and burial for the four core communes that were available to her in AD Morbihan, including data for family reconstitution for Tréal; and she did preliminary analyses of events for all four communes.
11. Baptism (*Baptêmes*), marriage (*Mariages*) and burial (*Sépultures*) records survive as follows: for Carentoir BMS 1668–1792, with B also for 1541–71 and 1588–1667 (WD used a microfilm of 532 leaves of complete BMS for 1642–75 in December 1985; these records were not available to Ms Ritchie a couple of years later and did not appear to be in AD Morbihan in 1995); Tréal BMS 1686–1792, also with BS for 1618–61 and M for 1621–60; Saint-Nicolas-du-Tertre BMS 1680–1792, also with B 1642–72 and 1577–1607 (the latter classified with Ruffiac); Ruffiac BMS 1668–1792, also with B for 1604–28, 1633–48 (also B 1577–1607 in Ruffiac *mairie*), M 1635–48 and 1658–68, and S 1635–48. AD Morbihan, 4E33/1-11 and 1MiEc033R01-15 (Car, Le Temple, La Haute Boixière); 4E230/1-3 and 1MiEc230R01-3 (S-N); 3E200/1, 4E200/1-7 and 1MiEc200R01-05 (Ruff); 3E253/1 and 4E253/1-5 (Tr). Most of the records are now microfilmed (1MiEc . . .).
12. Quelneuc BMS 1669–1792, B 1618–68 and 1672–77, M 1651 (ADM 3E183/1, 4E183/1-8); La Chapelle Gaceline BMS 1679–1792 (ADM 4E38/1-3); La Gacilly BMS 1669–1792 (ADM 4E61/1-14; 1MiEc061R01-4).
13. BMS survive for the eighteenth century and B for 1575–1669, 1683–92, M for 1628–63, S for 1633–69. La Haute Boixière has separate BMS for 1769–92 and also BM for 1796–1803 (taken by a priest who had refused to take the oath).

14. Records for the other parishes are missing for that year, which follows the Brittany-wide famine and disease years of 1625–6; mortality in Malestroit, just to the west, was high in 1626 (Croix 1981: 169, 289, 299, 300).

15. AD Ille-et-Vilaine C3909, C1734 (1776).

16. In most cases, there were far more burials in the months from September to April than across the summer. Precisely as Alain Croix, in his wider analysis of Breton seventeenth-century mortality, pointed out, crisis years tend to have a sharp upturn in death rates in August/September and often another peak in March/April (Croix 1981: 240–2).

17. Burial of 1–4-year-olds usually accounts for about 40% of the under-11 group.

18. Epidemics: AD Ille-et-Vilaine C1351-3, C3909, C1734.
Surgeons: *ibid.* C1392, C1391.
De la Bourdonnaye: *ibid.* C1353.

19. There are long periods when a high surplus of baptisms seems to have been sustained in Ruffiac and Tréal. It is likely that the parishes saw some small levels of out-migration at that time; if not, the implied rate of growth across the eighteenth century is beyond credibility. Out-migration is a better explanation of the surplus than under-registration of burials, since this was not a Protestant area, the crisis years coincide with regional trends and the detail of the records suggests exceptional care on the part of the recorders; further, the parishes do not feature in Croix's lists of under-registration cases (1981: 200). We should not overestimate the volume of out-migration; this was not an area that sent people to Canada (Charbonneau et al. 1987).

20. For comparison: 70 was the regional average of mid Devon in 1991; cf. 80 for north Devon and north Shropshire at that time.

21. Fabrics 17, 21, 42 in sample transects: respectively 1%, 27%, 19% of fields in Tr. R; 8%, 19%, 19% in Tr. M; 4%, 7%, 22% in Tr. P; 2%, 6%, 18% in Tr. N; Fabric 17 is therefore less common in all sample areas except M. Also note higher than core occurrences: 7% F28 in Tr. R, 6% F22 and 6% F28 in Tr. M, 7% F25 and 8% F28 in Tr. P.

22. The point is also true for all sample transects except Transect R, but the proportions vary: post-medieval sherds were collected from 47% of fields in Transect R (noticeably *more* than medieval fabrics), 45% in Transect M, 35% in Transect P and a very low 28% in Transect N (the latter three all have fewer post-medieval than late medieval findspots as well).

23. This is not too fanciful: we know that in the fifteenth century individual Breton potters, who had domestic workshops, made annual tours (Fichet de Clairfontaine 1988).

24. The exception is G74, which had 1.2 sherds per square; since this field is hard by La Métairie au Joly, along the back of the nineteenth-century houses, it is not surprising that it had higher quantities of material; see further below, pp. 191–2, on dumping.

25. In four places there are accumulations of post-medieval wares near chapels, all isolated sites: St Marc (east Car), St Jacques (south Car), St Adrien (west Car), and St André (west Ruff).

CHAPTER 9

Work and housing

In a period distinguished by rising population throughout the region, Carentoir's population density rose in the eighteenth century to levels half as much again as those of Ruffiac and of Saint-Nicolas. The tiny parish of Le Temple, within eastern Carentoir, had an exceptionally high density: its annual average of baptisms in the latter half of the century is comparable to that of Saint-Nicolas, an area more than three times its size; and, judging from the number of households listed in 1784, its density must have been well over 100 inhabitants per km^2 (see below, p. 200).

This demographic difference between the eastern and western halves of the core survey area is a development of the post-medieval period, and one of its most striking features. One would expect to see some reflection of it in settlements and the settlement pattern, and perhaps in the relationship between home and work.

Settlement and buildings

Settlement

Our best clues about settlement shape and location in the seventeenth and eighteenth centuries come from the cadastral record of the early nineteenth century. The cadastral data are comprehensive for the 1820s, clearly differentiating deserted from inhabited houses, and thereby giving us a picture of both the preceding and the existing situation at that time. Dated buildings of the seventeenth and eighteenth centuries still stand today in locations identified on the cadastral plan; and the distribution of seventeenth- and eighteenth-century pottery relates closely to the cadastral settlement pattern, with sherds of that period much more likely to be within 200m of cadastral settlements than are medieval fabrics (see above, pp. 185–8, 192–3). All this combines to make the cadastral record a relevant guide to settlement in the seventeenth and eighteenth, as well as nineteenth, centuries although a handful of settlements was clearly lost in the two generations before the 1820s.[1]

Of 362 distinct settlements in the core survey area in the 1820s, five were *bourgs* (the parish centres, including Le Temple), 199 were peasant hamlets and villages, 69 were isolated single buildings and the rest *château* and *métairie* complexes.

Peasant settlements are nearly always arranged in rows (*rangées*), most of which are oriented east–west, to give a south-facing aspect. The rows are sometimes grouped, so that a settlement may have one or more foci (see below, p. 219, for terminology). Settlements can be formed of both single and parallel rows, Carentoir and Ruffiac each having twice as many single as parallel row settlements (see Fig. 9.3). The steads which form the rows are not all of uniform size and many settlements (59%) have a larger stead at their centre or on their periphery.

There is a quite remarkable homogeneity of settlement form in this area and small and simply structured settlements are by far the most common (Fig. 9.1): 92% of peasant settlements had one, two or three foci in the 1820s, of which half had one focus only and a quarter had two (see Table 9.2, p. 214); 87% had no more than six rows, of which half had one or two only; and 86% had no more than 30 steads (and 68% no more than 20). Of the larger conglomerations (settlements with 20 or more steads), of which there are 65, most had many foci and very fragmented plans. The majority (59%) of these "larger" conglomerations were small, with 20-29 steads, and only ten had 50 or more. As might be expected, the *bourgs* of Carentoir and Ruffiac had the largest numbers of steads: 159 and 66 respectively. Not surprisingly, very few places look like a village of traditional English type, with continuous frontages; there are therefore few examples of classic nucleation.

Isolated buildings are uncommon (19% of settlements); most, like watermills and chapels, have a specialized function and are non-residential. The rarity of the isolated residence emphasizes a major aspect of the settlement character of the area: the isolated farm, so common in many other parts of Europe, is unusual. There was, however, a large number of settlements and an overwhelming majority of these was very small.

It is useful to compare this cadastral evidence of settlement size, shape and disposition with the *capitation* records of the late eighteenth century, since these give us some sense of the households who lived in the structures. These records list the people liable to pay tax and are in effect an updated

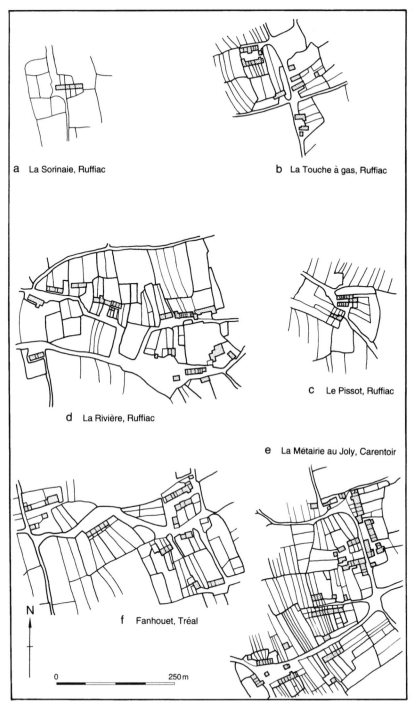

a La Sorinaie, Ruffiac

b La Touche à gas, Ruffiac

c Le Pissot, Ruffiac

d La Rivière, Ruffiac

e La Métairie au Joly, Carentoir

f Fanhouet, Tréal

N

0   250 m

Figure 9.1 *Some peasant settlements of the 1820s in Ruffiac, Tréal and Carentoir, showing single and parallel rows (a, d, e, f and c, e); staggered, interrupted, divergent and farm groups (b, e, c, f); larger conglomerations (d, e, f); and large buildings (d)*

version of the earlier *fouages*; like the *fouages*, they do not count heads or
households, for some persons were exempt and some households had more
than one payer; however, in naming those liable to pay, the record in effect
lists a good number of households and this gives us a rough guide to
relative hamlet size. Without making too much of the precise detail, given
the nature of the texts, some broad points can be made about Carentoir, Le
Temple and Tréal.[2]

In Carentoir in 1771 the *bourg* had by far the largest number of payers of
capitation; the parish also, as one would expect from the settlement
evidence, had very many places with small groups of payers: of 112
locations, 44 had fewer than five and 47 had five to nine payers. While Le
Temple in 1784 was counted by *frairie* rather than by separate hamlet, at
least 98 payers are listed for the parish; allowing for the exempt households,
this must represent a parish total of at least 98 households, a surprising
number for so small an area. The pattern for Tréal in the same year is quite
different from that of Carentoir or Le Temple: here the *bourg* did not have
the greatest number of payers (Le Plessis, with 31, had several more) and
there were proportionately far fewer small groups than there were in
Carentoir: of 21 places named, 13 had more than ten payers. Both in
Carentoir and in Tréal *métairie* settlements were different from the mass of
peasant settlements for they frequently had one or two payers only – as is
in any case implied by the cadastral maps.

These data broadly confirm the picture of settlement derived from the
cadastral maps, emphasizing the very dense settlement of Le Temple, the
difference between the *bourgs* of Tréal and Carentoir and the exceptionally
large number of small settlements distributed across the greater part of the
core survey area.

Houses

If we want to move from settlement to house, and get inside the structures,
we have both contemporary descriptions of buildings and a large number
of standing buildings. The descriptions occur in the many surviving *aveux*,
in sale and contract notes, and in surveys of tenancies. During the
eighteenth century, the survey area was dominated by the *seigneurie* of the
Marquis de la Bourdonnaye and we have descriptions of the lands and
métairies attached to La Basse Boixière (the Bourdonnaye seat) in 1708 and
again in 1727 (by which time the name of the seat had changed to La
Bourdonnaye). The *château* had four turrets and a wall surrounding its
courtyard, with stables, barns and grain lofts within and gardens behind
and alongside, together with a park and a meadow in front (Fig. 9.2).
There were six associated *métairies*, each with its own byres and stables,

Figure 9.2 *The Château de la Bourdonnaye from the southwest; photo: Pete Addison*

gardens, arable, meadow, pasture and *landes*: those of Chesne Tort, La Barrière, La Grée Rouleau, La Grée de Plaisance, La Charbonnière, Les Tanières; and there was also "forest", a windmill, and two watermills (cf. above, p. 11).[3]

From the sixteenth century onwards there are descriptions of other noble residences, all less grand than La Bourdonnaye but some more grand than others, with dovecots and other status indicators by the early seventeenth century (like the dovecot at La Ville Robert in 1628).[4] At La Ville Marie the house had hall and ground floor chamber in 1669, with a courtyard in front and garden behind, together with an "old house" called La Métairie, with its own garden, and woods. The house at Ruffiac Priory had kitchen, large hall, staircase to the upper floor and a latrine in 1688; it had a courtyard, separate foodstore with adjoining barn, tiled grain loft, byre and chapel.[5]

Peasant housing was described by length, measured by the foot, in explicit reference to the *rangées* that we see today and on the cadastral plans; 15 feet at La Ruaudaie (S–N), adjoining others on the east, west and south; twice times 12 feet at Rangera (Ruff), with slate roof, chimney and oven at the end of one; more grandly, 32 feet in the *bourg* of Ruffiac, with adjoining stable of 17 feet, all roofed in slate, fronting the street and with a garden behind. One-and-a-half-storey buildings are exceptionally common in older settlements (44% of all buildings recorded in the 1980s), and must have constituted the norm at this period; however, one of the Ruffiac houses had two storeys, and in 1634 the priest's house at Le Cleu (Tr) had three.[6]

Where roofing is mentioned, it is virtually always in slate (for peasant as well as noble housing): we have come across only one reference to (ceramic) tiles, and very occasional references to stone tiles and straw (thatch), as in 1609.[7] These documents very strongly imply that slate was the normal roofing material of the seventeenth century, doubtless replacing an earlier vernacular tradition of thatching, although some slate roofs are certainly evidenced in the sixteenth century. The earliest peasant stone housing may well have been thatched.

Some of the most interesting of these texts relate to dilapidation, with landlords' agents undertaking surveys and listing work that had to be done to make the houses good. Reading them makes it look as if many people lived in poor conditions, despite the external grandeur of some of the houses. The house at Ruffiac Priory was surveyed in 1736: the big window on to the courtyard had no glass and only two sections of the frame; the hearth and mantelpiece were broken; the courtyard door was rotten; the staircase to the bells in the chapel was rotten; and there were frogs (sic) eating the floor and the lime. A dispute about the upkeep of the noble house of La Nouan in eastern Carentoir brought a report in 1700 that windows on to the courtyard and the garden were rotten, with no shutters to close them and with panes of glass missing; the doors to the kitchen and entrance hall were rotten; the lathes of the roof were rotten so that the roof was in danger of falling in and two or three thousand (sic) slates needed replacing; in the barn the cider press was not functioning; the planking round the byre was rotten, the wall by the dovecot had already fallen down and that by the bakery was ready to fall.[8]

Despite the sense of dilapidation, it is fair to observe that most of the complaints – apart from missing slates – are about doors and windows rather than basic structure. Houses were stone-built; they were probably very damp but if they kept their roofs they are likely to have remained solid structures.

The dominant building tradition of the survey area uses roughly coursed inner and outer wall faces, of mixed local stone, with a rubble core of small fragments bonded by mud (Davies & Astill 1994: 145–8, 237–9). This construction technique was current for a very long period, from the twelfth to the nineteenth century, and was used for building noble and peasant houses alike in the sixteenth to nineteenth centuries (although grand buildings tend to be rendered, concealing the stone). Outbuildings of *petits châteaux* were often built of narrow fissile slabs in a more regular manner.

Of the 4,589 standing (stone) buildings recorded by Pete Addison in the core survey area in 1984–5, a quarter (1,213) are simple, single-cell houses (i.e. steads) within the single or parallel rows that constitute most peasant settlements (Fig. 9.3); a tenth (528) are long-houses (structures combining house and stabling) or long-house derivatives (see Meirion-Jones 1982: 191–249 for these long-house types): as late as 1757 wooden planking separated the kitchen from the stables and a wooden staircase led up to the grain loft at the *métairie* of the Château de la Ruée.[9]

Many of these standing buildings are of the seventeenth and eighteenth centuries; one has a precise sixteenth-century date (1579, at Le Bois Faux), 26 have precise seventeenth-century dates – of these nearly half lie between 1620 and 1650 and a third between 1680 and 1700 – and 45 have precise eighteenth-century dates (nearly half from between 1700 and 1730 and the rest spread fairly evenly across the century) (see Table 9.3, pp. 215–16). These figures are minima and refer only to those buildings which carry a date; others are typologically datable or datable by their physical relationship to dated buildings (39 are clearly of the seventeenth century and one clearly of the eighteenth; see above, pp. 23–5). Many of the long-

Figure 9.3 *Single-cell buildings (steads) within a rangée at L'Abbaye aux Alines (Car); photo: Pete Addison*

houses (a category which constitutes 21% of dated seventeenth- and eighteenth-century buildings) must derive from this period, or even before, which would add a further 206 structures.[10]

While there is no reason to suppose from these data alone that 1620–50 and 1680–1730 were periods of special building activity, these are known times of rapid population growth, and it may therefore be suggested that they do indeed mark notable periods of new building.

The dynamic of settlement change

Whether or not the sixteenth and seventeenth centuries saw widespread building in stone for the first time is a difficult issue. Pre-sixteenth-century evidence for the survey area suggests that stone building was, from the eleventh and twelfth centuries, appropriate for noble residences, whereas building in wood had been common in the ninth and tenth (Davies and Astill 1994: 143–51; see above, p. 98). This does not have to mean that building in stone was inappropriate for the rest of the rural population in the middle ages and we would not wish to rule out that possibility; however, it has to be said that the existing positive evidence suggests that *widespread* building in stone was a development of the sixteenth century in this area. So, whereas the buildings associated with peasant holdings are characteristically measured by the foot in seventeenth-century and later texts, that is not the case in the sixteenth century, even at the same locations.[11] The implication is both that there was a change in housing type and also that there was plenty of new building in the sixteenth and seventeenth centuries. Hence the *logis neuf* at La Ville Marie in 1698.[12] Changing housing arrangements are also implied by the changes in rubbish disposal practice indicated above (pp. 186–8): there must have been at least a greater separation of human and animal quarters, moving away from the long-house tradition, and perhaps some change in flooring.[13] It is also noticeable that there are few (foreign) stone scatters associated with dumps at medieval settlement sites (see above, pp. 191–3). There is no need to suppose that the new developments were dependent on the establishment of a stone supply industry; getting hold of stone was a very local business, and probably became part of the regular agricultural routine. Farmers dug small quarries, or even holes, all over the Brioverian shale for new stone, and Roman sites were robbed (there is Roman brick in a Marsac building and blocks of quartzite from the near-by Roman villa in La Touche aux Roux (both Car)) (Davies 1990b: 323). By the late eighteenth century texts comment that there were "quarries all around".

If it is right to see building in stone as a sixteenth-century development, this was not only a major cultural revolution: it was a change which fixed the settlement pattern. Hence, the patterns we see in the *cadastre* and in relict form in the landscape today are a creation of the sixteenth and seventeenth centuries. Pre-sixteenth-century settlements were not very far away from their successors but they were differently disposed, a disposition hinted at by the Fabric 1 and then the Fabric 4/6/23 clusters (see above, pp. 122–3, 129, 132). Most of the sites indicated by Fabric 4/6/23 and continuing Fabric 1 clusters *ended* in the sixteenth/seventeenth centuries; the settlements they reflect shifted slightly, as they were constructed in stone; medieval buildings were then sometimes used as dumps (above, pp. 191–3). The settlement pattern cannot have been significantly rearranged, for at least 80% of places named in the Carentoir *capitation* of 1771 were also named in fifteenth- and sixteenth-century texts. By contrast most of the new (*métairie*) sites established in the sixteenth century did not shift at all (above, pp. 135–6, 150).

When we look at the dated stone buildings that still stand, seventeenth-century buildings are distributed across the core survey area, but those of the eighteenth century are much more evident in Carentoir than farther west (Fig. 9.4, Table 9.3). The developing difference between eastern and western halves of the core is thereby reflected in standing structures, and suggests that it was the eighteenth century that was the period of divergence, with more building and rebuilding in Carentoir. There is also some evidence for extensions to buildings (some of which may have been for agricultural or industrial purposes): outshuts (small extensions to the *rangée*) were added to rear (total 257), end (total 147) and front (17) of the rows. Rear and end outshuts occur on buildings bearing sixteenth-, seventeenth- and eighteenth-century dates (largely the latter, but there are also two of 1799 and 1887); it is reasonable to see them as eighteenth- and nineteenth-century additions. Again, there are more in Carentoir, which has more than half of the rear and end outshuts (55% and 53% respectively, on 46% of the surface area of the core). The habit of extending existing stone buildings rather than beginning new structures is reflected in the mixed build of many *rangées*, which often have a series of additions.

It is in fact extremely difficult to identify completely new settlements of the seventeenth and eighteenth centuries. The new arable of the seventeenth and eighteenth centuries does not appear to be associated with new settlement; places nearest to these new fields virtually all have a documented medieval background. Only a handful do not have earlier references: from this handful it is reasonable to propose that one or two new settlements were created in northern Carentoir, particularly near the Bourdonnaye woods. Very occasionally a new form of settlement name (like "Terre de Bois Brun" as a domicile in 1762)[14] also implies the creation of new settlements. However, on the whole the evidence indicates expansion of the existing rather than creation of new.

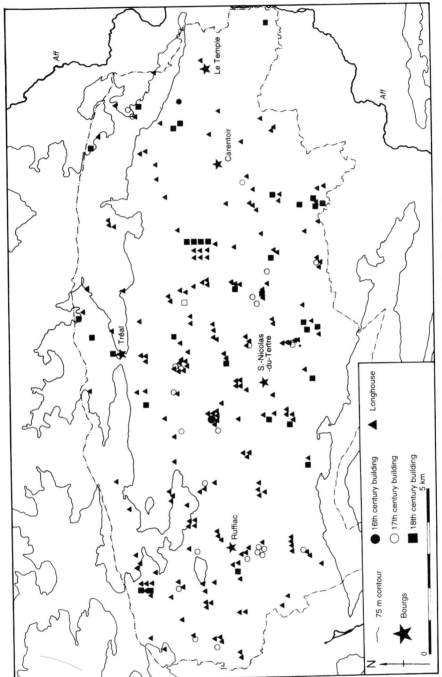

Figure 9.4 *Sixteenth-, seventeenth- and eighteenth-century dated buildings, and long-houses, in the core survey area*

In the 1820s the extent of the present commune of Carentoir visibly had a higher density of settlement, with 1.86 peasant settlements per km^2 compared with 1.26 in Ruffiac, 1.24 in Tréal and 1.47 in Saint-Nicolas. In Carentoir settlement is concentrated to the south of a northeast–southwest line through the *bourg*; here larger settlements (that is, those with more than 20 steads) are closely packed in the landscape, 0.5–1km apart where groups occur, as against 1–3km in Ruffiac. There are concentrations from Le Temple (reflecting its particularly high population density) to the present southeastern boundary of Carentoir commune and also south-southwest of Carentoir *bourg*. Interestingly, while no consistent trend in the rate of growth of settlements is implied by comparing 1447 *fouage* evidence with 1771 *capitation* records, at least eight settlements have a six-fold or greater increase in household numbers; these are largely located in eastern or southeastern Carentoir.

Work

The parishes of the survey area were strongly agricultural throughout their recorded history, and we would expect most residents, unless they were noble, to have worked on the land. The exceptional detail of the parish registers, which frequently classify principal actors by occupation, allows us to investigate work in the centuries before the systematic records of the nineteenth-century census returns. Although the registers do not provide a comprehensive record of occupations, nevertheless they supply a good deal of usable data. While there are years when no occupations are mentioned at all and years when almost everyone is classified by job, there are also years when fathers' occupations are systematically recorded in baptism records; whichever happens depends on the recording habit of the priest, but it means that in practice there are runs of years with consistently recorded information. What follows focusses on Carentoir as the parish of densest population, with Tréal for comparison and an occasional look at Ruffiac.[15]

As might be expected, an overwhelming proportion of people is described as *laboureurs*, peasant cultivators, who would have had a range of different tenancy agreements and a consequent range of social status; the term does not of itself imply that these people were poor. Where measurable, proportions vary on either side of 75%, for example 72% of Carentoir fathers in 1669, 71% in 1701, 83% in 1793 (cf. 74% in agriculture in Carentoir, averaged across the census returns for 1851, 1872, 1881); 72% in Ruffiac in 1736; 71% in Tréal across the 1690s, 70% across

1765–74; the term *cultivateurs* replaces *laboureurs* in the 1790s. To the *laboureurs* should be added the *journaliers*, those who worked for a daily wage (6% in Carentoir across 1701–6, ‹2% in Tréal in the late eighteenth century), and also peasant *métayers*, those who had contracted to farm noble lands (9% in Ruffiac in 1721, 4% in Tréal across 1765–74, and exceptionally rare in Carentoir); and finally there were *fermiers*, the term that came to replace *métayers* in the later eighteenth century – 2% in Tréal across 1765–74, but too rare to register in Carentoir. Overall the totality of those who were recognized as agricultural workers usually constitutes about 80%, although the proportion for Carentoir in 1701–6 is a low 70% and that for Le Temple in 1774–6 a very low 59% (see Table 9.1).

Table 9.1 Occupations in selected years in the core survey area

	Carentoir 1701–6	Carentoir 1793/7 /8	Le Temple 1774–6	Tréal 1695–1703	Tréal 1765–74	Ruffiac 1721	Ruffiac 1736
laboureurs	64.0	75.0	52.0	71.0	70.0	69.0	72.0
métayers	0.2	2.0	7.0	3.0	6.0	9.0	
fermiers				0.3	2.0		9.0
journaliers	6.0			0.3	1.0		
cultivateurs		4.0					
All agriculture	70.0	81.0	59.0	74.6	79.0	78.0	81.0
weavers	3.0	4.0	8.0	4.0	4.0	2.0	3.0
tailleurs d'habits	5.0	2.0		3.0	4.0	2.0	3.0
wool-workers				0.5	0.2		
couturiers	0.5	0.3					
shoe-makers	2.0	1.3	3.0	2.0	1.0		
All cloth/clothing	10.5	7.6	11.0	9.5	9.2	4.0	6.0
All construction	2.0	2.3		0.5	0.4		2.0
All other production	6.0	2.7	4.0	0.5	2.2		4.0
All food providers	4.5	4.0		1.3	1.0	2.0	2.0
All trade	1.0		0.3		0.8	2.0	
All professionals	1.0	1.3	4.0	0.5	0.7		2.0
Nobles	6.0		8.0	3.0	3.0	7.0	2.0
Number of records	707	459	39	378	423	47	64

Percentage by category of all fathers' occupations cited in Baptism records, in single years or groups of years; together with total number of references to fathers' occupations in the group. Construction includes roofers, carpenters, masons; other production includes blacksmiths, farriers, rope-makers, joiners, cart-makers; food providers includes millers, butchers, bakers; trade includes retailers, dealers and innkeepers; professionals includes municipal officers, army, lawyers, clerks, school-teachers.

We should not pay too much attention to precise percentages, given the nature of the record and the variation in the size of the parishes, but the broad picture is significant: the proportion working in agriculture was overwhelming, as might be expected; but it was not total: by any calculation about a fifth of these rural populations were *not* classified as farmers.

It is of considerable interest that the peasant community included a notable proportion of people who were non-agricultural producers. Whereas one might have expected that building, making implements, perhaps a little textile work, would have formed part of the agricultural routine, engaging most peasants for some part of the year, there were clearly people in these communities with more specialized occupations. It does not follow that they had no plots to cultivate, but they certainly spent enough time on their craft or service to be differentiated by the local priest.

By far the largest group was that which made cloth and clothing.[16] These constitute about 5% of those with a named occupation in Ruffiac but twice as many in Carentoir, Le Temple and Tréal. There is a very clear, and consistently maintained, proportion of cloth/clothing workers in Carentoir — a large parish with a mass of data. These workers included weavers, preponderantly, and makers of clothing, shoes and clogs (wool-workers also in Tréal) (Table 9.1). Weavers are present when the series begin in the seventeenth century and there is no indication that they are an introduction during the period; however, there does seem to have been some reduction in the numbers and proportions of *tailleurs* in Carentoir in the late eighteenth century.[17]

There are some 35 different occupations recorded at one time or another in Carentoir during this period. Of these, apart from nobles and cloth workers, the largest groups are of those who worked in food preparation and retail — butchers, bakers, millers — and in non-clothing production of one kind or another — blacksmiths, joiners, cart-makers (about 5% each in the early eighteenth century). Blacksmiths and millers, and farriers too, are a constant element from the start of the records, as one would expect, although numbers are small.

There are two changes across the period which, although small, appear significant: construction workers (masons, carpenters, roofers, stone-cutters) are present and identifiable from the start of the series but the numbers of individuals increase in the second half of the eighteenth century.[18] That the group was small is perhaps emphasized by the fact that the Ruffiac prior, or even the abbot of Redon himself, brought in masons, carpenters and roofers to give estimates when there were disputes about upkeep, as in 1611, 1688, 1748; and masons from Malestroit were used to repair Bodel bridge in 1767.[19]

The second change is that members of the professions (army, notaries, lawyers, schoolmaster, state officials, and a midwife) are only very rarely noted but become more evident from the 1790s: while the Revolution undoubtedly introduced officials into the communes (municipal officers and a *commissaire du pouvoir executif* of the Carentoir municipal administration), the trend was sustained in the nineteenth century (the professions comprised 2% of occupations in 1872–81). Those involved in buying and selling (merchants, retailers) were extremely rare throughout the series (less than 1%) but innkeepers begin to be noted in the later eighteenth century.

The latter trends are repeated in Tréal, with the appearance of officers, a dealer and a couple of innkeepers in the late eighteenth century.

Most of those with specialized occupations lived in hamlets, large and small, spread right across the parishes, although there were some settlements in all parishes, especially *métairies*, with none recorded; weavers occur as much at – for example – Les Feuges in the north of Carentoir as at La Vieille Abbaye in the south, at the large Bot Colin as at the very small Huno. The spread is particularly striking with reference to weavers, although there are also noticeable concentrations in Le Temple and eastern Carentoir – that is where settlement was itself most concentrated (Fig. 9.5). Cloth- and clothes-making must have been a common feature in rural communities in this area.

While people practising the less common crafts and trades could be domiciled anywhere, and most producers were scattered round the parish, there were nevertheless some concentrations: there was a rope-works at La Madeleine, 1 km west of Carentoir *bourg*, throughout the period. Innkeepers and members of the professions are found hardly anywhere except in the *bourgs*, and construction workers and food providers are common (indeed, tend to be focussed) in Carentoir *bourg*, especially in the Rue des Bouriennes. Some nobles resided there too. Given that, apart from nobles' agents, those with literacy skills lived overwhelmingly in the *bourg*, the parish focus must have had a markedly non-agricultural character. The *bourg* of Carentoir is also differentiated from the hamlets by its range of occupations – at least 12 – although hamlets like Bot Colin and La Danais had several.

In Tréal trades were similarly distributed across the parish, although it had a higher proportion of hamlets with several trades (and nearly 50% of all hamlets had some cloth and/or clothing workers); however, the *bourg*, like Ruffiac *bourg*, did not have Carentoir's distinctive character (nor did La Ville Lio, nor Bourgneuf); however, it did have a noble, an innkeeper, a noble's agent and public officers in the 1790s.

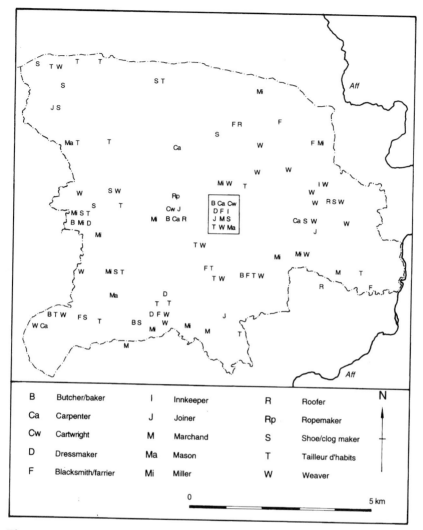

Figure 9.5 *Distribution of specialized occupations in eighteenth-century Carentoir*

Legend:

B	Butcher/baker	I	Innkeeper	R	Roofer	
Ca	Carpenter	J	Joiner	Rp	Ropemaker	
Cw	Cartwright	M	Marchand	S	Shoe/clog maker	
D	Dressmaker	Ma	Mason	T	Tailleur d'habits	
F	Blacksmith/farrier	Mi	Miller	W	Weaver	

N

0   5 km

Pre-industrial society

Two things appear to be especially relevant for understanding Carentoir's denser population: the high density of population in Le Temple, whose character – tiny parish that it was – was quite different from the other core parishes and was much less dominantly agricultural; and the small but significant proportion of professional clothworkers throughout Carentoir, especially noticeable in the eastern part of the parish. It is in this context that we see the significance of flax and hemp cultivation. Although there was some wool production in Tréal, weaving was overwhelmingly of linen and hemp cloth, clothing being made from both (cf. Jaubert 1773: ii.637). The "large buildings" which often occur in row settlements, with their associated large *clos*, could have been associated with flax and hemp processing, given the need for open curtilages to lay out the prepared thread for blanching.

Tréal's pattern of occupations was not quite the same as that of Carentoir but is nevertheless interesting: a parish with fewer but larger settlements per km^2; a parish with a higher density of population than Ruffiac and Saint-Nicolas, if the implications of the 1784 *capitation* are to be believed, and with many more settlements of complex form than Carentoir (more than 70%); it also had a greater number and range of occupations in many of its hamlets than did Carentoir. This is a different model of rural employment: this parish was not dominated by a central *bourg* with higher population and a wide range of occupations; rather, it was a parish in which people and occupations were distributed across a small number of substantial hamlets. Its employment pattern is varied, but quintessentially rural.

Of course, most of Carentoir's population did not live or work in its *bourg*; the place nevertheless had a distinctive, and non-agricultural, character. That there were nobles living in the *bourg*, as well as in rural houses, gives Carentoir something of an urban feel, quite apart from its wider range of occupations. While it might be stretching the point to call it a town, the centre did have some urban characteristics and it seems fair to say that it was on the road towards urbanization. That it did *not* develop to become a town has much to do with the fate of the Breton cloth industry in the nineteenth century (see below, pp. 237–8).

Can we observe any change in the relationship between work and settlement in the eighteenth century, as might initially be supposed from the increasing density of population? Broadly, no. Specialized work remained widely distributed across the parishes, all of them, and its practitioners lived beside agricultural workers, their occupations closely allied to the agricultural routine. To that extent the pattern is not urban at all.

How was the expansion of population accommodated? There is little to suggest the creation of new settlements since the sixteenth century. There was certainly new building in existing settlements: the location of dated eighteenth-century buildings in larger settlements implies expansion on the existing settlement base. There was clearly also a good deal of extension of existing buildings, whether as outshut or new stead at the end of a *rangée*.

(It is sometimes possible to demonstrate that *rangées* were extended at this time, as at La Lande Davide and L'Abbaye Blot (both Car).)

It is observable both that larger settlements nearly always had weavers and/or clothing workers, as did settlements with many outshuts (like Le Temple, La Gérossais, La Danais (all Car)); and also that those settlements *not* recorded in the 1447 *fouage* had cloth-workers. A good case can therefore be made that cloth-working was a factor leading to increasing settlement size and complexity. There were obviously major changes in the life and culture of the region during this period. However, the difference made by the rapidly increasing population was one of small-scale extension to existing settlements, not large-scale change of the settlement pattern nor whole-scale colonization of new areas.

Reflecting back on the material of the preceding chapter, we may recall that the proportion of land farmed as arable increased in this period (above, p. 189), and landlords turned some of their meadow, vineyards and orchards to arable (turning away from the charming backdrop). However, that increase does not seem to have matched the level of increase of population – perhaps 20% as against something approaching 100%. There is no indication that yields increased at this stage, although it is possible that less grain was exported and more imported than in the preceding centuries; nor are there indications of the diversification strategies adopted in the nineteenth century – reducing the fallow period, introducing potatoes, and so on. We therefore have to pose the familiar and crucial question: did people starve?

The population was obviously vulnerable to variation in the grain supply, and particularly susceptible to problems caused by the weather, aggravated by epidemics: there is a mass of evidence of calamities in food provision in the late eighteenth century in the survey area (see above, pp. 169, 176). Given the mortality patterns, and the incidence of crisis years, it looks as if there were recurrent food supply problems at that time. A fifth or so of the population had the flexibility that producing for retail can bring; others will have boosted their income with part-time domestic production; and perhaps another fifth could benefit from the charity of government, benevolent landlords and others. Despite these outlets, by 1789 the population was looking exceptionally pressured.

Table 9.2 Analysis of settlement elements in the 1820s

		Carentoir	Ruffiac	Tréal	Saint-Nicolas	Total numbers
Foci	1	56	41	46	42	**100**
	2	31	22	17	26	**53**
	3	9	22	17	26	**29**
	4	3	4	8	1	**8**
	5	1	9	13		**8**
	6		2			**1**
Rows	1	15	24	8	21	**33**
	2	32	20	21	32	**55**
	3	20	13	13	16	**34**
	4	14	9	21	5	**25**
	5	9	2	8	11	**15**
	6	2	15	8		**11**
	7	4	4	4	5	**8**
	8	3	2	4	5	**6**
	9	2		8		**4**
	10	1	2		5	**3**
	11		2			**1**
	12					
	13			4		**1**
	14		2			**1**
	15		2			**1**
	16		2			**1**
Orientation						
E–W		62	78	38	32	**119**
N–S		20	7	4	16	**29**
Other		19	15	59	53	**51**

Percentage of elements in each commune, with total numbers of each element

Table 9.3 Dated sixteenth-, seventeenth- and eighteenth-century buildings of the core survey area

Building no.	Commune	Settlement name	Date	Position of date
22	Ruffiac	la Touche Aga	1718	on wall stone
34	Ruffiac	la Touche Aga	1770	door lintel
75	Ruffiac	Tréleuc	1644	window lintel
163	Ruffiac	Digoit	1702	on ridge slate
191	Ruffiac	Kerhal	1727	on ridge
228	Ruffiac	Rangera	1688	door lintel
238	Ruffiac	Lodineu	1653	lintel
251	Ruffiac	Lodineu	1604	door lintel
252	Ruffiac	Lodineu	1684	door lintel
289	Ruffiac	Balangeart	1634	decorated plinth
321	Ruffiac	la Rivière	1728	ridge slate
424	Carentoir	la Métairie au Joly	1785	ridge slate
786	Carentoir	le Bois Faux	1579	chimney piece
833	Carentoir	Marsac	1633	interior timber
835	Carentoir	Marsac	1601	stone plaque inside house
890	Carentoir	Marsac	1798	plaque above loft access
1041	Carentoir	la Landriais	1733	door lintel
1188	Carentoir	la Rosaie	1723	door lintel
1195	Carentoir	la Rosaie	1707	stone set above window
1502	Carentoir	Galny	1799	on quoin
1537	Carentoir	la Lande David	1733	blocked door lintel
1538	Carentoir	la Lande David	1760	door lintel
1552	Carentoir	l'Hôtelais	1724	ridge slate
1620	Carentoir	Coetmorel	1788	stone inside byre doorway
1682	Carentoir	la Grand Ville	1711	ridge slate
1715	Carentoir	Brangolo	1719	door lintel
1722	Carentoir	Brangolo	1793	ridge slate
1723	Carentoir	Brangolo	1721	door lintel
1827	Carentoir	l'Abbaye aux Alines	1635	window lintel
2082	Carentoir	Trignac	1798	ridge slate
2105	Carentoir	les Touchettes	1701	lintel
2269	Carentoir	la Briancaie	1740	door lintel
2296	Carentoir	Pled	170?	door lintel
2312	Carentoir	Pled	1714	
2322	Carentoir	Pled	1717	
2390	Carentoir	la Ville Verte	176?	ridge slate
2449	Carentoir	Bonnais	1733	door lintel
2493	Carentoir	la Margandaie	1699	lintel
2497	Carentoir	la Margandaie	1622	lintel
2594	Carentoir	la Danais	1789	lintel
2616	Carentoir	la Rincelaie	1727	lintel
2623	Carentoir	la Rincelaie	1624	above window
2721	Carentoir	Henleix	1639	lintel
2797	Tréal	le Vieux Bourg	1624	plaque over blocked door
2807	Tréal	le Vieux Bourg	1750	virgin niche

continued

Table 9.3 Dated sixteenth-, seventeenth- and eighteenth-century buildings of the core survey area (*contd.*)

Building no.	Commune	Settlement name	Date	Position of date
2814	Carentoir	la Touche aux Roux	1770	door lintel
2849	Tréal		1750	door lintel
2871	Tréal	le Rocher	1647	door lintel
2916	Tréal	le Rocher	1665	door lintel
2970	Tréal	Fanhouet	1777	granite stone
3076	Tréal	Triguého	1726	door lintel
3107	St-Nicolas-du-Tertre	la Ruaudaie	1645	door lintel
3197	St-Nicolas-du-Tertre	la Châtaigneraie	1634	dormer pediment
3314	St-Nicolas-du-Tertre	la Bridelaie	1709	ridge slate
3344	Carentoir	l'Abbaye Blot	1747	door lintel
3345	Carentoir	l'Abbaye Blot	1727	door lintel
3368	Carentoir	Launay	1784	door lintel
3384	Carentoir	Sigré	1703	ridge slate
3503	Tréal	la Buardais	1660	window lintel
3519	Tréal	Château du Préclos	1610	stone set into wall
3545	Tréal	le Plessis	1697	window lintel
3719	St-Nicolas-du-Tertre	Lestrehan	170?	ridge slate
3754	St-Nicolas-du-Tertre	Villeneuve	1716	window lintel
3839	Tréal	Tréal	17??	ridge slate
3938	St-Nicolas-du-Tertre	le Carrefour	1750	door lintel
3976	Ruffiac	la Ville Hoyard	177?	ridge slate
4077	Ruffiac	la Chapelle St Jean	1701	stone cross in churchyard
4287	Ruffiac	la Sorinaie	1686	door lintel
4457	Ruffiac	la Hervaie	1681	ex site
4486	Ruffiac	Béculeu	1682	window lintel
4589	Ruffiac	Château de la Ruée	1687	door lintel
5031	Ruffiac	Lodineu	1684	door lintel

Notes

1. These are mentioned in parish registers during the seventeenth and eighteenth centuries, but not thereafter; e.g. *métairie* du Verger (near Quoiqueneuc) and *métairie* de Meriennes (near La Touche), both in Tréal.
2. AD Morbihan 21C513; Tréal and Le Temple (1784): 21C583.
3. AD Morbihan E1604.
4. AD Loire-Atlantique B1966. Erection of dovecots was strictly regulated to those of the appropriate status; Henry 1981: 71.
5. AD Ille-et-Vilaine 3H188 L5; 3H190 L3d (1688).
6. AD Ille-et-Vilaine 3H190 L5g (1754); 3H192 L6 (1695); 3H193 (1688 and 1758); 3H188 L5 (1669). AD Morbihan G981.
7. AD I-et-V 3H188 L4. Most of the houses mentioned in this text were slate roofed.
8. *Ibid.* 3H191[2] L2; 3H66.

9. *Ibid.* 3H190 L1.

10. While one cannot rule out the possibility that some long-houses were constructed after 1800, particularly since a couple carry nineteenth-century dates, nevertheless the available evidence overwhelmingly suggests that they are characteristic of a much earlier period, dropping out of fashion across the seventeenth and eighteenth centuries; witness the decline of long-houses and the increase of single-cell buildings in percentages of dated buildings by century: long-houses are 26% of dated 17th-, 18% of 18th-, 7% of 19th-, as against single-cell at 8% of dated 17th-, 36% of 18th-, 40% of 19th-, 33% of 20th-century buildings. It is also significant that there are equal numbers of long-houses in Ruffiac and Carentoir: they must date from a period *before* population expansion in Carentoir in the later seventeenth and eighteenth centuries.

11. E.g. AD Ille-et-Vilaine 3H188 L4, L5, L7 in the 1609, 1646 Priory rent-rolls, but not 16th-century rent-rolls for the same settlements; *ibid.* L10 for Lodineu in 1645, but not 1559. Measuring by the foot does occur in the sixteenth century, but relates to grander buildings: the *grande maison* at La Châtaigneraie (1571) or the Priory house in Ruffiac *bourg* (1583, but not 1497); *ibid.* 3H190 L2, 3H188 L10, 3H189 L6.

12. *Ibid.* 3H192 L6.

13. For comparison, note that at Le Yaudet in northwest Brittany, where there is a long excavated sequence within the rampart (which included stone buildings), stone building began outside the rampart in the fifteenth century, clearly a new departure in building tradition (Cunliffe and Galliou 1995: 59). Cf. Gallet 1983: 173 on the changing size of the *ménage*.

14. Tréal Baptêmes.

15. All the Tréal registers for the seventeenth and eighteenth centuries have been analyzed, also selected well-recorded years for Carentoir, and occasional well-recorded years for Ruffiac. Carentoir 1701–6 are particularly fully recorded, and 1793/7/8 nearly as well; Le Temple is well recorded in 1774–6 and Ruffiac in 1721 and 1736. The Tréal records are particularly good in the 1690s, 1760s and 1770s, and fathers' occupations are systematically recorded in Baptêmes 1695–1702, 1765–74.

    The figures cited in this discussion derive from a count of fathers' occupations, unless otherwise stated. Obviously fathers do not necessarily reflect the range of occupations of the total population, but they do provide a means of systematic comparison. (Occasionally potentially significant trends which are not reflected in the fathers material are suggested by the totality of data.)

16. The survey area does not feature as a linen/*toile*- (cloth) producing area in standard accounts of the subject. It is perfectly clear from the references to *tissiers/tisserands/texiers en toile* or *en linge* (cloth- and linen-weavers) throughout seventeenth- and eighteenth-century parish registers that there must have been some significant production of flax and hemp cloth; the 1845 edition of Ogée does in fact refer to the export of linen and hemp cloth from Carentoir.

17. *Tailleurs d'habits* (cutters of clothes) are here treated as makers of clothing; since they are occasionally recorded in the same years as *couturiers* they should be differentiated. (*Couturiers* are usually understood as makers of women's clothing.)

    Tailleurs (cutters) sometimes appear without the descriptive qualification; where the family cannot be checked it is just possible that these were *tailleurs de pierre* (stone-cutters); however, given the relatively small numbers of construction workers and the fact that the numbers of *tailleurs* reduced in the late eighteenth century, when building was on the increase, it is much more likely that the unqualified *tailleurs* were *tailleurs d'habits*; this is in any case the import of Rey 1992: 2076, *s.v. tailleurs*.

18. More individuals are mentioned, but the numbers remain too small for the increase to be reflected in the fathers' averages.

19. AD Ille-et-Vilaine 3H187 L6, 3H190 L3d, 3H191[2] L2; C2348.

A note on settlement types and terminology

Peasant settlements in the survey area largely consist of *rangées* or rows, disposed either singly or in parallel (see Fig. 9.1 a, d, e, f and c, e). These may be grouped in a number of ways: "staggered", where rows are not precisely opposed or where a part of a single row is set back from the block; "interrupted", where rows are separated by one or two small enclosed fields or curtilages; "divergent", where rows are set at right angles, or form two sides of a triangle (see Fig. 9.1 b, e and c). Where the gap between rows is substantial, so that some small fields intervene between them, each group may be counted as a separate "focus" of the settlement.

Groups of buildings sometimes constitute a farm, often arranged round a yard, involving a separation of residential, stock and storage buildings (see Fig. 9.1 f). It is rare for such groups to exist independently, since they are often a separate focus associated with a row settlement. A further settlement category is that of the "large building", identified not only by its size, but by the shape and size of its associated enclosure (see Fig. 9.1 d).

The size and character of settlements can be usefully discussed in terms of the number of rows and the number of foci as well as the number of "steads" (i.e. separate properties) (see Table 9.1). In English usage, settlements of 1–2 steads (farms) are often differentiated from those of 3–19 steads (hamlets) and from those of 20 or more (villages). For relatively large conglomerations, like the latter, see Fig. 9.1 d, e and f.

CHAPTER 10

After the Revolution

The French Revolution brought some rapid changes to the survey area, and did so surprisingly quickly: communes were formed in 1790, the Revolutionary language of *citoyen* and *bourgeois* was adopted in local records, and new officials were soon active. Commune minutes survive for Ruffiac from 1790–94 (ADM 204ES3); and although the miller of Bodel (just north of Ruffiac) was elected mayor of Caro, he quickly became involved in a complicated and protracted dispute with the Revolutionary authorities – and soon found himself ex-mayor (Kerrand 1988). Most of the local priests refused to take the oath, an issue on which the local population could have and express views – as did a man buying tobacco in La Gacilly in April 1791 (Marsille 1988). Many of the priests soon fled, although the priest of La Haute Boixière continued to register baptism and marriage for a few years. The lands and buildings of Ruffiac Priory, for so long a dominant seigneurial force in the core survey area, were sold between 1790 and 1792 (Le Mené 1904), within ten years of the Vicar-General's last visit from Redon to view and sign the parish registers.

But if there were sudden changes, there were also long continuities across the Revolutionary period. Although references to nobles tend to disappear, many old noble families were still in place in the early nineteenth century – like Tourtat, *sieur* of Pont Touchard, living at Tréal *bourg* in the 1780s, but known as Citoyen Tourtat *bourgeois* by 1801; and, after all, the Château de la Bourdonnaye, where de la Bourdonnayes have lived for much of the twentieth century, remains a striking residence in 1996 (see Fig. 9.2).

Changes to the structure of the agrarian economy did come, but it was late in the nineteenth century, and even the twentieth, before fundamental

220

changes began to be evident. There is of course a mass of detailed written evidence about rural change, particularly in material generated by the repeated and insistent (sometimes annual) government enquiries of 1850 and beyond. What follows is necessarily a brief look at the relationship between land-use and settlement in the nineteenth and twentieth centuries; it does not attempt to be comprehensive, for that would involve detailed studies that are beyond the range of this book.

The population

The enormous parish of Carentoir lost the southeastern zone of La Gacilly when it became a separate commune in 1790; it lost Quelneuc, on the eastern boundary, in 1863, and La Chapelle Gaceline, also southeastern, in 1874; but it included the parish of Le Temple from 1802 (see above, pp. 56–7). Quite apart from the effect of boundary changes which took populations to other units, the history of Carentoir in the nineteenth century is often marked by declining population levels, despite the existence of the several *bourgs* of Carentoir itself, Le Temple and La Chapelle Gaceline.

In 1801 Carentoir, Le Temple, Quelneuc and La Chapelle Gaceline had a combined population of 5,681; by 1861 the combined figure had dropped a little but by the end of the century there was a modest rise to 5,667 (1891), Carentoir's own share being 4,053, peaking in 1896 at 4,069. At 69 inhab/km^2 in 1896 this was much the same density as that of 1801 (70 inhab/km^2). Thereafter, beginning already before the First World War but accelerating during the war years, the pattern was one of decline to a population of 2,355 in 1975 (Fig. 10.1). The near-by town of La Gacilly, though showing some increase in the mid nineteenth century, and with a denser population in 1901, basically presented the same pattern: although numbers grew from 1801 to 1881, they dropped thereafter, reaching a low of 1,092 in 1962.

The other three communes of the core survey area shared these trends, to the extent that they demonstrated the small peak of the late nineteenth century and the long decline of the twentieth. However, Saint-Nicolas-du-Tertre and Tréal had much more buoyant population levels during the nineteenth century, with Tréal increasing by 22% between 1801 and 1906 (its high point) and Saint-Nicolas by 36% between 1806 and 1901. At their highest levels during the period of regular census returns, Ruffiac had a population of 1,877, Tréal 1,179 and Saint-Nicolas 724. By 1975 all had dropped significantly (see above, p. 52). Ruffiac and Saint-Nicolas

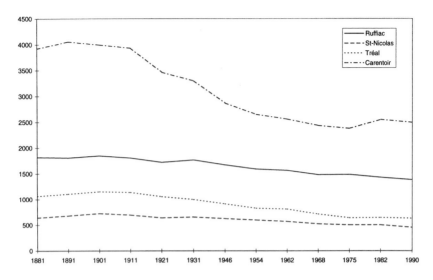

Figure 10.1 *Population levels in the core survey area 1881–1990*

continued to drop through the 1980s, Tréal remained stable, while Carentoir rose a little and La Gacilly rose rapidly to 2,269 in 1990 (107% increase since 1962). The density of populations in the core therefore changed between their late nineteenth-century high points and 1990 from 51 to 38 inhab/km^2 in Ruffiac, 56 to 35 in Saint-Nicolas, 61 to 33 and 69 to 42 in Tréal and Carentoir respectively; by comparison La Gacilly rose from 102 to 138 inhab/km^2 (see above, p. 6).[1]

This, then, is a demographic profile dominated by rural depopulation and outward migration, as is also particularly the case in the communes of sample transect N. It is a pattern shared by the town of La Gacilly until the industrial changes of the later twentieth century, although not by Malestroit to the west.

In the early nineteenth century the spatial horizons of this rural population were still limited. By looking at the locations associated with witnesses, we can analyze the domicile of nearly all the witnesses recorded at burials in Carentoir in Year XII (September 1803–September 1804). Witnesses were essentially drawn from neighbours and/or family, although very occasionally a "friend" is mentioned.

In Year XII there were 160 recorded burials. Witnesses came from 182 different locations, but almost every witness came from the same commune as the dead person, 57% coming from the same hamlet, 23%

from a near-by hamlet (up to 3 km away, or up to 5 km if the witness lived in the *bourg*), 4.5% from the neighbouring communes of Guer, La Gacilly and Saint-Séglin. Sometimes the birthplace of the deceased is given: of the 160 dead persons, only 3% has a recorded origin external to the commune (although this is a limited record and we should expect there to have been more); of the 3%, all but one arose from moves made by parents (that is in the generation previous to the subject). This material therefore provides some precise though slight evidence of inward migration to Carentoir in the late eighteenth century; the earlier eighteenth-century trend was clearly still continuing at that stage (above, pp. 177, 179).

In most cases it is the presence of neighbours that is recorded at the burial, but 160 family members are named as witnesses too. Since they are all assigned a domicile, we can also do a simple study of the spatial distribution of family members.

A majority of the family members named came from the same hamlet as the deceased. As might perhaps be expected, three-quarters of sons and daughters did so; but two-thirds of uncles, cousins and nephews did so too; while, not surprisingly, only half of sons- and sisters-in-law did so (and no brothers-in-law at all).[2] Only half the sisters and a third of the brothers did (Table 10.1). However, all but six of the relations who did not come from the same hamlet came from near-by hamlets within the single commune of Carentoir; five of the six came from neighbouring La Gacilly and one from

Table 10.1 Percentage of relations living in the same hamlet as deceased relatives in Carentoir in 1803–4

	Number of persons	*Percentage living in the same hamlet*
son	41	73
daughter	15	73
brother	26	38
sister	2	50
father	11	82
grandson	1	100
nephew	5	60
cousin	7	71
uncle	9	67
brother-in-law	7	0
son-in-law	20	55
sister-in-law	2	50
Mean percentage		63

neighbouring Guer. This very detailed evidence of domiciles provides a useful snapshot of family distribution in the early nineteenth century; many lived in very close proximity: the number of uncles, cousins and nephews living in the same hamlet is particularly striking.

Settlement and buildings

Limited mobility is not surprising given the nature of the communications system: although there was a plethora of small roads and paths between the hamlets, it was the 1950s and 1960s before the network of state roads was extended to all rural settlements; neither the near-by canal nor the more distant railway was close enough to make much difference in the late nineteenth century. By the 1820s the main road from Vannes to Rennes, through Malestroit and Guer, ran along the northern boundary of Ruffiac and Tréal; the main road from Malestroit to La Gacilly ran through Ruffiac and Saint-Nicolas, passing through the former and south of the latter *bourg*; a major road (*grande route*) ran from Carentoir *bourg* north to Guer and the north coast and south to Redon (through La Gacilly), as it had done for centuries, and another ran northeast from the *bourg* to Maur. Carentoir thus lay on a north–south axis, and Ruffiac on a northwest/southeast axis; there was (and is) no major road running east–west across the communes, linking Carentoir centre to Ruffiac centre, nor north–south through the middle of the core survey area linking Tréal to Saint-Nicolas centres. Both Ruffiac and Carentoir *bourg* locations were therefore related to major roads, but not to each other, and neither Tréal nor Saint-Nicolas had focal positions in this network.

From the late eighteenth century the provincial administration undertook extensive road works on the main routes, which were clearly in need of major repairs at that time. The Guer–Malestroit–Vannes road was repaired several times in the decade after 1758. Indeed, the *États* sent out many requests to the local parishes for *corvées* to present themselves to do roadworks (largely refused, on the grounds that parishioners were already paying enough *capitation*). Significant expenditure on roads within this locality really began in the later nineteenth century; in Ruffiac, for example, there was major expenditure on intercommunal as well as main roads between 1865 and 1892. Work on roads within the communes, from hamlet to hamlet, developed in the twentieth century: in Tréal the Département provided 2,490 francs towards a link to the intercommunal road in the 1920s. The main push, however, came after the Second World War: in the 1950s money came from the state, the Département and the communes themselves, as loans were raised for communal initiatives. In Saint-Nicolas the mayor wrote back vigorously when the Département refused to contribute to improvements in 1953, after the commune had already raised loans of 3,300,000 francs.[3] Communal councils were clearly energetic in pursuing a policy of local improvements at this point, but until then distribution of local products cannot have been easy.

From 1851 census data for the survey area (though sometimes incomplete) become more and more detailed, often recording population by hamlet and often differentiating houses from households, although different data sets survive for the several communes. In this period we have precise data on household size for the first time. In Carentoir the average size was 4.6 in the nineteenth century, dropping to 4.3 in 1911 and 3.9 in 1926 and 1931; it was the same in Tréal in 1931 and slightly higher (4.2) in Ruffiac and Saint-Nicolas. In the late nineteenth century there were houses with more than one household, especially in Ruffiac, where at least 100 households were sharing in 1881, nearly a quarter of the total. This was a relatively short-term phenomenon: by 1911, and 1926, sharing had dropped to 14 households (ADM 6M252).

Ferme and *métairie* settlements tended to be very small – one household only – just as they were in the eighteenth century, although these households were usually large, comprising eight or nine people. In Tréal, in particular, there was some redistribution of population between hamlets in the period 1836–81, with some (like Le Plessis) growing and others (like Le Cleu) shrinking; in 1881–1911, however, there was a clear tendency for small hamlets to shrink and larger hamlets to swell (Table 10.2). This tendency towards nucleation in the late nineteenth century is repeated elsewhere and is best demonstrated by the *bourgs*: in 1881 100 households (95 houses) are recorded in Carentoir, 59 in Ruffiac, 19 in Saint-Nicolas and 6 in Tréal. But the percentage of Carentoir's population living in the *bourg* rose from 10% to 13% between 1872 and 1931, of Ruffiac's 12% to 15% and of Tréal's 4% to 10%.[4]

In the twentieth century the shrinkage of the 357 hamlets continued, whether small or large, as the *bourgs* expanded, with plentiful building in new plots on their outskirts. A few new settlements were established where

Table 10.2 Number of households per settlement in Tréal, in 1881 and 1911

	1–5 households	6–10 households	11–15 households	16–20 households	21–25 households	>25 households
1881	22	6	4	2	0	0
1911	16	6	7	0	2	1

there had been none at the time of the cadastral survey. These new settlements almost invariably comprise a single, non-agricultural, well-built house, set back from the road in a well-maintained garden. Overall, however, the number of subsidiary settlements in the core survey area decreased fractionally between the 1820s and the 1980s.

Apart from the substantial shrinkage of some of the large early nineteenth-century hamlets (like Béculeu (Ruff), Le Rocher (Tr), La Métairie au Joly (Car), and La Ruaudais (S-N)), the most striking change to the settlement pattern in this period was the relocation of the *bourg* of Tréal. The (very small) medieval and early modern *bourg* lay in the northeast corner of the parish, on a confined space by the River Rahun, at the modern hamlet of Le Vieux Bourg. In the late nineteenth century the commune's focus was relocated 1 km to the southwest, at the hamlet of La Ville Lio, which had been associated with the *bourg* for centuries as a *métairie* of the *sieur* of Tréal (see above, p. 150). La Ville Lio already had more households than the *bourg* (which seems to have been losing population in the preceding generation) in the 1820s, and the presbytery was situated there at that date. In the old *bourg* the parish church was reduced to a simple chapel and a brand new edifice was begun at La Ville Lio in 1884, not far from the presbytery. This church was consecrated in February 1889. The *mairie*, school and some houses were built beside it and within five years Le

Figure 10.2 *A mid- to late nineteenth-century building at La Métairie au Joly (Car); photo: Pete Addison*

Mené was writing that the new *bourg* had soon overtaken the old (1891–4: ii.518).

Outside the *bourgs* there was of course some new building and there were many additions to existing houses (see above, p. 225). Of the dated or typologically datable nineteenth-century buildings in the core survey area, there is more evidence for building in the late nineteenth century than earlier (see above, pp. 24–5) (Fig. 10.2).[5] Of the dated or typologically datable twentieth-century buildings, more than a quarter date from the early twentieth century (see Fig. 2.6). About a third of the late nineteenth-century buildings lies in Saint-Nicolas-du-Tertre and there are rather few in central Ruffiac and in eastern Carentoir; there are few early twentieth-century buildings in eastern and in western Carentoir, perhaps reflecting the declining population outside the *bourg*, but there are plenty in central Ruffiac and central Carentoir, and again in the smaller communes. We know from agricultural census data that 41 new houses were built in Carentoir between 1919 and 1929 and 19 in Saint-Nicolas, but negligible numbers in Ruffiac and Tréal.[6]

As for materials, this was a period of some change: notable amounts of granite started to be used in rural housing in this area, largely for lintels; brick and tile came into use in the twentieth century, and not much then, although there was already a tile roofer living in Tréal in 1911 (ADM 6M305). The availability of new roofing materials, especially fine roofing slates from Angers and Rochefort, is also evident by the late nineteenth century. Ninety-four buildings have nineteenth-century dates on roof and ridge tiles; although there are examples from 1800 and thereabout, more than half post-date 1861, and more than a quarter lie between 1891 and 1899. There are more of these in the south of the core, and in southern Carentoir in particular, reflecting the distribution of eighteenth-century population and probably therefore reflecting upgrading of eighteenth-century housing: a dated structure of 1741 at La Bridelaie (S-N), for example, has a ridge tile dated 1904. Twentieth-century reroofing, where dated, is overwhelmingly a feature of the first decade of the century.

This material is therefore sufficient to suggest some redistribution of population and refurbishment or construction of dwellings within the core survey area, away from the hamlets and towards the *bourgs*, particularly in the period 1870–1910. This accords well with the demographic peaks and is unsurprising. In Ruffiac housing supply does not seem to have kept up with the peaking of population in 1906, with a significant proportion of households sharing. However, the rapidly declining population of the First World War period soon brought an end to any overcrowding.

Pottery

Sherds of pottery of the nineteenth and twentieth centuries can be found in and around settlements and on the surface of arable fields, as they can for all periods since the late Bronze Age. These are the fabric types classified as "modern" and they include a very high proportion of imports: the hard brown-glazed Fabric 49; hard red wares, like flower pot and modern tile (all called Fabric 26); Loire valley stoneware (Fabric 29); the hard yellow-glazed white ware of Fabric 35, which may be of Saintonge origin; and modern china and porcelain (all called Fabric 20) (Davies and Astill 1994: 208–9). All were available in the nineteenth century, but Fabric 29 seems to have begun in the late eighteenth and Fabric 20 occurs right through the twentieth century.

This material can be found across the surface of almost the entire core survey area, in fairly even quantities; this is in marked contrast to the occurrence of seventeenth- and eighteenth-century sherds, with their heavy concentration in Carentoir (see above, pp. 185–6). There are no striking zones of concentration or absence. However, the material is less common in western Carentoir, eastern Saint-Nicolas and Tréal, and western Ruffiac; and it is markedly absent from the neighbourhood of some settlements in southern Carentoir (Fig. 10.3).

China and porcelain (Fabric 20) is overwhelmingly the commonest of the fabrics, reflecting its wide availability in the twentieth century. Four-fifths of records which have modern fabrics have these types; however, despite its twentieth-century availability, it is far less common than the medieval fabric, Fabric 1, which occurs in 52% of all records and accounts for 24% by weight of all pottery collected in transect-walking (as against 26% and 5% for Fabric 20). Fabric 29 occurs in a fifth of fields with modern fabrics and Fabric 26 in a tenth, both tending to have been picked up near larger hamlets; Fabric 49 occurs in 3% of this group of records, and is commoner within 2 km of the *bourgs* than beyond; and Fabric 35 occurs in 5% of the records, almost half of the finds being recovered from the single commune of Ruffiac (Table 10.3).

In the sample transects, Transect R had a considerably higher proportion of Fabric 20; Transect P had considerably less Fabric 29; Fabric 49 was exceptionally rare in all (there was none in N or P); Fabric 35 was less evident than the mean in Transect M and did not occur in Transect R – emphasizing its more western distribution.

The quantities of modern ceramic collected in the core and in the sample transects are small by comparison with the totality of medieval sherds. This is as much demonstrated by the assemblage from individual fields as by

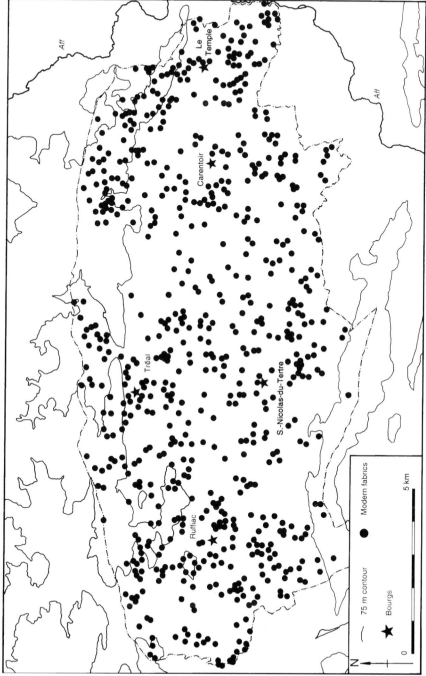

Figure 10.3 *Distribution of modern fabrics in the core survey area*

Table 10.3 Incidence of modern fabrics in the core survey area

	All modern fields	K	L	A	H	J	B	All fields
All modern fabrics	100	27	47	40	39	26	36	32.0
F29	21	7	12	9	6	5	7	6.8
F49	3	0	0	2	1	‹1	2	1.1
F35	5	1	2	5	1	1	1	1.6
F26	9	0	2	6	5	2	4	2.9
F20	80	21	37	31	34	21	29	25.5
F1	61	56	53	52	50	55	50	52.0

	All modern fields	C	F	D	E	G	All fields
All modern fabrics	100	26	38	38	48	43	32.0
F29	21	7	6	9	11	12	6.8
F49	3	0	3	2	1	0	1.1
F35	5	1	2	2	0	6	1.6
F26	9	0	6	2	2	8	2.9
F20	80	20	31	30	40	25	25.5
F1	61	70	68	55	57	100	52.0

Percentage of fields walked in which each modern fabric occurs, by transect (K the westernmost and G the easternmost transects); percentage of all fields and all fields with modern fabrics; Fabric 1 distribution for comparison.

global quantities: for example, 339.5g of medieval and late medieval sherds, 165g of post-medieval and 89g of modern came from D148, near Bot Colin (Car); and 298.5g, 102g and 72g respectively came from L107, some 500m east of Digoit (Ruff).

Modern fabrics are also less widely distributed than medieval, occurring in just under a third of all fields walked (32%). Sixty-eight per cent of arable fields of the 1820s in the core had no modern fabrics of any sort. Refuse containing modern ceramic waste cannot therefore have been spread on all arable, be it in the early nineteenth or late twentieth centuries, as it also clearly had not been spread in the seventeenth and eighteenth centuries (above, pp. 188–9). Indeed, two-thirds of fields which have medieval pottery do not have modern pottery, even though a smaller proportion of the surface was devoted to arable in the middle ages.

Where then do sherds occur and why do they occur where they do? In most respects, the vital statistics of records with modern fabrics are

Table 10.4 Topographic and cadastral characteristics of modern fabrics

	All modern fabrics	Modern excluding fields with F20 only	F49	F26	F35	F29	F20	All fields	F1
Arable	65	70	75	71	72	68	64	64	78
Lande	24	17	4	14	17	20	26	25	12
Meadow	4	6	8	10	6	5	4	5	5
Pasture	2	2	8	2	6	1	2	2	2
Château landscape	10	12	25	17	19	8	9	7	14
South slope	39	38	50	49	36	35	40	37	39
North slope	23	24	25	22	25	24	22	25	23
Contour:									
‹20m	1	1	0	2	0	1	1	2	1
20–60m	62	74	79	63	81	70	60	65	71
›70m	19	12	13	9	6	14	21	14	11
Stream:									
‹101m	32	32	50	29	33	31	31	33	36
‹201m	51	49	71	48	50	46	51	58	58
›400m	21	23	13	26	22	25	20	18	14
Settlement:									
‹51m	23	28	29	25	17	31	22	22	26
‹101m	36	43	46	43	36	44	36	35	42
‹201m	62	64	67	63	64	65	62	63	72
›400m	8	7	0	5	8	8	8	7	4

Percentage of each modern fabric, by cadastral land-use, château landscape, contour, distance from water, slope and distance from the nearest cadastral settlement; with all modern fabrics, fields with modern fabrics excluding fields with F20 only, Fabric 1 and all fields for comparison.

extremely close to those of the all-fields mean (see Table 10.4). However, they occur noticeably more frequently on land above 70m (and in Transect R noticeably on north-facing slopes); less frequently within 200m of water and more frequently at some distance from water (except in Transect M). Since more than half of the occurrences are within 200m of a settlement of the 1820s, modern ceramic sometimes occurs in the close neighbourhood of settlements and at others at some considerable distance from them; proximity to and distance from settlements are *both* characteristic patterns.

The scatters found on distant arable require a new kind of explanation. Although animal dung was still a principal fertilizer in the region in 1925/6, the canton of La Gacilly is recorded as purchasing 20,253m^3 of *boue des rues* – street soil – for fertilizing in 1852.[7] It makes most sense to suppose that this was put on newly and irregularly worked lands, with manure, for extra moisture and extra nutrients; one would expect street soil to contain sherds and this would explain their occurrence on new but not on "normal" arable. Of course domestic refuse from household dumps may well also have been taken to this arable and spread with the manure in the traditional way.

As we have said, most of the fields with medieval fabrics on the surface do not have modern fabrics, but the medieval fields which *do* have modern pottery too are more frequently sited at some distance from water and at higher altitudes – they emphasize the characteristic locations of fields with modern pottery (see above, pp. 119–22, 129; Table 10.5). Fields with modern fabrics that do not have post-medieval fabrics (nearly 70% of the group) are *much* more frequently a good distance from water and above 70m than the mean, and more than half are sited on cadastral *lande* or woodland. Fields with modern fabrics that have no other pottery at all (11% of "modern" records), are a quite unusual distance from cadastral settlements (only 15% are within 100m), are extremely often on cadastral *lande* or woodland, and tend to be high and some distance from water. Many of these fields indicating new arable were well away from the *bourgs*: there are small zones, for example, in south Saint-Nicolas (La Thiolaie/La Choulais to Les Grosses Nées), the north of Carentoir (Les Vignes to Trignac; Mauffrais to Maupas; Le Bois Faux); as also round Tréal. Twentieth-century farmers were going farther afield, to less obviously cultivable lands, and some lands that had never been cultivated before in historic time.

The accumulations of modern pottery which are near settlements (in fact, more frequently round the larger hamlets than the *bourgs*) must have

Table 10.5 Topographic comparison between fields with medieval and those with modern fabrics

	Medieval but no modern fabrics	Medieval and modern fabrics	Modern but no medieval fabrics	Modern fabrics only
Stream:				
‹101m	35	33	26	26
‹201m	57	52	43	41
›400m	16	19	31	29
Contour:				
20–60m	71	65	44	46
›70m	14	17	24	23
Settlement:				
‹51m	21	25	8	5
‹201m	67	65	48	44
›400m	5	8	10	13
Lande	16	19	49	54
Wood	‹1	‹1	5	6

Percentage of fields having medieval but no modern fabrics, medieval and modern fabrics, modern but no medieval fabrics, and modern fabrics only; by topographic category, by distance from cadastral settlement and by cadastral land-use as *lande* or wood derived from dumps, as they did in the seventeenth and eighteenth centuries (see above, pp. 191–3). There are at least 44 dumps with modern sherds in the core survey area.[8] Four are demonstrably located on the sites of early nineteenth-century settlements which have long since disappeared.[9] Another such field, E89, near Le Bourgneuf de Bas (Car), lies beside a building platform. Given the quantities of medieval material at some of these dumps (several hundred grams), and bearing in mind the differential distribution of medieval material discussed above (pp. 119–22), it is likely that at least 18 of the larger dumps are on the site of former medieval structures.[10] There are also smaller dumps, with little or no medieval material, and these obviously do not have the same import.[11]

Land-use

The surveys of the *ancien cadastre* provide a complete picture of land-use in the core communes in the 1820s, and a near-complete picture of land-use in the sample transects at the same time or in the 1830s and 1840s (see above, pp. 13–15) (Table 10.6). At that time the broad pattern of land-use in the core was 40% arable, just under 40% *lande*, 10% meadow (of which a significant proportion was water meadow), 6% pasture, and very varying amounts of woodland (including coppice, mature wood and chestnut plantation); the remainder was occupied by settlements and curtilages, and very small patches of unused land. Carentoir had somewhat less *lande* and more wood (including the substantial "forest" of La Bourdonnaye); and Saint-Nicolas rather less arable and more wood and *lande* (Fig. 10.4).

From the middle of the nineteenth century there exist very detailed statistics about agricultural change in the survey area, initially recorded by canton but soon by commune.[12] A fundamental change to the land-use pattern happened over the century from 1850 to 1950: there was a considerable expansion of the land under plough, with consequent reduction of both the *lande* and of water meadow – following, especially, the law of 1857 requiring drainage and utilization of the *landes*. Although

Table 10.6 Principal categories of land-use in the core survey area in the 1820s

	Arable	Lande	Meadow	Pasture	Wood	Settlement	Size
Carentoir	38.4	27.8	11.4	6.7	10.2	4.3	59.02
Tréal	40.5	37.3	9.8	5.5	2.7	2.7	19.28
Saint-Nicolas	28.4	42.5	9.0	4.7	10.8	4.6	12.93
Ruffiac	40.5	34.6	10.6	6.1	4.2	4.0	36.47

Percentage of each commune's surface area by category of land-use, with size of each commune (post-1874 boundaries) in square kilometres

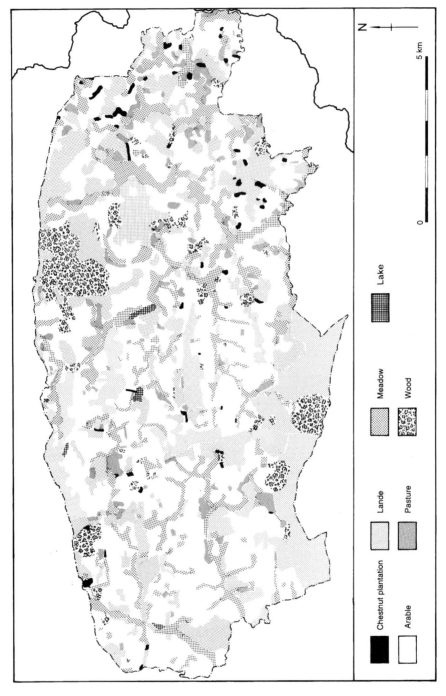

Figure 10.4 *Distribution of main land-use types in the core survey area in the 1820s*

Chestnut plantation

Arable

Lande

Pasture

Meadow

Wood

Lake

N

0   5 km

this change can be demonstrated in many parts of the core survey area, it is most dramatically demonstrated in sections of sample transect M, running due east from southeast Carentoir to the River Vilaine at Malon. Here a proportion of the commune of Bruc – now mostly arable – was a large tract of *lande* in 1831; and a large area of the commune of Pipriac, south of the *bourg*, was wet and water-logged in 1830 – the latter now drained and largely utilized as pasture, with a completely new road system and new settlements established.

Although clearance (*défrichement*) of the *lande* began in the region as a whole in the eighteenth century, in the core survey area it began in earnest in the later nineteenth century, with a decrease of nearly 50% in the cantonal proportions between 1852 and 1901. In Carentoir there was considerable activity in the 1860s, and thereafter, with partition and sale of common land to those with rights in it. By 1881 a slight increase in arable in all four communes begins to show in the records and by 1901 some decrease in the *landes* was being registered in Carentoir and Tréal, with rather more in Ruffiac and Saint-Nicolas. Between 1901 and 1939 most of the remaining *lande* was cleared – at different rates in the different communes – although the decades *c*.1890–1908 and the 1920s indicate the greatest activity.[13] Very broadly, the proportion of meadow and pasture remained constant at 15–20% in the nineteenth and early twentieth centuries; however, that proportion tended to increase everywhere in the 1920s and there was a huge increase in Ruffiac in the 1930s – matched by large increases in the number of pigs and cattle.[14]

The main consequence of the clearance of the *landes* was an increase in arable area, and cultivation was boosted by the use of chemical fertilizers from the early twentieth century (see above, p. 31). The principal trends in use of the arable were: a substantial increase in wheat production, especially in the period 1879-1908; a substantial increase in the potato crop, especially 1879–1923; a substantial drop in rye production 1901–8 and an uneven decline in buckwheat production; a substantial increase in growing animal fodder (*cultures fourragères*), especially between 1929 and 1952; and the disappearance of flax and hemp (the area under these crops was already very low in 1852) during the First World War, although they occur very occasionally thereafter (Table 10.7).

These were not of course the only products of the land. Production of timber (for fuel and building) had been significant since at least the sixteenth century and continued so into the twentieth; honey, wax and cider were still being measured in large quantities in 1929, but declined thereafter; and there had always been some sheep and cattle, the latter more important for traction and manuring than as a food source (Canévet 1992: 84). However, the later nineteenth century saw the beginning of massive

Table 10.7 Principal arable products in the core survey area 1879–1952

	Carentoir						Saint-Nicolas				
	1879	1901	1908	1923	1939	1952	1901	1908	1923	1939	1952
wheat	7	28	53	43	35	28	28	42	45	37	29
rye	13	25	4	3	‹1	1	33	8	3	3	‹1
oats	14	6	12	15	14	15	5	8	14	16	5
buckwheat	63	25	16	14	23	3	28	29	24	13	9
potatoes	2	6	9	14	10	7	3	5	11	19	9
flax/hemp	1	1	1	0	0	‹1	2	2	‹1	‹1	‹1
fodder	0	13	5	3	14	45	0	3	2	9	42

	Tréal						Ruffiac				
	1879	1901	1908	1923	1939	1952	1901	1908	1923	1939	1952
wheat	7	34	36	38	42	23	25	42	34	44	25
rye	40	30	23	‹1	‹1	1	11	5	2	1	‹1
oats	13	3	12	13	12	3	13	19	9	6	12
buckwheat	40	28	23	37	34	9	46	32	29	6	6
potatoes	‹1	1	2	5	1	7	4	2	23	21	9
flax/hemp	‹1	3	2	0	0	0	2	‹1	‹1	0	0
fodder	0	1	1	5	8	55	1	‹1	‹1	22	37

Percentage of arable, by crop.
NOTE: the total of areas under specified crops does not always match the stated totals under crop

growth in cattle-rearing, both for calf and milk/butter production, lasting over the period 1872–1939; a substantial decline in sheep (in 1841 Tréal had had three times as many sheep as cattle); and a large increase in pigs, particularly in Carentoir and Tréal (the increase was six-fold in Carentoir in the generation before the First World War) (Table 10.8).

Table 10.8 Animal product in the core survey area 1879–1952

	Carentoir						Saint-Nicolas			
	1879	1899	1913	1923	1939	1952	1913	1923	1939	1952
cattle	940	3118	3370	3310	3545	3400	527	588	1246	746
sheep	200	1306	540	330	186	105	40	108	27	71
pigs	120	1209	2010	1656	2898	2850	345	362	212	282

	Tréal						Ruffiac			
	1879	1899	1913	1923	1939	1952	1913	1923	1939	1952
cattle	430	1197	1206	990	928	1055	1670	2150	2085	1968
sheep	250	855	430	116	105	160	83	250	100	70
pigs	150	320	379	302	278	262	1284	600	1018	1000

By number of animals reported, including all categories of cattle

From 1950 the core survey area shared in the "agricultural revolution" of Brittany as a whole, as Canévet has demonstrated, with increases in wheat, barley, *cultures fourragères*, and cattle and pigs (the latter an enormous increase); decline in potatoes, rye, buckwheat and oats; and the introduction of maize (1991: 149, 157, 160–1, 177). Late to mechanize (oxen were still used for traction in the 1950s), tractors became widespread in the 1960s and 1970s (Canévet 1992: 322).

All of the core communes did not of course change in the same way or at the same rate: in Carentoir and Ruffiac the first decade of the twentieth century was the period of the largest shift in proportions of cereals grown, for example, Ruffiac then remaining very volatile until 1939. All except Saint-Nicolas saw a drop in cereal production after the Second World War.

Land, product and work

The agricultural changes which can be mapped in detail in the core survey area are consistent with the principal regional trends, although they lack the dramatic increase in production characteristic of northwest Brittany in the later twentieth century: a crisis and pressure period 1830–40, in the context of demographic rise and insufficient yields from the land (Canévet 1992: 84; O'Brien & Keyder 1978: 107, 121); a period of agricultural improvements and increasing production 1850–1900; technical progress and more production for the market 1919–39; and agricultural revolution 1950–90 (Canévet 1992: 85–96).

In 1851 there was still a noticeable proportion of cloth and clothing workers in the core survey area: 7% in Carentoir and 9% in Saint-Nicolas; while, for example, there were only two masons living in Saint-Nicolas, there were 21 *tailleurs d'habits*, 19 workers in linen or hemp cloth and two wool-workers (and two wool-working, eight linen/hemp, seven *tailleurs'*, three shoemaking establishments).[15] The fuller records generated by the census returns for 1872 and 1881 show that agriculture was still overwhelmingly the predominant occupation, much as it had been in the late eighteenth century (above, pp. 207–8). However, Carentoir had a noticeably lower proportion of agricultural workers than the other three communes, just over 70%; and correspondingly it had a much higher industrial component than the others, a component by no means dominated by cloth-working (Table 10.9); it also had more shopkeepers (1%) and more in the professions (2%). It still had a much wider *range* of occupations, as it had had in the eighteenth century. Contrast Tréal, where

Table 10.9 Nineteenth-century occupations in the core survey area

	Carentoir	Ruffiac	Tréal	Saint-Nicolas	Carentoir	Ruffiac	Tréal	Saint-Nicolas
	1872	*1872*	*1872*	*1872*	*1881*	*1881*	*1881*	*1881*
industrial	19	3	7	13	22	12	9	2
agricultural	73	91	88	83	69	83	86	93

Percentage of the population working in industrial and agricultural occupations, by commune

the entire industrial proportion arose from cloth-working (and where 79% of the population in 1866 could neither read nor write).

The numbers working in cloth and clothing declined across the later nineteenth century. By 1911 less than 1.5% of Tréal's population worked in cloth/clothing and 85% were working in agriculture (96% in Saint-Nicolas). By 1926 cloth/clothes working had declined to 0.8% in Carentoir (of which only four people were weavers), though the proportion remained 1.5% in Tréal (where only two were weavers).[16]

Cloth-working, once so characteristic of the rural work pattern, petered out, and the character of rural employment changed as textile workers went into agriculture. The result was the continuation, and even increase in the number, of very small farms: 54% of farms in Carentoir were no bigger than 1–10 ha in 1929 and only two were greater than 50 ha; 59% were cultivated by the proprietor (and family) alone; in Ruffiac a quarter were as large as 10–20 ha, a larger proportion than elsewhere, but 64% were cultivated by the proprietor (and over 70% in Saint-Nicolas and Tréal).

These were major social changes. In the century and a half after the Revolution there emerged a body of very small-scale peasant proprietors. Population, on the whole, continued to increase for a century, so that food supply was pressured and even less of the land's product was available for sale. As the textile industry collapsed, more and more of that population became dependent on working the land for its basic subsistence. Though increasing agricultural production in the area was evident by 1900 and the population began to decline before the disasters of the First World War, producing food for survival continued to occupy the labour effort of an overwhelming majority of the population. Most people were working small plots, generating little surplus for investment in agricultural improvement or in new industrial approaches. It was not until after the Second World War that nineteenth-century pressures and patterns were reversed. By the mid twentieth century there were considerably fewer people living in the survey area but much more of the land surface was cultivated; production had increased significantly and productivity enormously. From the 1950s the land was again managed for production for distribution, as it had been in the entrepreneurial days of the sixteenth and seventeenth centuries; some new industries developed (see above, pp. 53–4); and some people began to go outside their home communes to work on a daily basis.

Notes

1. In sample transects, Transects R and M broadly share the characteristics of peaking in the late nineteenth century, with a rapid drop in the twentieth – a drop more marked in Transect R and in western than in eastern M. Transect P was influenced by the steady rise of the small town of Malestroit and did not drop. Transect N is quite different: population peaked in early to mid-nineteenth century and declined thereafter to very low levels in the late twentieth century (e.g. 22 inhab/km^2 in Campénéac in 1975).

2. From the late eighteenth century there is a tendency for more marriage partners to come from outside: for example, in Tréal most came from within the parish until the 1780s but in the following 20 years they came from surrounding parishes like Réminiac or Ruffiac, as well as from farther afield (Sérent, Saint-Martin, Malestroit, Peillac, Saint-Congard and even once from Elven); two noble husbands came (ultimately) from Turin (via Vannes) and Paris.

3. AD Ille-et-Vilaine C2370, C4894. AD Morbihan 3ES200/10, 4W11783, 4W11761; cf. 4W11563.

4. AD Morbihan 6M18, 6M21, 6M71, 6M252, 6M282, 6M305. Saint-Nicolas does not show the same trend: 13% in 1881 *and* 1931, although there was clearly plenty of late nineteenth-century building in and around the *bourg*.

5. Taking into consideration only those buildings which are straightforwardly and uncontroversially assignable to a datable type.

6. AD Morbihan 7M235, 7M239, 7M238.

7. AD Ille-et-Vilaine 7M138; AD Morbihan 6M964. Cf. Dieudonné 1803: 398, for the value of street soil for improving *terres froides et humides*.

8. In the sample transects: 1 in P, 4 in N, 5 in R, 16 in M, in comparable locations to the core (e.g. M61 (La Guibourdaie), M387 (Pipriac), N201 (Château de la Touraille)).

9. B293 (Quilvain, S-N), A450 (La Nouette, near La Ruée, Ruff), H50 (Les Aulnais, Ruff) and K450 (south of Béculeu, Ruff).

10. L107 and E89, cited above, are such assemblages; D241, on the eastern outskirts of Carentoir, is another; cf. B313, near Le Doucet, east of Le Vieux Bourg (Tr), and E3, west of Marsac in northeast Carentoir.

11. For example, F178 (Bourboussé, Car), H105 (Villeneuve) and H111 (Le Carrefour, both S-N).

12. Despite the mass of data, comparison between communes and the identification of major trends is not without its problems: different questions were asked at different enquiries and the quality of the local replies is sometimes extremely suspect; there are obvious errors of notation and calculation: the quality depends very much on the individual practice of the local mayor or his secretary.

13. AD Morbihan $_2$O33/6; 6M964, 6M971, 6M980, 6M989, 6M1007, 6M1009, 6M1016, 6M1021, 6M1024, 6M1025, 6M1041, 7M235, 7M238, 7M239, 3P974, 2W10478.

14. There appears to have been just as dramatic a shift to arable in Ruffiac in 1901–8 and the figures look somewhat questionable, although of course both changes are possible; some adjustment of the figures seems to have been made in 1929 and hence the land-use shift in the 1930s may have been of lower magnitude than the recorded data suggest.

15. In what follows the figures are not strictly comparable, since the different reporters from each commune clearly responded to the (nationally formulated) questions in different ways; however, there is a mass of data and broad trends can be identified. AD Morbihan 6M11, 6M14.

16. AD Morbihan 6M18, 6M21, 6M71, 6M282, 6M305.

The *Longue Durée*

Methods

Our initial questions about *how* to investigate changes in land-use and settlement over a long period were answered as the East Brittany Survey developed: our methods, undeniably, evolved. With the benefit of hindsight, we would argue that what we ultimately did was – by and large – the right way to do it. We would certainly strongly recommend our starting-point: a detailed, localizable survey of the pre- (or early) industrial landscape, such as the Napoleonic *cadastre* for France or tithe and enclosure maps for England. This kind of source is particularly appropriate for investigating a much-used, as opposed to an uncultivated, landscape. However, archive work, field programme and buildings survey were all complementary and we could not have grasped thirteenth- to twentieth-century trends without all three.

Our methods got results, often unexpected results, but this study makes no claim to be comprehensive or definitive. There is no denying the fact that multi-disciplinary work needs a high level of resourcing if results are to flow; difficult choices therefore have to be made about the most productive of the many possible avenues to explore and some have to be left on one side (see further Davies and Astill 1994: 264–9); one can always do more. The desirable necessarily has to be balanced against the affordable.

Doing interdisciplinary work is exciting and intellectually stimulating, but it is difficult to do well and difficult to cross disciplines in a meaningful way. The historian, the archaeologist, the geographer all work within well-established codes that are rigorous and give meaning to any particular set of results that they derive; but the codes often do not overlap very much. Archaeology, geology, history, geography, architectural history all furnish interesting and valuable data within their own frameworks; but they cannot necessarily be put together. However, with respect to the questions posed at the start of this study, disciplines can be fruitfully crossed if data can be precisely localized, if there is sufficient material to establish spatial relationships, and if the spatial relationship can be economically expressed. Being able to localize – precisely – is critical: when a text tells us that there was a field in Carentoir that was arable in 1543, or that there was a place called Ran Riantcar in Ruffiac in 864, neither reference can tell us very much about land-use or settlement if we cannot place it on the ground. We can work with the seventeenth-century dated building that features on the cadastral map; or the Roman villa that lies on a road mentioned in the ninth century; or the meadow, located in sixteenth-century texts by reference to topographic features, that is also the site of a twelfth-century sub-surface structure; or the fourteenth-century pottery scatter on a fourteenth-century arable field located (textually) by reference to roads. Once we recognize the limitations, and pay attention – rigorously, precisely and systematically – to the areas where dialogue between disciplines is possible, we become able to derive useful results and address the tricky question of the changing use of space over time.

Some may say (indeed, many *have* said) that we cannot expect to gather anything more from archaeology than our texts already tell us about the thirteenth century and after; but in practice we can considerably enhance our understanding of the processes of rural change and development through archaeological fieldwork; and the sheer volume of the data in itself contributes an additional dimension (cf. Davies and Astill 1994: 274). The fieldwalking at wide (50m) intervals with which we began, though a crude instrument, enabled us to cover a wide enough area to achieve an overview of the landscape; it also yielded a remarkable amount of spatial information, especially of the location, size and shape of the changing arable. It was also a very practical tool for locating settlements; indeed, many of the "sites" identified in these very early stages of the fieldwalking programme turned out to be the location of documented fifteenth-century or other settlements; fields like A116, H132 and B409 stood out as archaeologically remarkable long before we unravelled their relationship to unusually powerful *seigneuries* in the former cases and to the near-by Roman villa in the latter. Fieldwork contributed results that could not have been derived from other techniques: plotting the arable of the late middle ages; demonstrating that refuse disposal and manuring practice changed in the seventeenth/eighteenth centuries and that collapsed medieval settlements became dumps in the modern period; showing how small were the property interests of the average fourteenth-century noble and how limited the range of pottery available to him (though not the quantity); and, especially, showing that rapidly increasing population did not lead to much increase in the area under cultivation.

There are also warnings from this study about the conclusions one might reasonably draw from archaeological or textual material alone, whatever the period: without texts, one might have thought that accumulations of seventeenth- and eighteenth-century pottery indicated settlement sites; without texts one might have thought that population declined in the nineteenth (as also in the ninth) century; without standing buildings one might have thought that increasing population meant new settlements rather than more crowded housing.

The core in regional context

Notwithstanding the survey area's location, notionally open to influences from the east and south, this project has demonstrated that – for much of its history in the last 2,000 years – the area was little subject to outside influence. It was not, of course, isolated in any real sense: it was not very far from the regional capital of Rennes, nor from the sea, nor from the great port of Nantes (70 km) and the lesser port of Vannes (35 km) (one or two days' walk) but most people did not go in for travelling, whether frequently or exceptionally. The core survey area is only 20 km from the major (navigable) route of the River Vilaine, but its basic material culture was overwhelmingly, and often exclusively, local for about 1,800 of the last 2,500 years.

Pottery is a sensitive indicator of the to-and-fro of exchange mechanisms, including the market: from the seventeenth century onwards, a wide range of foreign wares came into the area, as they had done in the first and second centuries AD; but both immediately before and for a long time after the Roman interlude they did not do so. Though social mobility was a fact of life, even in the seventeenth to nineteenth centuries spatial mobility was exceptionally limited for most individuals: some women certainly went to neighbouring parishes to find partners, but overwhelmingly people lived and worked if not in the hamlet in which they were born, then in a neighbouring hamlet. This may seem surprising: given the establishment of the Roman road system in the first century AD, there ought to have been means enough for people to move about with relative ease; but the very fact that the Roman east–west road along the northern boundary of the core fell out of use is enough to remind us that those roads did not continue to be walked.

The bulk of our detailed work has related to the core survey area but we have been careful to look at its relationship to the region beyond, using the sample transects, P to the west (to Malestroit and the River Oust), N to the northwest, R to the northeast and M to the east (to the River Vilaine) (Fig. 11.1).

The broad long-term pattern of change in the core is shared by the sample transects. However, there are differences, sometimes between core and sample transects, sometimes between sample transects, and sometimes within the core.

Firstly, the core lies on the eastern edge of the Morbihan, and beyond the northeast edge of the Vannetais. As such, it sometimes falls between cultural zones, whereas at other times it falls within a wider cultural zone and at others – especially in the middle ages – it was in effect a mini-culture zone in itself. Its relationship to culture zones in northwest France is not a constant.

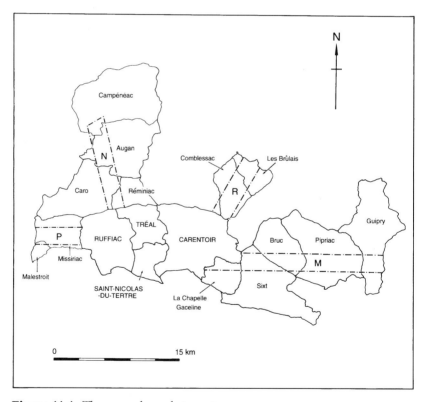

Figure 11.1 *The core and sample transects*

Secondly, it is striking that Transect N often exhibits different characteristics from the rest of the survey area: its stone is harder; it is much higher and steeper (71% of fields walked were above 70m, compared with 20% in the core); and there is, and has been, less arable and more pastoral farming (nearly three times as much meadow and pasture in the early nineteenth century as in the core). It also has marked cultural differences: concentrations of megalithic graves; more surface pottery of the Iron Age; a higher proportion of servile peasants in the early middle ages; much less pottery, and by implication fewer people, in the seventeenth to nineteenth centuries; and a population that declined more rapidly in the twentieth century (and began its decline much earlier than near-by areas). For all these reasons it belongs far more to central inland Brittany and to Porhoet than to the Vannetais or the *pays de Redon*.

Thirdly, in many respects the core became differentiated from the surrounding area in the later middle ages: it had more nobles, more settlements, more pottery; it was a highly productive zone by the sixteenth century, generating a significant surplus – thereby supporting an exceptional density of minor nobles and throwing up several great *seigneuries*, like that of Redon at Prieuré, as well as Coëtion, La Haute Boixière and Peccadeuc. It was far from being a backwater at this time; just as it had been far from being a backwater in the first and second centuries.

Fourthly, east–west distinctions become apparent within the survey area in the seventeenth century, marked by distribution and supply differences in imported pottery. Much more land was cultivated in Transect R to the northeast than in the medieval period and vastly more material was distributed on the surface of fields in eastern Carentoir. This is the time when eastern Carentoir became differentiated from western parts of the core, as well as from sample transects – particularly in respect of its denser population (focussing in the *bourg* and in Le Temple, La Chapelle Gaceline and La Gacilly, as well as the surrounding large hamlets); its wider range of occupations and its greater share of work in cloth and clothing industries (present elsewhere but at approximately half the level) also made it distinctive.

Quite apart from the latter development, the core was never itself an economic unity – a point reflected by its location in two different cantons. Even today, there is no direct road from Carentoir *bourg* to Ruffiac *bourg*, and travel by vehicle from east to west across the four communes is surprisingly time-consuming. Carentoir looks north–south rather than east–west; Ruffiac looks west to Malestroit and the River Oust. When the *curé* of Ruffiac died in June 1782, priests of Saint-Nicolas, Caro, Saint-Congard, La Bourdonnaye, Malestroit and Missiriac attended the funeral – but not the priests of Tréal and Carentoir. So too the uneven spread of epidemics in the seventeenth and eighteenth centuries: they would often capture a small zone without taking in the whole.

Long-term trends

Population

There is good reason to think that the population of the core survey area trebled over the 1,000 years from AD 900 to 1900, despite a 40% drop in the early fifteenth century; a particularly substantial rise marked the sixteenth, seventeenth and eighteenth centuries and a very rapid decline the twentieth.

There is no evidence to suggest any major immigration of people from Britain into the area in the fifth, sixth and seventh centuries, although it is possible that some limited numbers of incoming British settled there. There is therefore nothing to suggest demographic upheaval in the post-Roman period.

Although the survey area was sometimes at the centre of political action and was quickly involved in the complex of events that comprised the French Revolution, little effect of any political cataclysm can be detected on the rural farming population at any point before the twentieth century: whether the end of the Roman Empire, or Frankish raiding in the sixth century, or Viking ravaging in the ninth and tenth, or English campaigning in the fourteenth, or the Wars of the League in the late sixteenth, we see no trace of destruction of the population nor devastation of their lands and homes. It is reasonable to expect that goods were sometimes looted, stores commandeered, crops ruined, buildings damaged (the armies of the League and of the Royalists marched by western Ruffiac to Malestroit, after all);[1] but none of this impacted to the level of whole-sale dislocation nor caused the population to leave in large numbers until the disasters of the First World War. Crisis mortalities, however, recurred at least through the fourteenth, seventeenth and eighteenth centuries, and quite possibly in the intervening 200 years. The great pandemics came to an end in the late seventeenth century and by the late eighteenth many more people were cured than died from the recurrent epidemics; however, the population remained vulnerable to variation in the food supply throughout the nineteenth century and the threat of starvation continued to hover in the background.

These are issues of fundamental social importance. What conditioned population levels had far more to do with famine and disease than with politics, and the population shows signs of being seriously pressured in the late eighteenth century (as it may well also have been in the fourteenth).

The road to greater agricultural productivity was long and slow; it was in train by the mid nineteenth century but farms were tiny and did not generate sufficient surplus to invest in changing techniques; it was well into the twentieth century before yield per hectare and yield per inhabitant showed any substantial increase – a development closely associated with a massive increase in first cattle and then pig production (Canévet 1992: 12–13, 86–7).

In the nineteenth and twentieth centuries redistribution of population within the survey area began to be noticeable: the *bourgs* and the towns of Malestroit and La Gacilly grew as hamlets shrank. Outside the nucleations increasing demographic homogeneity marked what had been a rather more varied countryside 200 years before. Outward migration is also a major feature of the 50 years or so from 1914 – to the Wars, to Paris, to the larger Breton towns beyond the survey area. The shift of population from countryside to town – which characterizes English history, for example, from the fifteenth century and that of some regions of France from the eighteenth – came late in this area. As a result of the movement, however, overall population densities dropped to consistently low levels.

Landscape

Given that most of the natural woodland of the survey area had been cleared by the Iron Age, that is before the start of the two millennia that are the focus of attention of this book, the outstanding change that has occurred in the landscape in historic time has been the permanent cultivation of the *landes* in the later nineteenth and twentieth centuries. Since the *landes* accounted for some 40% of the land surface before the change, this can only have had a dramatic visual, as well as a major economic, impact during the last 130 years – even allowing that some parts of the *landes* were intermittently cultivated for centuries before.

There were also, of course, some other striking but less comprehensive changes. The most significant of these focus in the late medieval and early modern period and they are mirrored in the excavations through the lynchets T1 and T35 (see above, pp. 21, 22). They include the taking into cultivation of small-scale "blank" zones, including some that were lightly wooded, in the fifteenth and sixteenth centuries, filling out the farmed area; the creation of field boundaries, particularly in the fifteenth to seventeenth centuries, and subsequently their systematic removal in the 1970s; and the creation of château landscapes in the late sixteenth and seventeenth centuries, together with the deliberate planting of woodland, for commercial exploitation. All of these changes would have had a very clear visual impact, but they affected only a limited proportion of the total landscape. (Château landscapes accounted for about a tenth of the land surface of the core survey area.)

Notwithstanding these changes, the broad pattern of land-use changed relatively little from the late Roman period until the later nineteenth and twentieth centuries, although the long-term trend of the 700 years before 1900 was the slow increase in the area under arable cultivation. Despite some fluctuations there are very long continuities here.

If land-use was dominated by long continuities, there were nevertheless major shifts in the way the arable was managed, both in respect of changing crops and of changing field shape. The best guide to the sweep of long-term crop change comes from the palynological evidence: although there are no dated pollen cores from the survey area, the nearest suggest that the principal changes of crop came in the late Roman period, with the drop in cereals; in the central middle ages, with the rise in cereal proportions and the introduction of buckwheat; in the late middle ages with the huge increase in cereals, buckwheat and hemp (remembering also the introduction of chestnuts in the early modern period); and in the nineteenth century with the further huge increase in buckwheat (Marguerie 1992; Visset 1994; see above, pp. 114, n.13, 131).

Although field boundaries were systematically removed in the 1970s, there were plenty of open, subdivided fields in the 1820s: by no means all of this landscape was enclosed before *remembrement*. Our evidence suggests that there were very few field boundaries in the early middle ages and that the principal period of enclosure was in the sixteenth and seventeenth centuries, under noble initiative. It must be likely that subdivision of the unenclosed arable near non-noble settlements increased as population levels rose; the many references to *tenues* in fifteenth-century texts, and perhaps also the distribution of Fabric 1 near the *bourgs*, imply that this was happening already in the thirteenth and fourteenth centuries – that is, before the principal period of enclosure. There is no need to suppose that the existence of open fields implies common management, as in the classic midland English "open field system", whether in the ninth century or the nineteenth; the subdivided fields of southwest England are likely to provide a closer analogy (cf. Fox 1975).

Settlement

Throughout the last millennium and more, the settlement pattern of core and sample transects was essentially dispersed – as it still is. There was a scatter of larger and smaller settlements across the whole area: very few spots are more than 500m from some kind of settlement nowadays (only 44 of the fields walked – just under 2% – lay farther away) and not many more in the early nineteenth century (100 of the fields walked, 4.5%); this is no more than five to ten minutes' walk on a track or path or level ground. At the broadest level, therefore, there has been little change in settlement character since the Roman period.

We have no means of commenting on the overall Roman settlement pattern, but we can note that there were Roman villas scattered across the area, and – to judge from aerial photography – a scatter of other settlements beyond them. Even Roman villa sites (like medieval settlements) were associated with a cluster of surrounding farmland: this must indicate dispersed settlement at that time, for fields were near the residences of those who farmed them. There is therefore every reason to suppose settlement character was dispersed in the Roman period too.

Despite dispersal, there always seems to have been some element of nucleation within the scatter of hamlets. The crowding of structures and features at Le Mur, at the northeastern edge of Carentoir, together with the scatter of villas in its neighbourhood, looks very like a Roman-period nucleation – particularly given its position in relation to two major arterial roads (see Fig. 4.10). By the ninth century, both *plebes* of Ruffiac and Carentoir had village centres with churches and dwellings clustered round them; they were the forerunners of the later medieval and present *bourgs* of Ruffiac and Carentoir. New, though small, *bourgs* were established – for varying reasons – in the central middle ages at Tréal, La Gacilly, Saint-Nicolas and Le Temple; both Tréal and Saint-Nicolas had associated churches; La Gacilly grew up beside its castle and Le Temple beside the Templars' Commandery. None of the six *bourgs* was large: Carentoir, the largest, had fewer than 60 households by the late fourteenth century. We know little to nothing about the processes involved in their establishment – except to observe the presence of a major structure, whether secular or religious, at each site.

As we have noted, by the late nineteenth century there was some tendency for settlement to drain from the hamlets towards the *bourgs*. This was never of sufficient volume to contribute to real urbanization, until the large increase in La Gacilly's population in the generation after 1960, in the clear context of increased employment opportunities. Migration into Carentoir in the eighteenth century, however, seems to have related to a wider range of employment opportunities and to have contributed to an urbanizing trend; however, it was a trend that did not develop in the post-Revolutionary period, particularly as employment opportunities did not continue to develop and, indeed, were sagging by the late nineteenth century. Overall, during the last two millennia the level both of nucleation and of urbanization has been exceptionally low throughout the survey area.

There may not have been much change in settlement character, but there were certainly plenty of changes in settlement location in the area, especially before 1500. Small-scale settlement shift may already have been a feature of the Iron Age, was undoubtedly a feature between tenth and sixteenth centuries, and is implied between Roman and early medieval periods. Settlement shift of this kind was often simply to a near-by convenient location, not much more than 100m or 200m away; sometimes, however, settlement shift seems to have been determined by environmental conditions: tenth-century sites, for example, tend to be on higher land, and a fifth have no association with land-use of the central middle ages – just as there is little central medieval activity round the key Roman site of Le Mur.

Change in the number of settlements was a feature of the period from the thirteenth to the sixteenth century: there was about a 25% increase in the overall number, despite the disappearance of about a third of the older settlements. A high proportion of those with a pre-sixteenth-century background shifted slightly (within 100m or so) as they were rebuilt in stone. While some medieval house sites became dumps, the same is not true of sixteenth- or seventeenth-century houses: it is a sixteenth- and seventeenth-century pattern that we see reflected in today's settlement distribution and it was building in stone that fixed that pattern. Many of the new settlements of the sixteenth century had noble associations (in fact, in that period, over 50% of all settlements had noble residents or nobles' *métayers*) and noble enterprise was therefore in many ways responsible for establishing the pattern.

Despite the large population rise of the seventeenth and eighteenth centuries there were no further major changes in settlement distribution and pattern. *Rangées* were expanded and long-houses were converted, but the rise did not mean the establishment of new settlements – apart from the odd new *métairie*. The growing population was accommodated in extensions to existing structures, and by doubling up of households, rather than by building afresh. However, new building on the periphery of the *bourgs* is a particular feature of the twentieth century, preceded by the establishment of a new *bourg* for Tréal in the late nineteenth.

Building is difficult to characterize before the sixteenth century. Roman villa owners were using tile and hard, quarried stone in the first and second centuries AD; nobles were using miscellaneous local stone in the twelfth century, a building tradition that was to continue until the twentieth century. This tradition used materials gathered from the immediate locality – whether this was soft Brioverian shale dug out of a neighbouring field or Roman rubble gathered from a near-by villa site; it did not involve use of commercially quarried materials until the nineteenth and twentieth centuries (Davies and Astill 1994: 237–41). The likelihood must be that people used timber-based structures in the intervening early middle ages. Whether the change to stone was gradual or rapid we cannot know; as population increased, and wood became a marketable commodity, readily available local stone must have become more and more significant. Some noble buildings were clearly substantial by the fourteenth century (Davies and Astill 1994: 143–51), but no building of this period has survived into modern times; while the seigneurial structure at Couedic (Tr) has a fifteenth-century origin (Figs. 11.2, 11.3), it was the sixteenth century before most noble houses became durable. Slate seems to have been used in limited quantities for roofing as well as for structural walls and features from the twelfth/thirteenth centuries, but at that date mostly consisted of the locally occurring pink siltstone, k-o_1; large-scale introduction of the harder, black siltstone, o_{3-4}, still local but from slightly farther afield, was a sixteenth-century development (Davies 1993: 350): it was being used for the roofs of many *rangées* in the early sixteenth century.

Landscape, land-use and settlement

We cannot ignore the fact that, during the two millennia, there is one phase for which we have hardly any local information: $c.300$–$c.770$. This is a long time and it is particularly frustrating that there is no direct textual or material evidence for any kind of development or continuity. What we can say with confidence is that firstly, there is a marked degree of continuity of Romano-Gallic names in the area; and secondly, when detailed texts begin, $c.800$, it is perfectly clear that the area was heavily occupied and worked and that a number of then-current social and political institutions had changed since their initial establishment;[2] the society of $c.800$ was a long-settled and mature one. Even allowing for that maturity, it remains possible that there was some kind of dislocation in the late or immediate post-Roman period. In support of the argument for major dislocation of settlement and population is the fact that Roman villas of the third century concentrate in the north and east of the core, and relate to the focal settlement of Le Mur; by the ninth century, there were *bourgs* in the neighbourhood of present-day Ruffiac and Carentoir; and ultimately the Roman name of Le Mur (Marsac) was transferred to a hamlet in north Carentoir. Further, the Roman building tradition was not maintained beyond the Roman period, and some roads fell out of use (Davies and Astill 1994: 264). Against the argument for significant dislocation, on the other hand, although obviously there was *some* change, is the argument that the Roman villa economy may well only have involved a small proportion of the population. Many of the many settlements of the Iron

Figure 11.2 *The fifteenth-century house at Couedic (Tréal), from the east; photo: Gwyn Meirion-Jones*

Figure 11.3 *Couedic: the late sixteenth-century solar roof; photo: Gwyn Meirion-Jones*

Age must have continued into the Roman period, and beyond as well, with most people working the land in a small-scale, self-sufficient way, perhaps paying some tax (in kind) if and when the local *civitas* officials reached them: aerial photography increasingly reveals more small-scale enclosures across the core and its surround, revealing the presence of inhabitants who cannot have been villa owners.

Many villa sites cluster in the northeast corner of the core survey area, relating very directly to the road system and its junctions. Even if we assume that the identifiable 60-70 ha arable per villa is a minimum and double it, and then double it again to allow for other types of land-use, Roman villa farming can have affected only a third of the core survey area: the majority of the land was not touched by this particular form of exploitation. Given that Roman material peters out in the third century, it seems most probable that villa farming reflects the activities of a top level of agricultural entrepreneurs, who took off elsewhere when the political and currency problems of the third century began to be felt. Hence, it is unlikely that the late and post-Roman period saw any large-scale disruption of peasant economies.

Looking at the relationship between land-use and settlement over the longer term, at all periods for which we have evidence before the twentieth century, arable was located close to settlements, the majority within 200m: people walked a very short distance from their homes to their main arable. Although lands farther from settlements began to be regularly cultivated in the eighteenth century, it was the twentieth before people went a significant distance from home to daily work – be it agricultural, industrial or services. Industrial production was also home based, in an agricultural environment, in the seventeenth, eighteenth and nineteenth centuries. Overwhelmingly, then, the relationship between workplace and residence was very close; only in the twentieth century did it change.

It is notable that some relationships were different in the Roman period: a good number of villa sites were located in relation to the communications system, rather than to good arable land – indeed, while the "low status" sites were often near the latter, some villas lay beside the poorest soils.

Lastly, and most significantly, it is very striking that – although periods of well-documented demographic rise tended to see some extension of the arable, the percentage increase was small (much smaller than the percentage increase in population); nor did demographic rise provoke any immediate changes in approach to land-use. Increasing numbers of mouths to feed do not seem in themselves to have stimulated much agricultural change.

Rapid changes

Overall, there have been five periods of rapid change for the region during the last 2,000 years. These five are: the creation of a road network, importation of goods, quarrying, fine building and production for the market of the early Roman period; the collapse of that building tradition and of the associated economic exchange patterns, import and export, in the central to late Roman period; the establishment, with the foundation of the monastery of Redon, of a very large-scale proprietor with significant proprietary interests in the area, in the ninth century; the creation of a new nobility, with new ideas about comfortable living and about production for the market, in the late fifteenth and early sixteenth centuries; and the arrival of the modern road network, production for distribution and significant out-migration of the twentieth century. The major phases of post-Roman change are, especially, 850–70, 1480–1535, and 1946–60 – quite short periods. As argued above, it is more than possible that the Roman-period changes – the arrival and disappearance of Roman material culture – only directly affected a fraction of the local population: after all, more Iron-Age than Roman pottery was recovered in the course of the survey (despite the difficulties of detecting it on the surface) and everything suggests that the area had a thriving late Iron-Age culture.

It is perfectly clear that the impulses for rapid change were neither the rise and fall of crude demographic levels nor the impact of high politics (although, of course, the long demographic rise of the seventeenth and eighteenth centuries ultimately had a bearing on the fact of agricultural change in the later nineteenth and twentieth centuries). The periods of greatest change in land-use and settlement do not relate directly to the periods of greatest change in population levels. On the contrary, the periods of change do relate very distinctively to phases of short-term external influence and impact: Romans coming in from outside in the first centuries BC/AD; a few nobles coming in from outside in the late fifteenth and early sixteenth centuries; the road system entering into the hamlets in the mid twentieth century. Not hordes of people – in fact very small numbers – but new ideas rather than political cataclysm or demographic swing.

★★★★★★★

The unchanging landscape we thought we saw in 1978 was a complex of three very recent elements: the relict settlement landscape of the generation before the First World War, when population was at its highest and employment largely agricultural; an agricultural landscape of post-1930, after the *landes* had been cleared; and a communications system of 1950 and later. In response, therefore, to our original questions we must say: of course the farming communities of these communes are not timeless – far from it; of course there has been change in land-use and in settlement, and in their relationship, in the past – in several phases. But there are also some extremely long continuities.

Notes

1. Perhaps the mid-fourteenth-century hoard of 160 coins found in Ruffiac is a reflection of fears of, for example, the English on the loose (Duplessy 1981).
2. For example, the institution of the machtiern was clearly both ancient by the early ninth century and changed from its original form (see above, p. 93). Similarly, local recording practice must have had a sixth- or seventh-century origin; see Davies 1988: 175–83, 191–2, 134–8, and above, p. 112.

Bibliography

Addison, P. J. 1983. A study of the settlement names of four communes in East Brittany. Unpublished BA Archaeology dissertation (University College London).

Astill, G. G. & W. Davies 1984. Prospections dans l'est de la Bretagne, Résultats de la campagne de mars–avril 1984. *Les Dossiers du centre régional archéologique d'Alet* **12**, pp. 49–59.

Astill, G. G. & W. Davies 1985. Prospections archéologiques dans l'est de la Bretagne, Prospections de terrain en mars–avril 1985. *Les Dossiers du centre régional archéologique d'Alet* **13**, pp. 85–98.

Atlas 1990. Collectif, *Atlas de Bretagne* (Morlaix: Institut Culturel de Bretagne, Skol Vreizh, INSEE).

Bernier, G. 1982. *Les Chrétientés bretonnes continentales depuis les origines jusqu'au IXe siècle. Les Dossiers du centre régional archéologique d'Alet* E (Rennes: Université de Rennes Sciences).

Blayo, Y. & L. Henry 1975. La population de la France 1740 à 1860. *Population* **30**, pp. 71–122.

Blin, O. 1993. La *villa* gallo-romaine de La Démardais à Porcaro (Morbihan); rapport de fouilles. Unpublished report for SRAB.

Bois, G. 1992. *The transformation of the year 1000. The village of Lournand from antiquity to feudalism*, trans. J. Birrell (Manchester and New York: Manchester University Press) (French publication 1989).

Bonnassie, P. 1991. *From slavery to feudalism in southwestern Europe*, trans. J. Birrell (Cambridge: Cambridge University Press) (French papers 1968–90).

Brand'Honneur, M. 1990. *Les mottes médiévales d'Ille-et-Vilaine* (Rennes: Institut culturel de Bretagne, Centre régional archéologique d'Alet).

Brett, C. (ed.) 1989. *The monks of Redon. Gesta Sanctorum Rotonensium and Vita Conuuoionis* (Woodbridge: The Boydell Press).

Briard, J. 1989. *Mégalithes de haute Bretagne. Les Monuments de la forêt de Brocéliande et du Ploërmelais: structures, mobilier et environnement. Documents d'archéologie Française* 23 (Paris: Maison des Sciences de l'Homme).

Briard, J., M. Gautier, G. Leroux 1995. *Les Mégalithes et les tumulus de Saint-Just, Ille-et-Vilaine. Documents Préhistoriques* 8 (Paris: Ministère de l'éducation nationale, Comité des travaux historiques et scientifiques).

Brunskill, R. W. 1965–6. A systematic procedure for recording English vernacular architecture. *Transactions of the Ancient Monuments Society* **13**.

Brunskill, R. W. 1976. Recording the buildings of the farmstead. *Transactions of the Ancient Monuments Society* **21**.

Canévet, C. 1991. *40 ans de révolution agricole en Bretagne (1950–1990)* (Rennes: Institut culturel de Bretagne).

Canévet, C. 1992. *Le modèle agricole breton. Histoire et géographie d'une révolution agro-alimentaire* (Rennes: Presses universitaires de Rennes).

Carte géologique de la France à 1/50,000: Feuille X-20, Malestroit 1981. (Orléans: Ministère de l'Industrie, Bureau de Recherches Géologiques et Minières, Service Géologique National).

Charbonneau, H., B. Desjardins et al., 1987. *Naissance d'une population. Les Français établis au Canada au XVIIe siècle* (Paris: Institut national d'études démographiques and Presse de l'université de Montréal).

Charpy, J., B. Isbled, M. Maréchal, M. Mauger, C. Reydellet 1994. *Guide des archives d'Ille-et-Vilaine, vol. 1, Archives départementales 1ère partie, Archives hospitalières* (Rennes: Archives départementales d'Ille-et-Vilaine).

Chédeville, A. & H. Guillotel 1984. *La Bretagne des saints et des rois, V^e–Xe siècle* (Rennes: Éditions Ouest-France).

Chédeville, A. & N.-Y. Tonnerre 1987. *La Bretagne féodale, XIe–XIIIe siècle* (Rennes: Éditions Ouest-France).

Clout, H. D. 1973–4. Reclamation of wasteland in Brittany 1750-1900. *Bulletin de la société royale de géographie d'Anvers* **84**, pp. 29–60.

Clout, H. D. & A. D. M. Phillips 1972. Fertilisants minéraux en France au XIXe siècle. *Études rurales* **45**, pp. 9–28.

Collins, J. B. 1994. *Classes, estates and order in early modern Brittany* (Cambridge: Cambridge University Press).

Croix, A. 1981. *La Bretagne aux 16e et 17e siècles. La vie – la mort – la foi* [2 vols] (Paris: Maloine).

Croix, A. 1993. *L'âge d'or de la Bretagne 1532–1675* (Rennes: Éditions Ouest-France).

Cunliffe, B. & P. Galliou 1995. Le Yaudet, Ploulec'h, Côtes d'Armor, Brittany. An interim report on the excavations of 1991–4. *The Antiquaries Journal* **75**, pp. 43–70.

Daire, M.-Y., M. Gautier, L. Langouet 1991. Le substrat rural protohistorique en Haute-Bretagne. See Langouet, *Terroirs, territoires et campagnes antiques*, pp. 165–82,.

Darley, J. 1985. Human settlement and land-use history: a study of soil pollen from the Morbihan, east Brittany. Unpublished BA Geography project (University College London).

Davies, W. 1985. Priests and rural communities in east Brittany in the ninth century. *Études celtiques* **20**, pp. 177–97.

Davies, W. 1988. *Small worlds. The village community in early medieval Brittany* (London: Duckworth).

Davies, W.1990a. The composition of the Redon cartulary. *Francia* **17**, pp. 69–90.

Davies, W. 1990b. Field survey and the problem of surface scatters of building material: some east Breton evidence. *Revue archéologique de l'Ouest,* Supplément no. 2, pp. 321–32.

Davies, W. 1993. Surface scatters of building stone: enhancing field survey work. *Oxford Journal of Archaeology* **12**, pp. 337–53.

Davies, W. 1996. On servile status in the early middle ages. In *Serfdom and slavery: studies in legal bondage*, M. L. Bush (ed.) (Harlow: Longman), pp. 225–46.

Davies, W. & G. G. Astill 1994. *The East Brittany Survey. Fieldwork and field data* (Aldershot: Scolar Press).

de Clercq, C. (ed.) 1963. *Concilia Galliae, A.511–A.695. Corpus Christianorum Series Latina* 148a (Turnhout: Brepols).

de Courson, A. 1863. *Le Cartulaire de Redon* (Paris: Imprimerie national).

de Laigue, Comte R. 1902. *La noblesse bretonne aux XVe et XVIe siècles, Réformations et montres* [3 vols] (Rennes: Plihon & Hommay).

Dieudonné c.1803. *Statistique du département du Nord* (Brionne: Monfort).

Dobson, M. 1997. *Contours of death and disease in early modern England* (Cambridge: Cambridge University Press).

Duby, G. 1968. *Rural economy and country life in the medieval west*, trans. C. Postan (London: Edward Arnold Ltd).

Ducouret, J.-P. 1986. Croix monumentales du canton de La Gacilly. Étude typologique. *Mémoires de la société d'histoire et d'archéologie de Bretagne* **63**, pp. 73–101.

Dupâquier, J. 1988. *Histoire de la population française* [4 vols] (Paris: Presses universitaires de France).

Dupâquier, J. 1989. Demographic crises and subsistence crises in France, 1650-1725. In *Famine, disease and the social order in early modern society*, J. Walter & R. Schofield (eds) (Cambridge: Cambridge University Press), pp. 189–99.

Duplessy 1981. *Le trésor de Ruffiac (Morbihan). Trésors monétaires III* (Paris: Bibliothèque nationale).

Eveillard, J.-Y. 1991. Le réseau des voies romaines en Haute-Bretagne (Loire-Atlantique exceptée). See Langouet, *Terroirs, territoires et campagnes antiques*, pp. 19–25.

Favereau, F. 1993. *Bretagne contemporaine. Langue, culture, identité* (Morlaix: Éditions Skol Vreizh).

Fichet de Clairfontaine, F. 1988. La Poterie (Côtes-du-Nord). Le centre potier dans les comptes de la châtellenie de Lamballe au XVe siècle. *Mémoires de la société d'histoire et d'archéologie de Bretagne* **65**, pp. 81–91.

Fichet de Clairfontaine, F. (ed.) 1996. *Ateliers de potiers médiévaux en Bretagne. Documents d'archéologie Française 55* (Paris: Maison des sciences de l'homme).

Fleuriot, L. 1980. *Les origines de la Bretagne* (Paris: Payot).

Fox, H. S. A. 1975. The chronology of enclosure and economic development in medieval Devon. *Economic History Review* **28**, pp. 181–202.

Gallet, J. 1981. Une société rurale bretonne: Carnac en 1475. *Bulletin de la société polymathique du Morbihan* **108**, pp. 15–36.

Gallet, J. 1983. *La seigneurie bretonne 1450–1680. L'exemple du Vannetais* (Paris: Université de Paris-Sorbonne).

Galliou, P. 1983. *L'Armorique romaine* (Braspars: les bibliophiles de Bretagne).

Galliou, P. 1990. Commerce et société en Armorique à l'âge du fer. In *Les Gaulois d'Armorique*, A. Duval, J.-P. Le Bihan, Y. Menez (eds), *Revue archéologique de l'Ouest*, Supplément 3, pp. 47–52.

Galliou, P. & M. Jones 1991. *The Bretons* (Oxford: Blackwell).

Gautier, M., G. Jumel, G. Leroux 1991. L'occupation antique de la Haute-Bretagne méridionale. See Langouet, *Terroirs, territoires et campagnes antiques*, pp. 55–65.

Gebhardt, A. 1988. Évolution du paysage agraire au cours du sub-atlantique dans la région de Redon (Morbihan, France): apport de la micromorphologie. *Bulletin de l'association française pour l'étude du quaternaire* **4**, pp. 197–203.

Gebhardt, A. 1990. *Évolution du paléopaysage agricole dans le nord-ouest de la France: apport de la micromorphologie* (Thèse de Doctorat, University of Rennes I).

Gebhardt, A. 1993. Micromorphological evidence of soil deterioration since the mid-Holocene at archaeological sites in Brittany, France. *The Holocene* **3**, pp. 333–41.

Giot, P.-R., J. L'Helgouac'h, J.-L. Monnier 1979. *Préhistoire de la Bretagne* (Rennes: Éditions Ouest-France).

Giot, P.-R., J. Briard, L. Pape 1995. *Protohistoire de la Bretagne* (Rennes: Éditions Ouest-France).

Gouézin, P. 1994. *Les Mégalithes du Morbihan intérieur* (Rennes: Institut culturel de Bretagne, Laboratoire d'anthropologie-préhistoire, Université de Rennes I).

Guennou, G. 1981. *La Cité des Coriosolites* (Saint-Malo: Centre régional archéologique d'Alet).

Guigon, P. 1992. Les résidences aristocratiques de l'époque carolingienne en Bretagne: l'exemple de Locronan. *Mémoires de la société d'histoire et d'archéologie de Bretagne* **69**, pp. 5–42.

Guigon, P. 1993. *L'architecture pré-Romane en Bretagne: le premier art Roman* (Rennes: Institut culturel de Bretagne, Laboratoire anthropologique-préhistoire Université de Rennes I, Centre régional archéologique d'Alet).

Guillotel, H. 1982. L'Exode du clergé breton devant les invasions scandinaves. *Mémoires de la société d'histoire et archéologique de Bretagne* **59**, pp. 269–315.

Hamel-Simon, J.-Y., L. Langouet, F. Nourry-Denayer, D. Mouton 1979. Fouille d'un retranchement d'Alain Barbetorte datable de 939. Le camp des Haies à Trans (Ille-et-Vilaine). *Les Dossiers du centre régional archéologique d'Alet* **7**, pp. 47–74.

Henry, Y. 1981. Le colombier, un signe extérieur de noblesse. Essai sur les colombiers de Bretagne. *Annales de Bretagne* **88**, pp. 67–86.

INSEE, n.d. *État statistique de la population des communes du Morbihan (1806–1975)* (available in Vannes Archives Départementales).

INSEE, 1990. *Logements – population – emploi – évolutions 1975–1982–1990. 56 Morbihan (Recensement général de la population de 1990)* (Paris: INSEE).

Jaubert, l'Abbe 1773. *Dictionnaire raisonné universel des arts et métiers*, rev. edn (Paris: Didot).

Johnson, M. 1996. *An archaeology of capitalism* (Oxford: Blackwell).

Jones, M. 1988. *The creation of Brittany. A late medieval state* (London: The Hambledon Press).

Kerhervé, J. 1987. *L'État breton aux 14e et 15e siècles. Les ducs, l'argent et les hommes* [2 vols] (Paris: Maloine).

Kerrand, H. 1988. Les écrits "fanatiques" de Joachim Quérant meunier de Bodel et maire de Caro sous la Révolution. *Bulletin de la société polymathique du Morbihan* **115**, pp. 81–106.

Krusch, B. (ed.) 1896. Vita Melanii Episcopi Redonici. In *Passiones vitaeque sanctorum aevi Merovingici*, vol. 3 of *Scriptores Rerum Merovingicarum* (Munich: *Monumenta Germaniae Historica*), pp. 370–76.

La Borderie, A. le Moyne de 1888. *Le Cartulaire de l'abbaye de Landévennec* [2 vols] (Rennes: Imprimerie Charles Catel).

La Borderie, A. le Moyne de (& B. Pocquet) 1896–1914. *Histoire de Bretagne* [6 vols] (Rennes: Plihon & Hervé, Plihon & Hommay).

Langouet, L., D. Mouton, F. Nourry-Denayer, J. P. Pozzi, M. Ricq, H. Valladas 1977. La poterie carolingienne de Trans. *Les Dossiers du centre régional archéologique d'Alet* **5**, pp. 109–42.

Langouet, L. & G. Jumel 1986. Le milieu rural de la civitas des Coriosolites à l'époque gallo-romaine. *Revue archéologique de l'Ouest* **3**, pp. 91–106.

Langouet, L. 1988. *Les Coriosolites. Un peuple armoricain de la période gauloise à l'époque gallo-romaine* (Saint-Malo: Centre régional archéologique d'Alet).

Langouet, L. (ed.) 1991. *Terroirs, territoires et campagnes antiques: la prospection archéologique en Haute-Bretagne. Traitement et synthèse des données. Revue archéologique de l'Ouest*, Supplément 4.

Largillière, R. 1925. *Les Saints et l'organisation chrétienne primitive dans l'Armorique bretonne* (Rennes: Plihon & Hommay; reprinted edn Crozon: Éditions Armeline, 1995).

Leguay, J.-P. & H. Martin 1982. *Fastes et malheurs de la Bretagne ducale 1213-1532* (Rennes: Éditions Ouest-France).

Le Guen, G. 1985. L'évolution démographique de la région de Bretagne depuis 20 ans (1962-1982). *Bulletin et mémoires de la société archéologique du département d'Ille-et-Vilaine* **87**, pp. 71–80.

Le Lannou, M. 1950–52. *Géographie de la Bretagne* [2 vols] (Rennes: Plihon).

Le Mené, J.-M. 1891–4. *Histoire archéologique, féodale et religieuse des paroisses du diocèse de Vannes* [2 vols] (Vannes: Imprimerie Galles).

Le Mené, J.-M. 1904. Prieurés du diocèse. *Bulletin de la société polymathique du Morbihan*, pp. 41–92, 161–249.

Le Rhun, P.-Y. & J.-R. Le Quéau 1994. Collectif, *Géographie et aménagement de la Bretagne* (Morlaix: Éditions Skol Vreizh).

Le Roux, C.-T., Y. Lecerf, M. Gautier 1989. Les mégalithes de Saint-Just (Ille-et-Vilaine) et la fouille des alignements du Moulin de Cojou. *Revue archéologique de l'Ouest* **6**, pp. 5–29.

Le Roux, C.-T. & P. Thollard 1990. Bretagne. *Gallia Informations*, pp. 1–80.

Marguerie, D. 1992. *Évolution de la végétation sous l'impact humain en Armorique du néolithique aux périodes historiques (Travaux de Laboratoire d'anthropologie de Rennes, no. 40)* (Rennes: Laboratoire d'anthropologie de Rennes, Université de Rennes I).

Marguerie, D. 1995. Paléoenvironnement des monuments mégalithiques à Saint-Just. See Briard, Gautier, Leroux, *Les Mégalithes et les tumulus de Saint-Just*, pp. 129–42.

Marguerie, D. & L. Langouet 1993. Le déclin des activités agricoles au bas-empire en Armorique. Correlation des données palynologiques et archéologiques. *Les Dossiers du centre régional archéologique d'Alet* **21**, pp. 109–13.

Marsille, H. 1988. La constitution civile du clergé vue de La Gacilly. *Bulletin de la société polymathique du Morbihan* **115**, pp. 157–64.

Marsille, L. 1911. L'affaire du Pré-Clos, Tréal (Morbihan), 29 juin 1791. *Bulletin de la société polymathique du Morbihan*, pp. 34–58.

Marsille, L.1912. Les sépultures gallo-romaines de Foucherel, en Ruffiac (Morbihan). *Bulletin de la société polymathique du Morbihan*, pp. 77–87.

Meirion-Jones, G. I. 1982. *The vernacular architecture of Brittany* (Edinburgh: John Donald).

Ménez, Y. & P. Galliou 1986. La villa gallo-romaine de Kervéguen en Quimper. *Bulletin de la société archéologique du Finistère* **115**, pp. 43–78.

Meynier, A. 1976. *Atlas et géographie de la Bretagne* (Paris: Flammarion).

Minois, G. 1976. La démographie du Trégor au XVe siècle. *Annales de Bretagne* **83**, pp. 407–24.

Nassiet, M. 1993. *Noblesse et pauvreté. La petite noblesse en Bretagne XVe– XVIIIe siècle* (Société d'histoire et d'archéologie de Bretagne).

O'Brien, P. & C. Keyder 1978. *Economic growth in Britain and France 1780– 1914* (London: George Allen & Unwin).

Ogée, J. 1845. *Dictionnaire historique et géographique de la province de Bretagne*, A. Marteville & P. Varin (eds) [2 vols] (Rennes: Molliex).

Pape, L. 1995. *La Bretagne romaine* (Rennes: Éditions Ouest-France).

Petit, M. 1970. Les sépultures du Bas-Empire à Guer. *Annales de Bretagne* **67**, pp. 273–8.

Philipponneau, M. 1993. *Le modèle industriel breton 1950–2000* (Rennes: Presses universitaires de Rennes).

Planiol, M. 1893–4. La donation d'Anouuareth. *Annales de Bretagne* **9**, pp. 216–37.

Post, J. D. 1985. *Food shortage, climatic variability and epidemic disease in pre-industrial Europe. The mortality peak in the early 1740s* (Ithaca and London: Cornell University Press).

Provost, A. & A. Priol 1991. L'occupation gallo-romaine dans le bassin de Rennes. See Langouet, *Terroirs, territoires et campagnes antiques*, pp. 67–80.

Rey, A. 1992. *Dictionnaire historique de la langue française* [2 vols] (Paris: Dictionnaires Le Robert).

Roggero, S. L. 1984. East Brittany Survey 1983: pollen analysis. Unpublished BA Archaeology dissertation (University of Reading).

Sanquer, R. 1977. Circonscription de Bretagne. *Gallia* **35**, pp. 335–67.

Smith, J. M. H. 1992. *Province and empire. Brittany and the Carolingians* (Cambridge: Cambridge University Press).

SRAB 1993. *Archéologie et grands travaux routiers* (Rennes: Service régional de l'archéologie).

Sutherland, D. 1982. *The Chouans. The social origins of popular counter-revolution in Upper Brittany 1770–96* (Oxford: Clarendon Press).

Tanguy, B. 1980. La limite linguistique dans la péninsule armoricaine à l'époque de l'émigration bretonne (IVe–Ve siècle) d'après les données toponymiques. *Annales de Bretagne* **87**, pp. 429–62.

Thévenin, O. 1993. La vie matérielle dans le Vannetais rural au XVIIIe siècle: l'example de l'alimentation. *Mémoires de la société d'histoire et d'archéologie de Bretagne* **70**, pp. 263–77.

Tinevez, J.-Y. 1988. La sépulture à entrée laterale de Beaumont en Saint-Laurent-sur-Oust. *Revue archéologique de l'Ouest* **5**, pp. 55–78.

Tingle, M. 1994. Flint and prehistoric worked stone. See Davies & Astill, *The East Brittany Survey*, pp. 229–34.

Tonnerre, N.-Y. 1994. *Naissance de la Bretagne. Géographie historique et structures sociales de la Bretagne méridionale (Nantais et Vannetais) de la fin du VIIIe à la fin du XIIe siècle* (Angers: l'Université d'Angers).

Vallerie, E. 1986. *Communes bretonnes et paroisses d'Armorique* (Braspars: les bibliophiles de Bretagne).

Visset, L. 1994. Vegetation changes and development of agriculture at "Kerfontaine" (Sérent, Massif Armoricain, France). *Vegetation History and Archaeobotany* **3**, pp. 1–6.

Weir, D. R. 1989. Markets and mortality in France, 1600-1789. In *Famine, disease and the social order in early modern society*, J. Walter & R. Schofield (eds) (Cambridge: Cambridge University Press), pp. 201–34.

Index